BELOW THE POTOMAC

Wilson Dam at Muscle Shoals, part of TVA, whose surging power is so important to America's prosecution of the war.

BELOW

THE

POTOMAC

A BOOK ABOUT THE NEW SOUTH

By

VIRGINIUS DABNEY

KENNIKAT PRESS/PORT WASHINGTON, N. Y.

917.5
Da

TO MY FATHER
A SOUTHERNER FOR WHOM I WAS PROUD
TO NAME MY SON

CONTENTS

ILLUSTRATIONS

BELOW THE POTOMAC

I

THE SOUTH THAT NEVER WAS

THE New South is a perennial subject of vehement debate on both sides of the Potomac, but the misunderstandings concerning it remain. It is belabored, all too often, as a reactionary and backward land, incredibly sleazy and down-at-heel, inhabited by degenerates drooling tobacco juice, whose penchant for lynching is exceeded only by their predilection for divers varieties of lechery. Fantastic as this picture is, except for a limited segment of Southern society, it is no more so than the South of mockingbirds, magnolias and mammies, of crinolined belles and burnt-cork Negroes with which the public also is occasionally regaled. Neither is typical, of course, nor could any thumbnail vignette of so huge a section of the globe illumine more than one facet of the picture. Consider that the region under examination in this volume—comprising the eleven states which formed the Confederacy, plus Kentucky—has an aggregate area of nearly 800,000 square miles, or more than the combined area, in 1938, of France, Belgium, Holland, Switzerland, Denmark, Germany, Italy, Austria, Hungary, Czechoslovakia, and Yugoslavia. The South's population of 34,675,000 is, on the other hand, only a small fraction of that which lives in the European countries referred to—is, indeed, less than that of pre-war France or Italy. Obviously, then, the South is a sparsely settled region by comparison with older lands, and although it is becoming industrialized at an increasing tempo, Southern civilization takes on the social coloration of the rural and small-town community. The fourteen largest American cities are all in other parts of the country, and New Orleans, which ranks fifteenth, has fewer than 500,000 inhabitants.

Many of the misconceptions concerning the New South stem from earlier misconceptions concerning the Old South. It seems hopeless, for example, to attempt to disabuse the minds of most Americans of the notion that ante-bellum civilization was compounded well-nigh exclusively of great slave-owning planters in pillared mansions. As one example among many which might be cited, let us take the opening words of the prologue to the motion picture, *Gone With the Wind:* "There was a land of Cavaliers and cotton." What could be more grotesque? As a consequence of this single sentence, the milieu of Miss Mitchell's fine novel became badly distorted from the moment it was transmuted into celluloid. Another typical pronouncement in the same tradition emanated not long ago from Mr. Earl Carroll, a gentleman less celebrated as an historian than as an impresario of feminine pulchritude. Mr. Carroll revealed that the most beautiful American girls are found in the South because "you must remember that the South was settled by the patrician Cavaliers, and that their descendants still form the great body of the population." The fact is that scarcely any authentic Cavaliers came to America in the early days; moreover, it might be slightly disconcerting to those who did if they were told to-day that their descendants were disporting themselves under Mr. Carroll's aegis, garbed in little more than powdered epidermis. As for the great plantations, fondly imagined by many to have existed in all parts of the ante-bellum South, they were to be found only in certain limited areas. Less than one-fourth of the white Southerners had any slaves at all in 1860, less than 3 per cent had as many as twenty, and only two-tenths of one per cent as many as one hundred.

It is partly because so many latter-day Americans are unable to disabuse their minds of the myths which have grown up with respect to the Old South that such a large body of phantasmagoria has developed in the public consciousness concerning the current South. It explains the naïve notion entertained in some other areas that Dixie is swarming with goateed gentlemen in broad-brimmed black hats, whose conversation consists chiefly of a reiterated "Suh, suh," and "By God, suh!" and who sit on their verandahs in the honeysuckle-laden air, inhausting mint juleps to the strains of *Old Black Joe*. Such a concept of the Southern scene finds its origin partially in the basic fallacy that nearly everybody in the South is descended from the English aristocracy, as well as from more immediate forebears whose every whim was catered to by hundreds, if not thousands, of slaves. As we have seen, more than 75 per cent of the white persons living below the Potomac and the Ohio in the year before the Civil War began, possessed not a single chattel. Their ancestors were either small farmers, urban tradesmen, clerks or mechanics, or members of the large group of despised unfortunates known as "poor whites." The last-named element was by no means as numerous as many believe, but it formed a substantial percentage of the ante-bellum population.

Latterly, the "poor whites" have received much attention from students and interpreters of the social scene in the former Confederacy, and rightly so, for their underprivileged status and lack of hope for the future, especially prior to the advent of the Roosevelt Administration, made them a natural object of solicitude on the part of humanitarians and students generally. Yet it is apropos of this very group of sharecroppers, common laborers and marginal workers that some of the worst misconceptions with respect to the New South have arisen. Thousands who have seen Erskine Caldwell's powerful play, *Tobacco Road,* have gained the impression, for example, that the generality of Southern poor whites are as filthy and depraved as Jeeter Lester and his libidinous entourage. This and other works of Mr. Caldwell, and similarly preoccupied Southern writers, such as William Faulkner, quite naturally lead one to believe that countless "poor whites" in the cotton belt are murderers, sadists, and idiots of the most revolting sort. There are persons of this stripe among them, needless to say, but they are decidedly exceptional. The "poor whites" frequently live in great squalor, under physical conditions similar to those enjoyed by the characters in the Caldwell play, but in other respects that picture of them is accurate for only a limited number.

Dwellers in the North and West would never learn from *Tobacco Road* that the average white Southern sharecropper or other marginal worker comes of sturdy Anglo-Saxon yeoman stock, that many of these underprivileged people are proud and self-reliant, if given half a chance to break out of the cycle of poverty and disease which has held them for so long in its vise-like grip, and that about all they need is rudimentary medical attention and some instruction in agricultural and dietary fundamentals, together with enough credit to enable them to shake off the shackles of the one-crop "furnishing-merchant" system. Until the New Deal attacked this situation by means of Federal legislation, no comprehensive effort to ameliorate it had been made. While many of these "poor whites" are undoubtedly beyond redemption, a decided majority are capable of marked improvement, once they are made physically whole and educationally receptive. After all, Abraham Lincoln and Andrew Johnson sprang from this same class of society.

The belief is widely held that the traveler through the South is sure to encounter numerous moronic degenerates of the sort depicted in the ultra-realistic literary and dramatic studies already referred to. Such is far from the case. On a recent trip of nearly two weeks' duration through Georgia, Alabama, Mississippi, Louisiana, and Tennessee, the writer failed to see more than two persons who approached this condition, even remotely. They were not observed in or near any of the countless tumbledown shacks which stand on the edge of forlorn cotton patches; they were walking on the streets of an Alabama city. It is important to note, however, that I, like the average traveler in the region, had little opportunity to view these types at close range. The visitor to the South does not usually leave the main highways, nor does he enter the cabins where Mr. Caldwell's Jeeters and Ty Ty's are to be found. The researcher in quest of such human wreckage will come upon it in the little shanties off the beaten path, on badly eroded land or amid sandhills and pine barrens. Mr. Caldwell's *You Have Seen Their Faces* presents some such types, although there are also faces in his pages which bespeak an innate dignity and a finely tempered integrity, evidence of a valiant but hopeless struggle against insuperable odds. Yet those who conclude that his arresting volume contains physiognomies typical of "the South," will discover that they are mistaken, and that *You Have Seen Their Faces*, for all its incisive documentation, is hardly more representative of the region as a whole and its people than is *Faces You See*, the antidote issued by Southern cotton mill interests, and depicting invariably smiling, exuberant, well-nourished and prosperous-looking mill hands. Both books are definite overstatements, in so far as they may be deemed applicable to Southern farmers or Southern laborers as a class.

There is no intention here of minimizing the evils which have grown up as inevitable concomitants of sharecropping and one-crop farming in the South. Yet the South is misunderstood in the important respects noted, just as the North is misunderstood by Southerners in certain particulars. For example, Northerners are regarded in some Southern circles as spiritual descendants of William Tecumseh Sherman, and as no less ruthless in their personal and business relationships than the diabolically efficient gentleman who marched through Georgia, burned Atlanta and Columbia, and made himself generally *persona non grata* to the Confederate States of America. Northern businessmen are considered by some sectionally conscious Southerners to be less trustworthy than Southern businessmen. They also are regarded by the same uninformed Southerners—most of whom have never traveled north of the Potomac and the Ohio—as mere money-grubbers, intent on piling up dollars, to the neglect of culture and the amenities. While it is probably true that in Charleston, South Carolina, for instance, the business tempo is slower than in any Northern center of population, and while there is nothing in the South comparable to the mad rush and febrile atmosphere of New York City, there are fewer divergencies between cities of similar size in the two sections than is commonly realized. One injustice done the North when such matters are under discussion emerges in the Southern propensity to regard New York as typical of Northern civilization and Northern society. It is nothing of the sort, but unfortunately it is the only city beyond the Mason and Dixon line which some Southerners ever visit, just as it is almost the only one which Europeans see when they dash over to "do" the hemisphere in three days.

New York and Charleston certainly have little in common, but then nothing like either is to be found anywhere else in the world. Lusty, dynamic, sprawling, polyglot Gotham is as different as could well be imagined from languourous, sleepy Charleston, dreaming beneath its moss-hung live-oaks of the days when John C. Calhoun spoke for the slave states. It would be almost equally futile to seek similarities between Natchez and Youngstown or between Savannah and Paterson. But if one chooses cities in some measure comparable as to population, and not wholly dissimilar with respect to economic interests, the divergence is much less marked— as in the case of, say, Birmingham and Pittsburgh, Dallas and Des Moines, or Atlanta and Indianapolis.

Do the men and women who live in the North and West concern themselves to a greater degree with mere money-getting and to a lesser degree with the things

of the mind than do those of the South? On the contrary, the evidence points in precisely the opposite direction. What regions have the best universities and
libraries? Which enjoy the best living-standard? Which
buy the most books per capita? Which have the best
symphony orchestras, the most adequate art galleries?
The answer, in every instance, is "the North and West."
The propensity of certain Southerners to change the
subject when these unflattering facts are mentioned is
not particularly creditable. Others speak of the Civil
War as though this constituted an adequate and satisfying explanation, but it may be observed that, as a
continuing alibi for all Southern deficiencies, the War
is growing rather tiresome. Unquestionably certain pon-
derous obstacles were placed athwart the path of the
South by the war and its terrible aftermath, but some
of them should have been surmounted long ago. The
effects of others, it must be conceded, are being felt un-
avoidably, even to-day.

It is everywhere recognized, however, that the South
is making progress. The literacy rate has been raised
until it is beginning to approach the figure enjoyed by
other sections. Southern writing is commanding the attention of both America and Europe, and Southern art
is giving convincing evidence of vitality. There are art
museums of an extremely high order of excellence in
Dallas and Richmond. It is noteworthy, too, that Atlanta, New Orleans, and Dallas have regular seasons of
Metropolitan Opera each year. On the material side,
the South can take pride in many things, such as New
Orleans' possession of one of the world's finest airports,
and Birmingham's erection of an office building which
the London *Times* has described as one of the three

Parker Griffith photo, Dallas, Texas

The Dallas Museum of Fine Arts, which houses a permanent collection of paintings and sculpture valued at over three million dollars.

Bellingrath Gardens near Mobile, Alabama, showing giant live oaks festooned with hanging moss.

best-designed office structures in existence. Yet it is manifest that much remains to be done in raising the standard of Southern prosperity and Southern living, and in promoting a keener and more lively Southern appreciation of cultural values and cultural endeavor.

One of the much-debated aspects of civilization below the Potomac is the cuisine. Does Southern cooking deserve the reputation it has enjoyed in some quarters, or is the skepticism concerning it justified? Conversely, do Northern gourmets have more satisfying opportunities to indulge their gustatory preferences in their native habitats than when traveling below Mason and Dixon's line?

Those who call down all-inclusive objurgations upon Southern cooking—such as one which seared the pages of the *American Mercury* in 1939, and evoked heartfelt expostulations from all sections of the former Confederacy—are not to be taken seriously. The Northern lady who penned the blast in question informed her public that Southern "Epicureans subsist for the most part upon ... meat, meal and molasses"; that "goat meat" is the "South's common substitute for lamb"; that "the best Virginia ham in the world is served in New York restaurants"; that in the South "all meats, poultry, and fish are consigned to swim endlessly in deep pools of smoky, smelly grease"; and that "flies infest all restaurants," while cockroaches are "usually to be seen scurrying across the floor." There was much more in the same vein. Some of the irate Southerners who unbosomed themselves in epistolary retorts to the magazine seemed to think that they had to be as egregiously absurd as the party to whose exaggerations they were objecting—as, for example, the correspondent who asserted that Arkansas has "the best cooking in the South and also in the world." But those who reacted in this bizarre fashion did so not without provocation.

It must be conceded that there is ground for some of the criticisms made of Southern cookery. In the first place, the scarcity of large cities naturally reduces the number of first-class Southern restaurants. It is manifestly not fair to compare and contrast the best restaurant in, say, Plant City, Florida, or Corpus Christi, Texas, with the best in Chicago or Philadelphia. There are some excellent caravanseries in the South, and they are to be found in places like Williamsburg, Virginia, Augusta, Georgia, and Mobile, Alabama, as well as in such centers of population as Louisville, Atlanta, and New Orleans. On the other hand, there is ground for the criticism that grits are served too often in the far South, that good cuts of meat are sometimes difficult to get, and that in the Southeast pork is found on menus with excessive frequency, and the lowly collard is occasionally too much in evidence. One need not pause unduly to adjudicate the controversy launched by the late Huey Long over whether one should dunk or crumble his cornpone in his potlikker, for potlikker is more of a canine than a human delicacy, and the dunkers and the crumblers can fight the matter out among themselves. An encouraging phenomenon of the culinary situation below the Potomac is to be found in the fact that Tuskegee, the Negro institute in Alabama, inaugurated in 1936 a four-year course for stewards, chefs, and caterers, as well as less intensive and prolonged instruction for family cooks and others. The addition to the curriculum proved popular at once, not only with the matriculates, but with hotel men, restaurateurs, and housewives throughout the South who were more than glad to have Tuskegee-trained majordomos preside over their kitchens.

The foregoing brings to mind the traditional "Southern hospitality," and the question whether it is, in truth, largely tradition, or whether it is rooted in actuality. Is there, for example, more hospitality in the South than in the North? One would judge so, from the fact that openhanded Southern hosts and hostesses have become proverbial. It may be doubted, however, whether one section of America is, on the whole, more hospitable to visitors than another. While it is true that the graciousness of Southerners is often noteworthy, such graciousness stems sometimes from the fact that the visitor is armed with the proper credentials, not to mention the proper ancestors. There is, for example, no more delightful city in which to visit than Charleston, provided one has introductions to the right people. The Charlestonians are proud of their patrician heritage and they are careful not to offer the keys of the municipality to those whom they consider interlopers. Their attitude here resembles that of those ultra-refined Bostonians who are in the habit of conversing exclusively with one another and the Deity. But on the Battery, as in Back Bay, the possessor of adequate forebears who comes bringing the requisite evidence thereof virtually is handed the town. There is scarcely any limit to the warmth of his welcome. In certain other areas of the South, and of New England, family is likewise regarded as the *sine qua non,* but in the North and West as a whole, one finds considerably less of this sort of thing than in the South. In other words, hospitality is apt to be more uninhibited outside of Dixie than in it.

The above is set down in the full knowledge that in most areas of the South the cult of ancestor-worship is fading steadily. As long ago as the middle twenties it was aptly stated that in Virginia, to paraphrase a famous saying, "Banknotes are more than coronets, and simple flasks than Norman blood." Moreover, if the South devotes most of its thoughts to past glories, why are its historic shrines less well preserved than those of New England? Is it conceivable that Massachusetts, for example, would allow the home of one of its heroes, with a name comparable to that of Raphael Semmes in the annals of Alabama, to fall into such dilapidation and decay as shocks the visitor to the Semmes home to-day on one of Mobile's principal streets; or that Connecticut would permit the one-time dwelling of a President born within its borders to lapse into the disgraceful condition of the James Monroe home in Fredericksburg? Even a professional Southerner might have a difficult time justifying such neglect as this, for men of the stature of Semmes and Monroe are entitled to better treatment. The apparent fact is, however, that they are more likely to receive this treatment in the North, and especially in New England, than in the South.

Our reference to that obnoxious species of Southern fauna, the professional Southerner, leads to the question whether he is ubiquitous as some believe. There are still parochial and unreconstructed Southerners among us, but they are gradually growing less articulate, and also less numerous. Fewer inhabitants of the former Confederacy spend their time in uncritical ravings anent the splendors of ante-bellum and post-bellum civilization, in full-throated ululations alleging the superiority of Southern horses, women, dogs, oboe-players, fly-fishermen, and flagpole-sitters over those of any other section of the globe.

The professional Southerner is, of course, a sentimental and narrow-minded person who is congenitally incapable of seeing anything bad in the South or anything good in the North. He is the sort of individual who is largely responsible for the backwardness of the South in certain fields, for the region's excessive sensitiveness to criticism, and for an occasional propensity on the part of Southerners to regard even the most valid Northern demurrers to Southern attitudes and *mores* as nefarious plots hatched by descendants of William Lloyd Garrison. And in the memorable words of the late Grover C. Hall, the professional Southerner is also "ever ready to protect the honor of any woman against all men, except himself." This species of Southerner is responsible, needless to say, for many of the misunderstandings concerning the region which he inhabits, for he is apt to be more vocal than his fellow citizens. His fatuous opinions are regarded, therefore, by the uninformed, as representing the entire section, instead of merely its lunatic fringe.

There are professional Northerners, too, but it should be said, in all fairness, that Northerners are perhaps, on the whole, more tolerant of the Southern viewpoint than Southerners are of theirs. Fortunately, there is relatively little intolerance on either side in this fifth decade of the twentieth century, but the North's attitude should be viewed in the light of the fact that, unlike the South, it did not have to taste the bitter hemlock of defeat, or to endure thereafter a decade of extortion and humiliation. Consequently, a detached viewpoint is, for it, more readily attainable than for the section which suffered the calvary of the sixties and seventies. The South put up a magnificent battle for four years against overwhelming odds, but Appomattox and Reconstruction left deep scars. Those scars are fading, but some Southerners, even to-day, exhibit a tendency toward morbidity in their intersectional attitudes—a morbidity which makes it difficult for them to view issues involving the North and the South objectively. It should be said, to the credit of the North, that its more well-informed citizens often make a genuine effort to understand their fellow-Americans who dwell below Mason and Dixon's line. The Abolitionist point of view is not yet extinct in the land which gave the Abolitionists birth, but it is dying fast.

True, there is a regrettable tendency on the part of some Northerners to regard nearly all Southerners as unlettered and provincial persons—the males as addicted to chewing tobacco and profanity, and as acquainted only mildly with cultural matters, and the females as semi-literate and given to petting. There are such men and women on both sides of the Potomac, but it would be difficult to prove that they are more numerous on one side than on the other. Chewing tobacco sales are not skyrocketing in Dixie, and if there are accomplished wielders of expletives in the region, as there undoubtedly are, it remains to be demonstrated that their virtuosity in the field is markedly superior to that of their Northern rivals. As for Southern girls and young women, Mary Boykin Chesnut, the South Carolinian who kept a diary in the sixties, described the Southern belles of that era as "soft and sweet, low-toned, indolent, graceful, quiescent." These adjectives are much less applicable to the Southern girls of to-day, but even so they probably are more accurately descriptive than some care to admit. The rather saccharine passivity which seems to have been the hallmark of a certain type of Southern womanhood in the mid-nineteenth century, if Mrs. Chesnut is to be believed, is not wholly lacking more than three-quarters of a century later. Yet the Southern girl of the 1940's is a totally different animal from her great-grandmother. If she is apt, on the whole, to be less intellectual than her Northern contemporary, partly because the North has rather better women's colleges than the South, she can evince a lively curiosity concerning things political, literary or artistic without risking social ostracism. As for the notion that Southern girls have a greater propensity for petting than other girls, it remains only a notion, and is quite insusceptible of proof.

Whatever the truth of the foregoing, there is certainly one sphere in which the Southern demoiselle is by no means the revolting creature she is sometimes represented to be. I refer to her accent, the same "Southern accent" which has been caricatured and lampooned and parodied in a hundred dramas of the stage and screen, with the result that the simpering, hideously drawling "Southern girl" of those ghastly travesties is enough to make an authentic Southern male run a mile in the opposite direction. Producers should remember that there is seldom anything more obviously synthetic than synthetic Southern argot. The film version of *Gone With the Wind* was a miraculous exception, but such miracles are extremely rare. The fact that this one was achieved largely because Miss Susan Myrick of Macon, Georgia, was retained by the producer as special consultant on accent, ought to be taken to heart by all those who, in the future, wish to portray typically Southern characters on the boards or in the films.

Miss Mitchell, who had no part in the adaptation of her book for the screen, expressed a high degree of pleasure at the way in which the job was accomplished. She said she was agreeably surprised at not finding the film full of pseudo-Southern talk like "Now you po' cully-haided little lamb, res' yo' haid on mammy's breast." She was annoyed, on the other hand, at the profusion of white columns on the Georgia plantation homes, put there by Hollywood as a concession to traditional notions about the South, despite the explicit statement in the book that Tara was a rambling old farmhouse, and the further fact that it was situated in a section of Georgia where columns were almost non-existent.

Miss Mitchell must have offered up orisons to the Deity for the fact that nobody in the motion picture perpetrated that abominable slander against the fair name of Southern civilization, the use of "you all" to denote only one person. It seems futile to protest that such usage exists only as a figment of the Northern imagination. Declarations of this character are greeted all too frequently with indulgent smiles by visitors below the Potomac, who are absolutely certain that they have heard Southern acquaintances say "you all" when addressing an individual. Strangely enough, this is correct, as far as it goes, but they fail to realize that the party thus addressed is never the only person connoted by the phrase. For example, when a Southerner says, in parting from a friend on a street corner, "You all come to see us," he means "You and all the rest of the family come to see us." When a customer asks a clerk behind the counter, "Have you all got a sale on neckties to-day?" he means "Have you and the rest of the people who run this store got a sale?" As used in the South, the expression "you all" is entirely grammatical, and, moreover, our savants point out that it was used similarly in England hundreds of years before the South was ever heard of. Even the early Anglo-Saxons of Beowulf's time employed an equivalent phrase, and in much the same sense in which the Southerner of to-day employs it. So let's have an end to "you all," as currently uttered before the footlights by such a "Southern" character as bewhiskered old Colonel Breckinridge Taliaferro Bougainvillea, who is customarily made to address his Negro butler in some such terms as: "Sambo, yo' all fetch me a tumblah of likkah and brahnch wahtah heah on the verandah."

Many sincere inhabitants of other sections really believe that educated Southerners speak in the manner of the aforesaid colonel. Sometimes, however, there is a deliberate effort in the North to distort and misrepresent an episode, or even the customs and habits of a whole region. Agitators who seek to use arrests or convictions in the South as propaganda against Southern attitudes and prejudices, or Southern laws and taboos, are the chief culprits in this regard. Sometimes they have genuine grievances, grievances which ought to be corrected, but even in such cases they are apt to make wildly unfounded charges, in order to impress the uninformed. Take, for example, the behavior of one such organization in connection with the recent killing of a white tenant farmer by a Negro sharecropper. Uncontradicted testimony had it that the sharecropper went to collect his share of the wheat crop from the tenant, on whose land he was working, and that after a brief parley, the sharecropper shot the tenant four times, twice in the back, although the tenant was unarmed. It may be that the death sentence was too severe, since the killing may not have been premeditated. But some of those who espoused the sharecropper's cause in the North not only pronounced the killing justified and demanded a new trial, but they made the case a sounding board for propaganda against the sharecropping system, as practised in the South, against the poll-tax system, and against what was described as the prevailing attitude of Southern white men toward colored men. Even this might not have been objectionable in all respects, if the agitators had stuck to facts. But they didn't. They misrepresented the case in their inflammatory literature, and never mentioned once that the sharecropper shot the tenant twice in the back when he was unarmed, but proclaimed that the Negro killed "in self-defense." Moreover, one of the printed circulars which was distributed all over the United States asserted that a Negro sharecropper "has no rights in the American South." One can acknowledge the vulnerability of the South to some of the criticisms made against it here and elsewhere, without condoning such flagrant distortions as these.

Misrepresentations of a somewhat different character occurred in connection with the so-called "slipper slaying," which took place in the mountains of Southwest Virginia in 1935. According to the internationally publicized version of this case, Edith Maxwell, a young mountain school-teacher, killed her drunken, backwoods "pappy" when she hit him with her dancing slipper in self-defense, because he berated her and tried to spank her for coming home one night after the nine o'clock "mountain curfew." The "curfew," according to stories published throughout America and England, was part of the "mountain code." Edith had not only violated the code by remaining out after nine o'clock, but she had gone to teachers' college, she wore "store boughtened clothes," and she knew "the lure of the movies." That, it appeared, was enough, and the "jury of grim-faced mountaineers" gave her a heavy prison term, not because she was guilty of second-degree murder (although that was the verdict), but because they wished to uphold the "archaic code of the mountains" against the "encroaching freedom of modern youth."

There had been much confusion everywhere immediately after the killing, concerning the basic facts in the case, for the crime took place in the little mountain village of Pound out near the Kentucky line, where experienced newspapermen were either hard to find or non-existent. Then the Hearst papers had seized upon the murder, and had run a series of sensational articles, thereby adding to the confusion. Honest mistakes were made in the early stages by commentators who found it difficult, if not impossible, to ascertain the most elementary facts.

But leaving the typically Hearstian performance out of account, there was no excuse for the lurid coverage given the killing and the two trials by at least one reputable press association and one reputable Eastern newspaper. Someone observed that the correspondents who went to Wise Courthouse to report the trial evidently wrote their stories in hotel rooms with a bottle of "corn" in one hand and a copy of *The Trail of the Lonesome Pine* in the other. Their primary purpose seemed to be to depict that section of Virginia as the domain of unlettered hill-billies, the slaying as justifiable homicide, perhaps even an accident—since Edith had merely tapped her intoxicated pappy with a slipper —and the convictions at both trials as gross miscarriages of justice. What are the facts?

In the first place, Miss Maxwell was never convicted of beating her father to death with a slipper, for the jury did not believe that version, one of several explanations given by her of the manner in which her father died. She was convicted twice of beating Trigg Maxwell to death with an ax, a flatiron, or some other such instrument—and not in self-defense, either. Moreover, numerous witnesses testified at both trials that Maxwell was not drunk, but that he was cold sober when they saw him shortly before the fatal altercation. Had he invoked the "mountain code" against his daughter? There isn't any such code, nor is there a "mountain curfew." Edith herself finally admitted that, without having the least effect upon the highly imaginative scribes who continued to refer to these non-existent phenomena, in order to stir the emotions of humanitarians throughout America, and thus to secure contributions to the defense fund being raised by the Hearst papers.

By the time the second trial took place, a few newspapers sought to counteract the nonsense which had been broadcast to much of the world, but it was impossible to eradicate impressions which had taken such a deep hold upon the public consciousness. It was pointed out that Wise County, where the slaying took place, is a rich coal-mining county, with three modern towns, nine high schools, 100 school buildings and 400 young men and women off at college; but in the mind of the average American it remained the last stronghold of backwoods pappies. Completely unbiased persons who attended the second trial, concluded that the twenty-year sentence was justified (Miss Maxwell got twenty-five years at the first trial), particularly since there was abundant testimony that she hated her father and had frequently threatened to kill him. All of which means that the effort to transform this ordinary criminal case into "a dramatic struggle between the archaic family code of the mountains and the encroaching freedom of modern youth" was so much balderdash, unless one takes the view that it is all right to hit your father in the head with a flatiron anywhere except in the mountains of Southwest Virginia.

Not content with such flagrant misrepresentations as the foregoing, certain professional Northerners delight in reading lectures to all Southerners for their "narrow-mindedness," their "provincialism," and their general lack of decency and intelligence. Such criticisms of the South are heard most often with respect to its handling of the race problem. Fantastic statements in Northern magazines and newspapers, by self-constituted authorities who know little or nothing about the subject, naturally contribute only slightly to intersectional goodwill. For example, the following pontification appeared not long ago in the editorial columns of the Lowell, Massachusetts, *Sun:* "Any Negro in the South who dares go near a polling booth on election day invites a bullet through his brain. That is fact, not fiction." A Virginia editor promptly pointed out that many thousands of Negroes vote every election day in the South, without any such retribution as the Lowell paper declared to be universal, and three Northern-born residents of Virginia protested the *Sun's* extravagant assertion. The Massachusetts daily promptly modified its charge with respect

to Negro voting, but was equally absurd in its comment
upon one of the above-mentioned letters. The author of
the letter, a native New Englander, had declared, on
the basis of residence in both Florida and Virginia, that
"the lot of the Southern Negro is no worse than that
of the average Northern laborer." This declaration, it
is true, was distinctly vulnerable, but the *Sun's* editor
went to the extreme length of saying, in rebuttal, that
"no Northern laborer would for one moment tolerate
conditions under which the Southern Negro lives." He
should have read the series of newspaper articles by
Harry Ashmore, a young South Carolina newspaperman,
lovingly describing the unspeakably foul slums of various Northern cities—a series which was published with
gusto in 1938 by more than a score of Southern dailies
grown weary of excursions by Northern journalists into
the cabins and back alleys of the cotton belt.

Almost simultaneously with the controversy in the
columns of the Lowell *Sun,* the New York newspaper,
PM, carried a long account of how two drunken white
men from the South abused a Negro red cap at the
Pennsylvania Station and tried to get him fired. Near
the close of the article, the newspaper explained why it
carried no photograph of the colored man. "He was
scared to have his picture taken for *PM,* scared of being
singled out for persecution by other white men from
the South with a few drinks under their belts," said the
writer, thereby creating the impression that the Pennsylvania Station is swarming with ruffianly Southern
drunks, itching to slap down red caps. Then there was
the account distributed by the Associated Negro Press
of the commendable action of six Greenville, South
Carolina, Negroes, who dragged another Negro to jail

on a charge of raping a ten-year-old colored girl. They carried him to jail, said the dispatch, "instead of following the usual procedure in the South for such crimes." And what is the "usual procedure"? During the year when this account was written there were five lynchings in the South, while nineteen lynchings were prevented there by the authorities, and in numerous other cases no attempt at lynching was made. Roughly, the same proportion had obtained for several years previously. In other words, the "usual procedure" is to protect the prisoner from would-be lynchers, precisely the opposite of the impression created in the newspaper dispatch referred to.

Other misunderstandings which have arisen concerning the South seem to be cultivated by Southerners themselves. One of these has to do with the cost of living within the region. Nearly everybody appears to assume that one can live far more cheaply in the South than in any other section of America. This widespread misapprehension seems to be based mainly on the fact that the average Southern income is only about half that for the rest of the nation. Unfortunately this simply means that most Southerners have a lower living standard than Northerners or Westerners. They have become accustomed, through stern necessity, to getting along with less.

The unanimity with which competent and disinterested analysts of regional living costs have arrived at almost identical conclusions over a period of two decades, cannot fail to be impressive. Beginning with 1919 and 1920, when the National Industrial Conference Board found that such costs in certain typical Southern cotton mill centers were *higher* than in certain corresponding Northern centers, on through a dozen other studies by public and private agencies, the greatest differential found to exist in favor of the South has been 5 per cent, and usually no differential at all was discovered. True, the studies seemed to indicate that small towns and rural communities everywhere are apt to have lower living costs than cities. Since more Southerners live in such semi-rural and rural regions than Northerners and Westerners, they do appear to enjoy a small advantage in this one respect. But the prevailing impression that it is much cheaper to live in a city or town of a given size below the Potomac than elsewhere, is not well founded. Business men, professional men, college professors, farmers, and ditch-diggers all receive lower average incomes in the South than outside it.

Is the South slow and unprogressive? The answer depends on which aspects of Southern civilization one subjects to scrutiny. For instance, the census of 1940 revealed the South as sharing with the Far West the distinction of being America's fastest growing area. Every Southern state, except Alabama and Arkansas, was in the class which had a population growth of between 7.2 and 14.9 per cent, and Florida was in the highest class of all, reached by only four other states, each of which showed a rate of growth in excess of 15 per cent. The solid belt of states running northward from Oklahoma to North Dakota suffered a net loss for the decade, and the next poorest showing was made by the entire northeastern area of the country, from the Maryland-Pennsylvania line to Maine. Not only did nearly all the Southern states exhibit a rapid rate of increase, but of the seventeen cities in the country with at least 100,000 inhabitants which grew at least 10 per cent in the decade, the South had eight—Miami, Jacksonville, Houston, Charlotte, Memphis, Dallas, Atlanta, and Norfolk. The first three listed had population increments of over 31 per cent.

Is the South's rapid growth due to a high Negro birth rate? Only in part, for the white birth rate is higher than the Negro, especially in urban areas. Moreover, the census showed that the South has a younger population than the other sections, so that its sons and daughters would seem to be more ready and able, from this point of view, to cope with future problems and difficulties. While other less favorable aspects of Southern civilization tend to vitiate this advantage to a considerable degree, it may be surprising to many that the supposedly decadent and backward South is actually one of the most lush and fecund portions of the earth's surface.

Moreover, some of our outlanders may be astounded to learn that Southerners wear shoes. It will be recalled that Secretary of Labor Frances Perkins, in the early 1930's, exhorted Dixie to put on shoes, apparently oblivious of the fact that thousands of denizens of the region actually have arrived at such a state of civilization that they wear shoes all the year round, even in summer. There are other surprises in store for those who think of the former Confederacy exclusively in terms of hookworm and pellagra, illiteracy, and fundamentalism. How many of them know that Dallas has a five-story air-conditioned bookstore that is second to none in America in the quality of its stock and the excellence of its appointments? How many know that Richmond enjoyed by far the greatest percentage of industrial growth of any large American industrial center between 1929 and 1937, and that the same city has a larger percentage of persons with wealth of at least $5,000, and also more with at least $50,000, than any city in the country, except Cincinnati? How many know that the American fur trade is heavily dependent upon the far-Southern state of Louisiana, which produces more fur than the whole of Canada? And finally, how many know that the percentage of farms operated by tenants in certain Middle Western states is considerably higher than in certain Southern states? The percentage, to wit, in Illinois, Iowa, South Dakota, Nebraska, and Kansas is much higher than in Florida, Kentucky, and Virginia, and about the same as in North Carolina and Tennessee.

The more one studies the South, therefore, the more one discovers novel and curious facts concerning it, and the more one finds that he who generalizes with respect to any large region of America will come to grief. There are melancholy and lamentable misconceptions in many minds concerning both the South and the North, but the South is the greater sufferer here, for there is a propensity for limning its attitudes and its *mores* in either rose-tinted or Stygian hues, with scant, if any, middle ground. Too often, in the popular mind, the Southern people are devouring possum and watermelon, or they are becoming rachitic on cornmeal and sowbelly. The student of the South who would pluck out the heart of its mystery must view the regional canvas in its entirety, focusing upon its social penumbra no less than upon its brightest coruscations and its blackest depths. Fortunately, there is in America an increasing tendency toward this more balanced view of the Southern scene.

II

POLITICS AND PURGATION

POLITICAL mimes, clowns, and zanies have been hatched more numerously in the New South than in any other region of the United States. Where of late, except in Georgia, has a candidate taken off his shoes before addressing a country audience? Where, except in Alabama, has an aspirant for office removed his silk socks and harangued the sovereign voters sockless because his opponent taunted him for wearing silk hose? Where, except in Arkansas, do members of the state legislature customarily slug one another on the floor with fists and ink-wells?

It would be unfair to assume, however, that Southern politics is compounded wholly of such antics. On the contrary, it is often dignified and restrained—too much so, in fact. But the not infrequent emergence of Southern crackpots can scarcely be wholly accidental. The explanation must lie somewhere below the seething surface of Dixie politics.

There are several fairly obvious reasons for the South's proliferation of political mountebankery. For one thing, the region's illiteracy is still considerably higher than that of other sections. The general level of education among the Southern masses is well below what it should be. To this should be added the fact that these same masses are inadequately cared for in various other important respects. Consequently, the

27

demagogic appeal is more effective here than elsewhere. In the second place, the heavy percentage of Negroes in the populations of most Southern states gives the low-grade spellbinder an "issue" with which to rouse the Negro's chief economic rival, the "poor white." Fortunately, this sort of campaigning is considerably less blatant than it was a quarter of a century ago. Even the lower orders of whites are becoming relatively immune to the brutal Negrophobia exemplified by such a man as the late Senator Vardaman of Mississippi. Now that the Negroes are outnumbered in every Southern state by a race which freely admits its own vast superiority, the old prejudices and passions, the old fears of "Negro domination," are less readily aroused. Yet the race issue emerges with considerable frequency, even today. A third explanation for the South's political backwardness is to be found, of course, in the one-party system, which everywhere tends to stifle initiative, to encourage political inbreeding, to remove the incentive for party achievement, and to discourage the most enterprising and intelligent young men and women from seeking public careers.

Such are the chief reasons why demagoguery flourishes unduly below the Potomac. It should be emphasized, however, that the demagogues are distinctly in the minority here, as everywhere else. They merely make the most noise, and consequently are the recipients of the most publicity. As striking as the prevalence of these political bladder-wielders in the South's public life, is the prevalence there of certain ultra-conservative gentlemen who seem largely out of touch with current thinking, and whose social concepts apparently are roughly identical with those of Chester A. Arthur. Whence come

these exemplars of nineteenth-century economics and
ideology? How do they manage to get themselves elected
year after year, in a region which is overwhelmingly
behind the New Deal of President Roosevelt? If these
men were catalogued purely on the basis of their economic and social attitudes, one would assign them un-
hesitatingly to the Republicans. Yet they occupy key
positions in the Democratic party, and are extremely
influential in shaping its course in the Senate and
House.

The remarkable phenomenon is to be explained
largely on three grounds. The first is the one-party
system already referred to. Where there is little or no
inter-party competition within a given state, and a single
party has a virtual monopoly on the offices, it is much
easier for a political leader to set up a well-nigh invincible personal machine than where control of the
state oscillates every few years from the Democrats to
the Republicans, or vice versa. Moreover, after the
Southern Democrats have sent a given senator or representative back to Washington for several terms, and he
takes senior ranking on his committees, he is able to
make the argument that he can do more for his state
or district than any newly elected Democratic rival, and
the difficulty of unhorsing him is thereby increased. The
second reason why so many conservative, if not reactionary, Southerners are in strategic positions in Washington
is that the poll-tax and other franchise restrictions in
eight Southern states prevent a large percentage of their
constituents from voting. Hence the machine, plus the
business, industrial, and financial interests, usually can
combine to defeat any rival who challenges the incumbent's hegemony. The third reason is that the South

has long been the most conservative section of the country with respect to social and labor legislation, and its individual states are all backward in this regard. In choosing their senators and representatives, the people of these states tend to reflect state, rather than national, attitudes.

It is hardly pertinent to assail the motives or the integrity of the conservative Southerners at the national capital. The violent opposition of Senator Glass of Virginia, for example, to nearly everything President Roosevelt has done on the domestic front, and to the whole philosophical basis of the New Deal, is no more to be taken as proof of insincerity on his part than the staunch support accorded the administration by, say, Senator Pepper of Florida is to be regarded as evidencing the sincerity of Mr. Pepper. One can disagree with nearly all the views of Senator Glass and those whose thinking on current economic and social issues parallels his, and still acknowledge that he and some of his fellow-conservatives are not infrequently more courageous and more intellectually honest than their critics.

The important committee chairmanships held by a number of these anti-New Dealers, and the opportunities enjoyed by others for sabotaging the President's legislative program, led Mr. Roosevelt to attempt to "purge" several of them in 1938. He made the effort over the protest of his wisest and most seasoned political adviser, Postmaster-General James A. Farley, who felt that it would fail, and would contribute heavily to intra-party bitterness. Mr. Roosevelt apparently preferred the counsel of such political neophytes as Thomas G. Corcoran and Harry Hopkins, who reportedly felt that the Southern conservatives could be beaten, if the President would throw all his influence and prestige into the fight.

Two prominent Southern senators accordingly were marked for a political garrotting in the Democratic primaries, along with another from a border state and a representative from New York City. The Southerners were Senator Walter F. George of Georgia and Senator E. D. ("Cotton Ed") Smith of South Carolina, while Senator Millard Tydings of Maryland and Representative John J. O'Connor of New York were likewise slated for the guillotine.

There was an immediate nationwide uproar from enemies of the President, who claimed that Mr. Roosevelt was trying to make himself a dictator. Such unheard-of meddling in the affairs of the states ought to be condemned by all right-thinking Americans, said these patriots. Nothing of the sort had been tried before, and the great Democrats of the past would revolve in their sarcophagi at the news of such arrogance and audacity. So the argument ran. It soon developed that Woodrow Wilson, as President, had successfully pursued an almost identical policy in 1918 with respect to two Southern members of the Senate who had fought his efforts in the international sphere, Senators Hardwick of Georgia and Vardaman of Mississippi.

There was, however, one valid argument against the Rooseveltian attempt to liquidate Senators George and Smith, which could not have been by any means so pertinent or persuasive twenty years previously, when Woodrow Wilson achieved the defeat of two of his senatorial adversaries. This was the argument that it is even more objectionable for a President to use Federal patronage and the Federal machine to defeat a candidate for office from a single state than it is for him to throw them into a nationwide election. In Wilson's day, these Federal mechanisms were infinitesimal by comparison with those which were available to Mr. Roosevelt. The thousands on WPA, the other thousands who were getting agricultural and social security benefits and other largess, and the enormously expanded blocs of Federal functionaries all presented a temptation to the White House in the summer of 1938. It must be said to the administration's credit, however, that only a spasmodic and feeble attempt seems to have been made to swing this Federal vote into line for the New Deal candidate in Georgia, and that no such effort appears to have been made in South Carolina. Moreover, this vote went heavily to the anti-New Deal candidates in both states.

An attempt was made by anti-administration elements to show that Senator George was really a New Dealer at heart, and that in seeking his defeat, Mr. Roosevelt was exhibiting a rule-or-ruin attitude. The point was stressed that the Georgian had voted for nearly all the major administration measures during the first term, and for others in the second. Mr. Roosevelt was depicted as having failed to abide by his statement that he would not oppose a candidate because of "a disagreement on a single issue," and Mr. George was depicted as having provided "general support of progressive trends." The fact is that whereas the Georgian is a high-minded and able man, he was never a progressive, and he not only opposed the public utility holding company bill, the Wagner housing bill and the Guffey-Snyder coal bill during the first Roosevelt term, but he fought the President's five favorite bills during the second term. These were the Supreme Court enlargement bill, the wage and hour bill, the Federal reorganization bill, the Wagner housing bill, and the farm bill. He voted reluctantly for the last-named, but before he did so, he described it as "not a farm bill . . . any more than a bill for the relief of the Indians."

It is a little difficult, therefore, to blame Mr. Roosevelt for wanting someone else in the Senate from Georgia, his "adopted state." He had similar reasons for wishing to defeat "Cotton Ed" Smith in South Carolina. Senator Smith's attitude toward the New Deal was roughly analogous to that of Senator George, and his windy ranting and bellowing on the floor of the Senate had long been calculated to make the judicious grieve. A man of less character and capacity than the Georgian, one of his favorite appeals to the electorate was his unctuous recital of how he walked out of the Democratic National Convention at Philadelphia in 1936, rather than permit a Negro minister to lead the gathering in prayer. "White supremacy," it appeared, had been endangered, and "Cotton Ed" was never a man to betray that sacred cause, nor yet the cause of Southern womanhood—two of the major "issues" of his campaign. The Senator was sometimes interrupted when discussing his New Deal record or the price of cotton with some such ejaculation from the audience as: "Come on, Ed, tell us about Philadelphy!" It is said that he never failed to respond. Hill-billies spat tobacco juice and leered, as "Cotton Ed" described, in well-embroidered detail, his refusal to be prayed over by a "nigger."

While President Roosevelt called openly for the defeat of Senator George and for the election of Lawrence Camp, a Federal district attorney, he did not make quite such an unequivocal fight on Senator Smith. True, he permitted Governor Olin D. Johnston to announce his senatorial candidacy from the White House steps, and he attacked Smith as "one who thinks in terms of the past," but he never asked specifically that Smith be defeated, although every one realized that such was his desire. Nor did he formally endorse Johnston.

In both Georgia and South Carolina, the anti-New Deal incumbents were renominated by thumping majorities. It was fairly obvious that this would happen, for the people of both states resented the intervention of the President in these elections. Although Georgia was Mr. Roosevelt's part-time residence, and his popularity with the Georgians was, and is, great, and although he has always carried Georgia and South Carolina by huge majorities, his attempt to oust two senators there who had been generally hostile to his program was repudiated in resounding fashion. The same thing happened in Maryland, where Senator Tydings was triumphantly returned, despite a record which was more hostile to the New Deal than that of most Republicans. The only successful presidential purgation carried out in these contests of 1938 was in New York City, where the victim was Representative O'Connor, who had fought Federal reorganization, the enlargement of the Supreme Court, and the President's attitude toward business.

Why did the effort to defeat Senators George and Smith fail so miserably in states which had voted heavily for the New Deal? Aside from the resentment at presidential "interference" in matters deemed to be primarily local, the candidates sponsored by the White House were not the strongest who could have been selected. That was especially true in the case of Lawrence

Camp, who had no state-wide following in Georgia, and whose selection as the man to run against Senator George was greeted with incredulous amazement by the politically informed. Mr. Camp was a poor third in the race, and by an ironic twist, his chief contribution was to insure the reëlection of Senator George. It is reliably declared that if President Roosevelt had not come to Georgia and made a speech for Camp, Eugene Talmadge, the third candidate, would have won. Since Talmadge is a considerably more aggressive foe of the New Deal than George, this constituted a slight gain, but the overwhelming defeat of Camp was a heavy blow to the President's prestige.

In South Carolina, Governor Johnston seemed a much stronger aspirant to the Senate than Camp did in Georgia. But although he had been elected to the governorship twice, he was running against a man who had been in the Senate for nearly thirty years, and who somehow managed to get the support of most of the Federal officeholders, despite the administration's strong preference for his adversary. Moreover, Johnston was by no means as effective a campaigner as his opponent, who was able to draw upon a large fund of anecdotes, quotations from Mother Goose and verses from the Bible, and to apostrophize Southern womanhood on the slightest provocation. Since South Carolina has the astounding requirement—a hangover from the horse and buggy era—that candidates for state office must appear jointly on the hustings in each of the forty-six counties, the man with the best political bedside manner and the most indestructible vocal cords enjoys a marked advantage. In addition, Johnston had angered and alarmed many South Carolinians by calling out the militia in an

effort to depose hostile highway commissioners—an illegal and high-handed performance. So he was over-
whelmed by "Cotton Ed," and the New Deal suffered
another setback.

Compounding the administration's loss of prestige in
the South and the country during the summer of 1938,
were the political campaigns in Kentucky and Tennessee. If the Federal jobholders and check-receivers were
not marshaled behind the New Deal candidates in
Georgia and South Carolina, they were herded into line
like cattle in the other two states mentioned. Senator
Alben Barkley of Kentucky, Democratic floor leader,
was opposed for reëlection by Governor "Happy"
Chandler. Mr. Barkley had enjoyed the administration's
aid shortly before in defeating the first Hatch Act, which
would have made the use of Federal patronage in such
contests more difficult. Since the bill was beaten, the
Federal office-holders and reliefees were mobilized as
promptly and as solidly as possible for the sitting senator, while Governor Chandler put all the pressure he
could command on the State employees, notably the
highway force, and the old-age pensioners, whose benefits came partly from the State. Barkley won, but his
victory can hardly have brought much satisfaction to
any one with a political conscience who had a hand in
it. The same thing would have been true if Chandler
had been successful.

In the neighboring state of Tennessee, the situation
was virtually duplicated. Prentice Cooper, candidate for
governor, and Tom Stewart, candidate for senator, enjoyed the support of the Federal machine, efficiently
swung into line by "Boss" Crump of Memphis and Senator McKellar. These political virtuosos did the job

with such thoroughness that a correspondent for the New York *Times* who surveyed the results on the ground reported that the thousands of Tennesseans on WPA had been whipped into line as though they had been a political army. Many were wearing Cooper-Stewart buttons. The other ticket, comprising Gordon Browning and George Berry, gubernatorial and senatorial candidates, respectively, tried to even up matters by raising a war chest from forced contributions "donated" by state officials and employees. The Cooper-Stewart ticket proved the stronger on election day, but the triumph was achieved, as has been indicated, by one of the rankest exhibitions of patronage jobbery the country has seen.

If further evidence is needed of the wholesale skulduggery resorted to in these Kentucky and Tennessee primaries, consider the report made before the vote was taken by the Sheppard committee of the United States Senate, following a careful inquiry. Although headed by the late Senator Morris Sheppard of Texas, a staunch New Dealer, the committee did not soft pedal its findings. It reported that in Kentucky "organized efforts have been made and are being made to control the vote of those on relief," and that in Tennessee "apparently every scheme and questionable device that can be used in a political contest to raise funds and to influence votes" was employed. While no one can excuse such methods, it should be said, in all fairness, that they were not typical of the South or of the country. We have seen that nothing remotely comparable took place in either Georgia or South Carolina during the same summer, although the Roosevelt administration was vitally interested in the primaries there. Nor have there been any comparable scandals involving relief and Federal patronage elsewhere in the United States.

While the issue of pro- and anti-New Deal was crystallizing in the four above-mentioned Southern states, there had arisen some years previously in a fifth state one of the most arresting political figures in American history, a man who built a dictatorship of devastating strength and lethal effectiveness. This most menacing of all the public characters to arise in the United States in modern times was, of course, Huey P. Long of Louisiana.

The story of how Long rocketed to national prominence while in his thirties, and became a definite threat for the presidency at the age of forty-one, is one of the most significant of American political sagas. It is a saga especially meaningful for the South, since the conditions which made Long's Louisiana dictatorship possible could have been almost duplicated in half-a-dozen other Southern states, given a leader with the astounding ability, industry, and ingenuity which Huey exhibited.

Long's birth, of poor parents, on a farm in Winn Parish, an infertile, gully-washed region in the Northern part of the state, gave him an appreciation of the hours of back-breaking toil and the years of battling against well-nigh hopeless odds which blight the lives of so many thousands of Southern families. His youth was spent under the rigorous conditions which afflict the homes of the great majority of Southern farmers. While it would be inaccurate to say that his background was "poor white," since his parents were from a somewhat higher social stratum, Huey Long knew the pinch of poverty throughout his formative years, and the fact should always be kept in mind. It serves to explain many of his later attitudes.

Long might be termed the final flowering, the epitome, of all the Southern rabble-rousers from "Pitchfork Ben" Tillman and Tom Watson down to the present day. His point of view was roughly similar to theirs, and as with them, his appeal was to the dispossessed masses. If he was what is commonly termed a demagogue, as he certainly was, it must be conceded that he knew how to strike a sympathetic chord in the hearts of share-croppers, tenants, and other Southerners whose economic disabilities were plunging them deeper and deeper into poverty and hopelessness. Long was in many ways one of the most revolting and despicable personalities of his time. He was vulgar, he was crude, he was crass, he was oafish, he was obscene, and he was, withal, a physical coward. Few of his contemporaries inspired such unbounded aversion. Yet it must also be conceded that few inspired such loyalty. The toilers of the Louisiana cane brakes, the illiterate Cajuns of the swamps and bayous, regarded him, and not without reason, as their deliverer, and were ready and anxious to follow him to the end.

By virtue of transcendent ability, coupled with demoniac energy, Huey Long rose to be master of Louisiana, after forging the only absolute dictatorship established north of the Rio Grande since the carpet-bag era. From the day when he successfully completed a three-year law course at Tulane University in seven months, it was evident that he was cast in an uncommon mold. He was to prove this time and again during the public career which began soon thereafter. Shrewd, sharp and unscrupulous, he outsmarted his opponents with monotonous regularity. Ambitious for power, impervious to criticism, and utterly ruthless, he was elected to the Louisiana Public Service Commission at the age of twenty-five. As a member of that body, he demonstrated a constant concern for the interests of the people, and an equally constant aversion for the corporations. His service there was a springboard to the governorship, and once he attained that office, he began building the machine which ultimately made him *Fuehrer* of Louisiana. Although he went later to the United States Senate, he remained the complete master of his state, directing its legislature, choosing its governors, and controlling its affairs from the smallest township to the city of New Orleans, and from the parish courthouse to the great capitol he built at Baton Rouge. It was all done, of course, under the terms of laws which he rammed through the Louisiana legislature, chiefly in 1934 and 1935, the same legislature whose members he openly boasted he could "buy like sacks of potatoes." Every policeman, fireman, school-teacher, school superintendent, and election commissioner, clerk, and watcher in Louisiana was appointed by the Governor, under this legislation, and the Governor, after Long went to Washington, was simply Long's stooge. The Senator also controlled the State Supreme Court, and his Attorney-General was empowered to supersede any local district attorney at will. Long, or the aforesaid stooge, could call out the militia at any time, contrary to the wishes of the local authorities, and the courts were specifically forbidden to interfere. Those who helped to promote the political fortunes of the "Kingfish," as Long styled himself, were practically immune from punishment of any kind, as witness the legislature's action in pardoning no fewer than 510 New Orleans election officials who had been indicted on charges of making fraudulent returns. Three of them had actually been convicted, but prosecution was rendered impossible by legislative fiat.

It would be inaccurate, however, to suggest that the Long machine in Louisiana was purely and solely an instrument for the perpetuation of its members in power. Even when all its vicious attributes are admitted, even when it is noted that Long had more than three-score relatives on the state payroll, even when it is conceded that he escaped impeachment before he had risen to absolute power simply because fifteen state senators refused to vote for impeachment under any circumstances (they were handsomely rewarded later with jobs for themselves and their families)—when all this is admitted, the fact remains that the poor people of Louisiana idolized Huey Long, and they had reason to idolize him. Why? Because he was their friend, because he had their interests at heart, because he saw that they "got a break" for the first time in generations.

The conservative gentlemen who had run Louisiana since the Civil War, had run it in the good old-fashioned tradition, which is to say that they ran it for the benefit of a small minority. As for New Orleans, the last stronghold in the state to fall before the assaults of the Kingfish, it had been corrupt and contented for half a century, when the city's better element set up its monumental howl against the ill-mannered upstart from Winn Parish.

New Orleans elections were proverbially rotten, the police were in the pay of vice rings, and the picturesque and charming city had been something of a political cesspool for decades when Huey tackled it and its mayor, the Hon. "Turkey Head" Walmsley.

So the situation both in New Orleans and in Louisiana as a whole was ripe for Long, when he rose to the governorship. The good burghers of the Crescent City were naturally revolted by his boorishness in receiving a distinguished European caller in pajamas, and throwing oysters on the floor of a fashionable restaurant, because he didn't approve of the manner in which they had been fried. They resented his loud-mouthed attacks on corporations, and his obvious concern for the submerged elements of the population. For years they kept New Orleans as an anti-Long citadel, and the war between its city machine, which was determined to get him, and the Long-controlled state machine, was war to the knife. When Huey finally overcame New Orleans, his revenge upon the town was sharp and bitter. The once-proud city was deprived of its right to tax, its local affairs were all placed under the Governor at Baton Rouge, and it was reduced to the status of a minor appanage of the State government.

Other localities which crossed Long's path were treated with the same ferocity, but many of the smaller communities and rural districts felt that he had been a benefactor, for his administration increased school attendance by 15,000 and provided free textbooks, taught about 100,000 illiterates to read and write (Louisiana had next to the highest illiteracy rate in the Union when Long took office), built thousands of miles of highways, shifted some of the tax burden from the poor to the well-to-do, gave the state a fine new capitol at Baton Rouge and a badly needed bridge more than four miles long, with its approaches, over the Mississippi at New

Orleans, and developed Louisiana State University so markedly as to make its rise one of the period's most striking educational phenomena.

But while Long was achieving these things he was not only forging the shackles of his dictatorship upon Louisiana, but he was raising the State debt to $150,-000,000, almost the highest in the Union, and the per capita cost of government to approximately twice the average cost for all the other states. Nevertheless, the thing which impressed the typical one-gallus Louisianian was that Huey Long was seeking ways in which to help him, and was making a genuine effort to improve his level of living. Finally, when the Kingfish promulgated his "share-the-wealth" program on a national scale, it made him a doughty challenger of President Roosevelt himself. Here was a program which struck a ready response in the breasts of the underprivileged elements everywhere, and speedily made Huey Long the most talked about senator in Washington, with several times as much office space as any of the others, and a large force to handle the 15,000 to 30,000 letters a day which his radio addresses on national hookups were bringing him from persons in all corners of the country.

President Roosevelt had sought the backing of these same elements, but the practical demonstration which Long had given in Louisiana of his ability to aid them, coupled with his wealth-sharing plan, which called for a $5,000 homestead for all, a minimum income of around $2,000, old-age pensions, and other benefits, made undoubted inroads on Mr. Roosevelt's following. This was especially marked after Long was able to demonstrate that a twelve-month of the New Deal had brought a

large increase in the number of millionaires, but a substantial reduction in the number of persons with $5,000-
a-year incomes. The fact that Federal agents began
giving his own tax returns a going over, caused him to
redouble his assaults on the administration. Mr. Roosevelt, who liked to travel on Vincent Astor's yacht, became "Prince Franklin, Knight of the *Nourmahal*" in
Huey's blistering broadcasts, while Secretary of Agriculture Wallace was "Lord Destroyer," and Secretary of
the Interior Ickes, "Lord High Chamberlain, the
Chinchbug of Chicago." The New Deal was just a "St.
Vitus' dance."

As Huey became an increasingly dangerous challenger
to the President, the administration was stampeded
into enacting a hastily put together and half-baked
tax program designed to take the edge off the Long
"share-the-wealth" plan. This didn't stop Huey. In addition to keeping up his attack on the New Deal, and
calling the President "a liar and a faker," he launched
a *panzer* attack on Postmaster-General Farley, with virtual charges on the Senate floor that he had used his
office for private gain. He also threatened to invade the
states of two administration stalwarts, Senators Joseph
T. Robinson of Arkansas and Pat Harrison of Mississippi, and to beat them for reëlection. These two elderly
gentlemen became intensely nervous at the prospect, for
they knew that Long had gone into Arkansas single-
handed with a sound truck in 1932, and after campaigning for one week for Mrs. Hattie Caraway had sent her
to the United States Senate with more votes than the
combined total of her four experienced male opponents,
although she had been confidently expected to run last.
Carrying out a speaking schedule which would have sent

a lesser man to the hospital in a state of collapse, Long spoke six times daily in Mrs. Caraway's behalf, and every district in which he appeared went for her overwhelmingly. After such an exhibition, it was not surprising that Huey's colleagues in the Senate and his other foes in Washington conceived a profound respect for his astounding powers as a campaigner.

It was Long's appeal to the people which was the secret of his strength; for, although he broke many of the accepted political rules, the people's interest in him waxed steadily. One of his heterodoxies was to have the bodyguard which he kept with him at all times, hold a personal or political enemy, while he pummeled the hapless and helpless wight. He ran away from elderly former Governor J. Y. Sanders following the gubernatorial campaign of 1927, during which Long had applied to Sanders various profane and obscene epithets. Sanders, about twice Long's age, sought satisfaction in a New Orleans hotel lobby, but Huey sprinted for the elevator. Sanders caught up with him there, and landed a few wild swings before they were separated. Then there was Huey's well-known fondness for alcohol. Although he practically stopped drinking after he got to Washington, as Governor of Louisiana he had frequently carried out his prodigious labors while in a semi-intoxicated condition, and the unseemly brawl in which he engaged in 1933 at the Sands Point Bath Club on Long Island, alone would have been enough to wreck the career of an ordinary man. But none of these imbroglios and peccadilloes even slowed him up.

"He is far abler than Hitler," one of his senatorial colleagues said of Long during the last year of his life, and while comparisons are proverbially odious, it would be difficult to prove that there was in America a more devastating combination of organizing ability, shrewdness, political prescience and diabolical, well-nigh superhuman driving force than Huey P. Long exemplified.

Such a man was clearly a threat for the presidency, and while Long had decided not to offer for that post in 1936, but to run again for Governor of Louisiana, he said openly that the presidency would "come later." Having built up a nationwide following in less than a year, on the basis of his rapidly growing "wealth-sharing" plan, it seemed that Long would be a factor on the national political scene for decades.

And then came the assassin's bullet. Whatever the precise circumstances which surrounded Long's death—and there are certain aspects of the killing which may never be entirely cleared up—his passing removed one of the most significant political figures of modern times. Wherein lay his significance? It lay in the fact that here was a man who could set up an ironclad dictatorship on American soil, without arousing such resentment that his rule became intolerable to the majority. And why was his iron-fisted control tolerable? Because he gave large groups of oppressed people benefits to which they were entitled, but which they had been denied. The average Louisiana swamp dweller, who found his taxes lightened and his children furnished with free schoolbooks, and who looked forward to that $2,000 income and $5,000 homestead which Huey said he would try to get for him, didn't care particularly whether he was free to criticize the Long régime, or whether that régime had the power to raise his taxes at will, if he became cantankerous. So long as the regnant machine evidenced

a fairly constant concern for his well-being, he had no
desire to criticize it, anyway.

Haven't we here the pattern for a domestic brand of
Fascism? Wasn't the system which Long established in
the Pelican State actually totalitarian rule, masquerad-
ing as democracy? Precisely, and therein lay its danger.
One of the ironic aspects of this situation was that
Senator Long himself told Dorothy Thompson, the
columnist, that if Fascism ever came to America, it
would come under the guise of democracy. The sort of
bogus democracy he himself had set up in Louisiana?
It would seem so, although he pretended to be oblivious
of the fact.

Huey Long never had a chance to extend that type
of "democracy" to the rest of the United States, but if
he had lived, there is no telling over what portions of
the republic his oriflamme might have waved. His profound understanding of the yearnings and aspirations of
the Southern masses—millions of whom did not during
his lifetime, and do not now, have the opportunities for
a better life to which they are rightfully entitled—enabled him to appeal to them as few men have done.
Moreover, his appeal seemed almost equally strong in
other sections, to judge from the enormous response to
his wealth-sharing program. It is readily conceivable
that he would have been President of the United States,
if he had survived.

The Long machine fell upon evil days, after the death
of its leader in 1935. The heirs of the Kingfish played
fast and loose with the dictatorial powers he bequeathed
to them, and in 1939 scandals broke with a resounding
roar. Thanks to the vigilance and unterrified independ-
ence of the New Orleans *Times-Picayune* and *States,*

a whole series of revelations was set in motion, and one
Long henchman after another was sent to the peniten-
tiary. On top of all this, Sam Houston Jones was elected
Governor on an anti-Long platform, and he set about
cleaning up the mess.

One would surmise that such a repudiation as this
for his organization would have besmirched the memory
of Huey Long beyond hope of redemption. Not so. The
Cajuns of the bayous and the sharecroppers of the cane
brakes swear by him to-day no less devotedly than they
did a decade ago. Nobody ever caught him with his
hands in the till, they say, and even though he did some
highhanded and illegal things, even though he may have
taken money which didn't belong to him, he distributed
most of it to the poor, who needed it. After all, they
point out, Huey left only $153,000 when he died, over
$58,000 of it in life insurance, and $20,000 more in his
law library. When one considers his almost unparalleled
opportunities for graft, and the manner in which his
successors seized those opportunities, it is arguable that
the contrast between Long and those who came after
him was considerable.

Even in New Orleans, for so many years the focus
of anti-Long feeling, his memory is kept wrapped in
bay leaves. Not that there is any less aversion for him
on the part of his onetime enemies there—the upper
crust of New Orleans society and the business, banking
and industrial interests, which always had excellent reasons for despising him. But as late as 1941 one could go
down to what once was called the Place d'Armes, the
lovely square near the Mississippi, which is the heart of
old New Orleans—where artists sun themselves beneath
the palms, the dulcet accents of France are heard along

the walkways, and the bells of St. Louis Cathedral summon the faithful to matins. One turned into the Cabildo, that fascinating repository adjoining the cathedral, where the story of the city is told in thousands of relics, from the time of 'Sieur de Bienville, the founder, down through the revolutionary and ante-bellum eras to the present day. And after one had lingered over the statue of mighty Bienville, who laid out Nouvelle Orléans in the name of the Sun King, and had looked into a hundred showcases with their rusty swords of long-dead warriors and their faded gowns of dark-eyed Creole belles who once roamed the streets of the Vieux Carré, one came suddenly upon a room on the topmost floor which was unlike anything which had gone before. It was the room dedicated to Huey Pierce Long, "the martyred governor."

There was the desk at which Governor Long worked, and the original manuscript of a law course which he outlined for a friend, several records of songs which he wrote or helped to write, including *Every Man a King,* and many photographs showing him leading cheers at L.S.U. football games, campaigning with Hattie Caraway in Arkansas, exchanging banter with Governor O. K. Allen, and in other characteristic poses. There was also a picture of his rather unpretentious home in Audubon Place, with the announcement that it was open to visitors daily, without charge.

It seemed rather incongruous that these relics should be housed in the Cabildo—as redolent otherwise of ante-bellum New Orleans as the Musée de Cluny in Paris is of pre-revolutionary France. When, therefore, the collection was removed to the former Long residence in Audubon Place, the change appeared salutary. It is visited there by a steady stream of admirers from many parts of the Union.

So the memory of Huey Long is not fading in the state which gave him birth. Some of his chief henchmen are wearing prison stripes, and the voters have smashed the remnants of his machine at the polls, but the thousands who poured into Baton Rouge for his funeral back in 1935, with mud on their shoes and a few coppers in their jeans, still look upon him as a Messiah, who would have provided them with a $5,000 homestead and a $2,000 income, if fate had not intervened.

"There would be a revolution in Louisiana, if anybody tried to move Huey Long's grave from the capitol grounds at Baton Rouge," one of the state's best-known and best-informed newspapermen told the writer recently.

The disturbing lesson of Long's career is that many voters are willing to forego certain of their civil liberties, in return for a measure of economic security. Jonathan Daniels has said cogently that "democracy is bread," and someone else has pointed out that "you can't eat the Bill of Rights." All-important as that document is, a hungry man can hardly be expected to attach undue importance to, say, his right of free speech, if the only answer to his pleadings for food is that he is still free to criticize those who deny it to him.

So the danger that someone like Huey Long will rise to power in America remains, as long as there are enough of the destitute and near-destitute to listen to his siren song. The surest means of avoiding such a catastrophe lies in affording the people reasonable economic security and economic justice through democratic means. Then the incentive to follow the next pied piper

Leon Price Picture Service

Living room of the Huey P. Long home in New Orleans, now a museum, and visited by tourists from all over the Union.

A.P. Photo

Governor Eugene Talmadge of Georgia, red suspenders
and all, in action before his constituents.

who promises the New Jerusalem will be reduced to a minimum.

Is there any Southerner above the political horizon to-day with the potentialities for arousing the type of enthusiasm on the part of the dispossessed which was evoked by Huey Long? The only possibility appears to be Governor Eugene Talmadge of Georgia, and Talmadge's deficiencies as an organizer appear to make him only a minor threat outside his cracker bailiwick. It also seems highly doubtful that he approaches Long in abilities of other sorts. Described acidulously by one observer as looking like "a cross between a ventriloquist's dummy and a sour-faced owl," Talmadge has always made his chief appeal to the "hick" element in Georgia. To that end, he exploits his double negatives and his red suspenders. Like Tom Watson before him— who had a residue of 17,000 followers in Georgia, even when his political fortunes were at their lowest ebb, and he himself had descended to the bathos of racial and religious vituperation and abuse—Gene Talmadge has a much larger nucleus of from 80,000 to 100,000 who are with him in victory or defeat. The depth of their devotion is symbolized in the action of one of them, who walked the forty-two miles from Cartersville to Atlanta carrying a possum for Gene under each arm.

Governor Talmadge was serving his third term as chief executive of Georgia in 1942, and apparently planning to run against Senator Richard B. Russell for the Senate, or to seek reëlection to the governorship. He had riveted his control upon the administrative machinery of the State, with the aid of an overwhelmingly friendly legislature. That legislature made him an absolute czar over all Georgia finances in 1941, empowering him to give such funds as he desired to any department, and to withhold monetary support from any other department. This made it possible for him to eliminate completely any state activity or agency which was politically obnoxious to him, thereby nullifying the act of the legislature which created the agency in the first place. Have such powers ever been exercised before in any American state, with the exception of Louisiana under Long?

Governor Talmadge, it is true, has always stood for economy, in contrast to the vast program of spending instituted by Long. He slashed automobile tags to $3 by executive order—many said his action was contrary to law—and cut the salaries of numerous state officials. And while both Talmadge and Long forced utility rate reductions, and both appealed primarily to the "ill-fed, ill-clothed and ill-housed" of whom President Roosevelt speaks so often, both denounced the New Deal. Talmadge said it was run by Socialists and Communists, and was woefully extravagant, and that its social security program was a "fraud." He expressed vigorous aversion to Mr. Roosevelt's relief program. "Let 'em starve!" he bawled to an interviewer from New York. "Any man can find a job, if he really wants to work." When his interlocutor protested that more than 1,000,000 persons were jobless in New York City, Gene retorted: "What you need in New York is not LaGuardia but Mussolini. A little castor oil would go a long ways toward starting the wheels of industry goin' again."

Talmadge's own record as Governor explains his invocation of the name of the Italian *Duce*. He used the Georgia National Guard to smash strikes and to oust political opponents, and he suspended constitutional requirements and nullified prerogatives of the legislature on his own motion, before the latter body collaborated with him toward that end in 1941. But his violations of the Georgia Constitution did not prevent him from serving as the key figure in a weird gathering held at Macon, Georgia, in 1936 under the auspices of something called the Southern Committee to Uphold the Constitution. Talmadge was invited by this motley aggregation of malcontents to become its presidential candidate, and thus to "split the Solid South." The convention had been called by John Henry Kirby, wealthy Houston lumberman, who had been investigated six years previously by Congress with something less than flattering results, and it was harangued by two notable spell-binders, in addition to Talmadge, namely, Thomas Dixon, Negro-baiting author of *The Clansman,* and the Rev. Gerald L. K. Smith, who was posing as leader of the "Share the Wealth" movement, and hence as inheritor of the Huey Long mantle. Although 10,000 delegates from seventeen states were announced as on the way, 2,400 persons actually showed up, nearly all of them henchmen of Talmadge from Macon and other points in Georgia. This "Grass Roots" convention of anti-Roosevelt Southerners turned out, therefore, to be a dismal fizzle, and nothing further was heard of it, or of the presidential aspirations of its "candidate." If and when he gets to the United States Senate, he may occupy the national spotlight again.

There are other exhibitionists among the South's public men, such as Senator Robert R. Reynolds of North Carolina, whose organ, the *American Vindicator,* gives off definitely Fascist overtones, and whose ravings on the Senate floor about "aliens" serve subtly to inculcate anti-Semitism. Among the governors there

is the chief executive of Texas, W. Lee O'Daniel, who
entered the campaign of 1938 as a rank outsider, and
by means of a sound truck, a hill-billy band which
specialized in the ditty *Pass the Biscuits, Pappy,* and
a promise of $30 a month for everybody over 65, per-
formed miracles as amazing as those of Huey Long in
Arkansas six years before. He was triumphantly elected
over eleven opponents, most of whom were far better
known than he was when he entered the campaign a
few weeks previously. He never delivered the pensions
he promised, but similar campaigning brought similar
results in 1940, and again he got more votes than all
his opponents combined. His victory in 1940 was won
despite the fact that a crooner and a guitar player were
weaned away from him by one of his rivals for the
nomination, a snuff-dipping former bell-hop, but
O'Daniel made himself invincible by adding "Texas
Rose," a girl ballad singer, to his troupe. The following
year he was elected to the United States Senate in a
campaign as bizarre as any that had gone before.

Such antics, as we have stated, are the exception,
rather than the rule, in Southern politics. More numerous below the Potomac than political medicine men
like Talmadge, Reynolds, and O'Daniel are the dignified ultraconservatives, such as Senators Bailey of North
Carolina, Glass and Byrd of Virginia, and George of
Georgia, not to mention more progressively-inclined
senators like Barkley of Kentucky, Hill of Alabama, and
Pepper of Florida. In the House, the Southern Democrats run the gamut from Rankin of Mississippi, with his
fulminations against Wall Street and his occasional anti-
Semitic outbursts, and more enlightened and civilized

liberals, like Rayburn of Texas, Sparkman of Alabama and Priest of Tennessee, to the erratic Dies of Texas, with his blunderbuss technique of investigating "un-American activities," and such reactionaries and labor-baiters as Smith of Virginia and Cox of Georgia. The great majority of Southern House members fall between the two extremes, although they tend definitely toward the conservative side.

The reasons for this conservatism have been examined, and the point has been made that the one-party system has been detrimental to the South. Yet it must be conceded that when the Democrats are dominant nationally, and there are Democratic majorities in both branches of the Congress, certain salutary results accrue to the South from the one-party system. During most of Mr. Roosevelt's sojourn in the White House, for example, the great bulk of the choice committee chairmanships in the Congress have been held by Southerners whose long tenure has given them seniority. During periods of Republican dominance, on the other hand, such as the country experienced most of the time prior to 1932, the South got little or no consideration. On the whole, the South would gain from both parties, if it could no longer be counted as bound to either. Presidential and vice-presidential candidates are chosen customarily from politically doubtful states, while cabinet posts and other important Federal positions usually go to appointees from areas whose party allegiance is in the balance. Nor is the South's influence in the Democratic National Convention commensurate with its long record of adherence to Democracy. Its consent to the abrogation of the two-thirds rule in 1936, under which for a century a united South was able to block any presidential candidate deemed obnoxious to it, has not been adequately repaid by the party. The convention of 1940 decided that hereafter each state which goes Democratic in a presidential election will receive two extra delegates in the succeeding national convention, but at conventions which follow a Democratic sweep, the South will be relatively weaker than it was in 1940. The Democratic National Committee will report on this matter further in 1944, and may recommend a more equitable plan.

Since Mr. Roosevelt's reëlection to a third term, the South has enjoyed a relationship to the Democratic party unlike any which has gone before, for the party in the North and West became in that election, predominantly the party of the urban masses. Whereas New York, Boston, and certain other northeastern cities had been Democratic for many years, the agricultural South and West had for a century been the party's traditional strongholds—with intervals, such as the two Cleveland administrations, when the Democrats appealed primarily to the financial centers of the Northeast. But in 1940, Mr. Roosevelt carried all the large cities of the country except Cincinnati, while losing many of the rural areas, and his victories in such states as New York, Pennsylvania, Illinois, and Ohio were attributed to his huge city majorities. In other words the rural, "dry," Protestant, Anglo-Saxons of the South found themselves in the same political bed with the urban, "wet," Catholic, foreign-born laborers of the Northern and Western metropolitan areas, not to mention the Negroes, who voted overwhelmingly for Roosevelt, as did nearly everybody on WPA. In the second of these two groups are substantially the same elements which caused four Southern states to bolt the Democratic presidential candidate in 1928.

The South has given no sign of restiveness under this situation, and perhaps it will give none. But those Southerners who feel that their section now is bedded down with uncongenial elements, have at least a partial remedy at hand. That remedy lies in working for the establishment of a strong Republican party in the region. From every standpoint, such a development would redound to the ultimate benefit of a section which has adhered overlong to traditional thinking. Many Southerners who currently profess allegiance to the Democratic party would be far more congenially situated as Republicans if they could but forget Thad Stevens and Ben Wade, and put out of their minds the fact that to their grandfathers the Democratic party was only slightly less sacrosanct than the Army of Northern Virginia. A South divided politically on the basis of principle is far preferable to an eternally solid South, ordering its political allegiance in accordance with issues which were vital in 1875, but which have been well-nigh defunct these forty years. However, if such a South is in the making, there are few signs of it. Much of the region is still wrapped in the apathy and decay that is the inevitable concomitant of one-party rule. It would seem that strong political purgation is what the South needs, after all.

III

DIXIE AND THE NEW DEAL

NO President since the Civil War has revealed the understanding of, and the concern for, the South's problems that Franklin D. Roosevelt has evidenced. Woodrow Wilson was a Southerner by birth and upbringing, but his preoccupation with the first World War and its aftermath seems to have made him relatively unaware of regional problems, and he may well have hesitated before addressing himself too vigorously, as President, to the needs of his native section. But Mr. Roosevelt, whose part-time residence in his "adopted state" of Georgia has given him a deep interest in Southern social and economic relationships, and whose birth and official residence in New York lends a flavor of nonpartisanship to his regional predilections, has been interested for a good many years in the well-being of the South, and more specifically in that of its underprivileged elements. He finds no validity in the dictum enunciated by a cynic of another day, that "the masses" are indistinguishable from "them asses."

This is not to say that all measures instituted under the New Deal actually have brought improvement in Southern levels of living. On the contrary, some of them missed fire, as a consequence of having been poorly conceived or ineffectively executed. Waste and overlapping characterized certain of these efforts, especially in the early years of the New Deal. For example, during

Mr. Roosevelt's first term a prominent Southerner, intimately familiar with the needs of Southern agriculture, and sympathetic to New Deal objectives, counted the number of separate Federal agencies which were trying to help the farmer in one Southern county, and reported finding no fewer than twenty-seven! He also asserted that too many of those who were endeavoring to administer this multiplicity of criss-crossing bureaus were incompetent. However, it was well-nigh inevitable that the comprehensive program of farm relief built under pressure from the ground up by the Roosevelt Administration should have suffered from a goodly number of infirmities. This would be almost unavoidable in the case of agencies established in the middle of an unprecedented depression, and designed to cope with urgent and widely ramified situations. However, a large proportion of the duplication and lost motion now has been eliminated.

The early and continuing interest of President Roosevelt in all matters pertaining to the Southern states was nowhere more evident than in the New Deal's program for agricultural rehabilitation. His concern for the South was emphasized again in 1938, when he requested the National Emergency Council, of which Lowell Mellett was executive director, to provide "a statement of the problems and needs of the South." When formulation of that statement was begun, the President wrote: "It is my conviction that the South presents right now the nation's No. 1 economic problem—the nation's problem, not merely the South's. For we have an economic unbalance in the nation as a whole, due to this very condition of the South." The President said this with a view to aiding the region toward a constructive solution

of its difficulties, but he aroused a certain amount of
Southern ire, for there were residents of the region who
felt that he had reflected on the former Confederacy by
focusing attention upon it as a domain of poverty,
illiteracy, and inequality of opportunity. They pointed
quickly to the huge Federal relief payments made to
such states as New York and Pennsylvania, and argued
therefrom that these centers of unemployment were the
nation's major economic problems.

It is undeniable, however, when the complete picture
is taken into account, that Mr. Roosevelt was right in
terming the South "the nation's No. 1 economic problem." While the depression naturally caused havoc in
such highly industrialized regions as the Northeast and
the manufacturing areas of the Middle West, this was
a temporary phenomenon, whereas the economic disabilities of the South have a different derivation. In
good times and in bad, the South has the lowest per-
capita income, the most inadequate educational facilities, and the worst health and housing in the country.
True, the South's poor statistical showing is related importantly to the fact that its population is about one-
third colored. If the Negro population of the other
regions of America was proportionately as large, their
rankings in the statistical indexes probably would be
not greatly unlike that of the South. The Negro sections
of the Northern cities are uniformly below those of the
white sections with respect to these same indexes. This
is not said in derogation of the Negroes—who have had
numerous handicaps to surmount since emancipation
and whose poor showing is attributable, in no small
measure, to the whites—but it is a simple statement of
fact. While the white population of the South also ranks

below that of other sections in various categories, the regional rankings would be much more nearly equal if the Negroes did not pull down the Southern averages all along the line.

The economic retardation of the South was well-known to students before the above-mentioned compilation was made by the NEC in 1938, which explains Mr. Roosevelt's early concern for the formulation and execution of a program designed to bring relief. Basic to any large-scale plan for raising levels of Southern living was, of course, a comprehensive approach to the South's agricultural problem, for in a predominantly rural region, dependent in so large a measure upon the one-crop economy, such a plan was fundamental. It was especially incumbent upon the Federal Government to provide a solution, for its failure to do so after the Civil War was responsible to a considerable degree for the rise of the single crop, tenancy, and sharecropper system, with its "furnishing merchant" and its all too frequent cycle of hopelessness and poverty for the small tenant or share-cropper without resources. The ruined planters, whose cash was wiped out by the War, naturally turned to the small farmers who were willing to work their lands in return for a share of the yield. It was a natural development, under the circumstances, and no more blame attaches to the South because of it than to the North, by virtue of its failure, through government aid, to make possible the establishment of a more equitable, more workable, and fairer system.

The fact that there were many inequities became clear in the eighties. The story of the Southern agrarians' struggle for better prices and more just legislation is almost the political history of the last decade and a half of the nineteenth century. Beginning with the Farmers' Alliance and continuing until the emergence of the Populist movement, the resurgent "wool hat boys" became more and more articulate. This was the period when such political leaders as "Pitchfork Ben" Tillman of South Carolina and Thomas E. Watson of Georgia voiced the South's agrarian discontent and championed the rural population against the railroads and the era's other industrialist exploiters. The Charleston *News and Courier* referred to Tillman as "the leader of the Adullamites, a people who carry pistols in their hip pockets, who expectorate upon the floor, who have no toothbrushes and comb their hair with their fingers." This organ of the lowland aristocracy did not feel that the Tillmanites had any genuine grievances. Henry Grady and his Atlanta *Constitution* were similarly skeptical with respect to Watson and the Georgia farmers. Grady painted a glowing picture in his celebrated Dallas speech of how "plenty rides on the springing harvests," but Watson remarked sourly that "plenty rides on Grady's springing imagination." He added that on the average Georgia farm, "a billygoat would have to labor twelve hours a day for his living."

The agrarian revolt on which Watson, Tillman, and the rest rode to power in the South brought substantial improvement in the farmer's lot. Yet the one-crop system and its concomitant evils remained largely unchanged. Grover Cleveland's presidential interests were largely urban, and after he left the White House a steady succession of Republicans held sway there. Woodrow Wilson's first term brought certain enactments for the benefit of Southern agriculture, notably a rural credits law and lower tariffs, but in his second term he was concerned almost wholly with the first World War and its aftermath. His three Republican successors in the presidency took little or no interest in the Southern farm problem. It remained for Franklin D. Roosevelt vigorously to espouse the cause of the South's underprivileged tenants and 'croppers.

There are those, of course, who contend that the sharecropping system is far from the atrocious form of of near-slavery which some have pictured. For example, the late William Alexander Percy expressed the view in his beautiful book of reminiscences, *Lanterns on the Levee,* that "it is one of the best systems ever devised to give security and a chance of profit to the simple and unskilled." Mr. Percy pointed to the average annual income of $437.64 enjoyed by the 124 families on his plantation in the Mississippi Delta, and drew the conclusion that the iniquities of the system not only had been grossly exaggerated, but were non-existent.

Such an opinion is quite unsound. Mr. Percy was led into the unfortunate error of assuming that nearly all other large Southern plantations were like his "Trail Lake," and that other Southern landlords were like himself. Would that they were! It is not unfair to the average Southern cotton grower to say that while he is as just, as able, and as conscientious as his counterpart in any other section of America, he is not the man to make such a system function successfully and equitably. Mr. Percy obviously was a humane, understanding, and tolerant person, whose success with sharecropping was comparatively rare. It should not be forgotten that his plantation was in one of the richest agricultural sections in the world, where erosion has not taken the frightful toll which so often is a notable feature of the Southern landscape. Moreover, the families at "Trail Lake" evidently belonged to a different genus from the hundreds of thousands of migratory tenants and 'croppers, both white and black, who are almost constantly on the move in the cotton belt, dragging after them a few dented pots and pans, a few sticks of battered furniture, and half a dozen or more ragged children. The stability of those at "Trail Lake," with their average annual income of $437.64, was in dreary contrast to the debt-ridden one-gallus farmers of most of the cotton states, over one-third of whom move every year from tumble-down shack to tumble-down shack, carrying their irresponsible farming methods with them, and exhausting the soil to the limit of their abilities, since they have no incentive to do anything else. Many are diseased, and hence are without energy or ambition. One of their number has been quoted as describing his daily routine as follows: "Sometimes I sets and thinks. Sometimes I just sets." (The terms "tenant" and "sharecropper" are used interchangeably by many persons, although in reality a tenant usually is better-circumstanced than a sharecropper, since normally he is able to supply a larger percentage of his requirements, such as work stock, feed, tools, and seed.)

Mr. Percy conceded that the system under which he and thousands of other cotton planters operated their plantations had one drawback—"it must be administered by human beings to whom it offers unusual opportunity to rob without detection or punishment." That is certainly a "drawback," to put it mildly, especially since there is hardly ever a written contract between the landlord and the tenant or 'cropper. Another objection is that the entire system is geared to one-crop farming, with the single crop as the basis of credit for both landlord and tenant, so that the landlord too often encourages, or requires, the tenant or 'cropper to raise only the cash crop and not to utilize any of the land in planting vegetables or fruit trees. Still another objection lies in the 35 to 40 per cent interest rate charged the tenant or 'cropper by the "furnishing merchant." It may be remarked that the uncertainty of one-crop farming makes the landowner likewise a poor credit risk and causes him to pay interest rates as high as 20 per cent— further evidence that the South's cotton and tobacco economy is far from ideal, either from the standpoint of the landlord or that of his tenants.

The Roosevelt administration decided in 1933 to attack this unsound system through a varied program. By the time that program had evolved completely, it included government credit and debt-adjustment aids for the farmer, crop control, soil conservation, parity payments, crop loans, rehabilitation of farm families through loans and education, constant emphasis on subsistence farming, encouragement of farm coöperatives and group medical care, and aid to tenants in the purchase of homes. As already noted, there were serious imperfections and duplications in parts of this program. Undoubtedly too large a share of early AAA payments, intended for both landlords and tenants, found its way into the pockets of landlords. The extent to which this occurred approached the level of a scandal in many areas. Moreover, in 1934 a group of thirty-three nominal farmers received no less than $38,000,000 in government checks. In addition, AAA crop restrictions threw thousands upon thousands of tenants and sharecroppers on relief. Subsequently the system was tightened up, and the farmers who are lowest in the economic scale have been benefiting to a larger degree from crop control, soil conservation, and parity payments.

It must be conceded, however, that, in some respects the farm program for the South, like that for the nation, is unsound. The measures devised for the relief of that long-suffering individual whom David L. Cohn terms "the man with the woe," have conflicted, at times, with one another. For example, in 1941 there were no feasible means by which the Federal system of parity loans and payments could be reconciled satisfactorily with the principle of cash crop limitation. On the other hand, it is indisputable that much of the Federal farm program has been of distinct and lasting benefit to the South.

Let us glance at the record of the Farm Security Administration, which has done much to point the way to greater opportunity for the tenants, sharecroppers, and migrant laborers of the cotton belt. Tens of thousands of these once-despised agriculturalists have shown that they have ability, ambition, and the capacity for achievement, once they are given an incentive to better their lot. A total of $570,000,000 was loaned to over 900,000 needy farm families, about half of them in the South, from 1935 to 1941, for rehabilitation purposes. Although every one of these borrowers was considered a "bad credit risk," when judged on the basis of the usual business criteria for determining such things, there are sound reasons for believing that 80 per cent of the loans will be repaid. Most of the uncollectible 20 per cent were made in such sections as the Dust Bowl, where the elements have combined to thwart the best inten-

FSA photo by Marion Post Wolcott

Alert farm men and women at an evening class conducted by a vocational home economics worker, Mt. Zion School, Coffee County, Alabama.

Photo by *North Carolina Department of Conservation and Development*

Clingman's Dome, North Carolina, highest point in the Great Smoky Mountains National Park.

tions. Nearly $200,000,000 of the principal had been repaid by August, 1941, although much of it was not yet due. About 222,000 families had taken care of their loans in full by that date, FSA officials said.

What could be more constructive than a service of this character to one-crop farmers whose chances of breaking out of the dreary round of cotton raising, and of escaping from their diet of meat, meal, and molasses, would otherwise have been virtually nil? These rehabilitation loans, averaging around $600 per family, have made it possible for tenants and share-croppers to acquire the livestock and the simple equipment needed to produce a diversified food supply, as well as feed for the stock; to develop farm enterprises producing food for the market, and to adopt methods which build soil fertility. A recent FSA survey of 360,-000 families which had had such loans for periods ranging from one to five years showed that they had increased their average net incomes by 43 per cent, their net worth, over and above all debts, by 26 per cent, and the worth of foodstuffs raised for home use by 66 per cent. Milk, fruit, vegetables, and meat produced on these farms were quadrupled or quintupled, with corresponding improvements in health and living standards. The FSA has bettered the health of its borrowers further by aiding in the setting up of county medical plans, in coöperation with local medical societies and state medical associations, under which participants pay a fixed sum annually for medical care. It also has established farm debt-adjustment committees composed of local farmers and businessmen who arrange for a meeting between a farmer and his creditors where an effort is made to arrive at a solution satisfactory to both par-

ties. The FSA likewise encourages small farmers to
band together for the purchase of relatively expensive
farm equipment or breeding stock, such equipment or
stock to be owned coöperatively by the group.

The FSA calculated recently that this entire service,
plus the estimated 20 per cent of uncollectible loans,
is costing the Federal treasury annually less than $75
net per family rehabilitated. The figure includes all administrative overhead. Consider what this means. Hundreds of thousands of farm families are being put on
their feet permanently, are being taught how to feed
themselves decently, how to clear up their long-standing
health problems, how to diversify their crops and to preserve the soil, and greatly to increase their net incomes
and net worth—all for only a fraction of the cost of
keeping them on relief, assuming the FSA figures to be
correct.

A recent development of the FSA program in Alabama, Georgia, Florida, and South Carolina, growing
out of the current "food for defense" effort, is particularly interesting and exciting. More than 52,000 "hard-
scrabbling, ragged-edge patch farmers" of those states
who already were FSA borrowers, were loaned an average of $87.50 each additional with which to buy 50
more chickens and one brood sow or two milk cows.
If they preferred not to take the sow or the cows, they
could double the number of chickens, and get 100. The
results were almost instantaneous as well as extraordi-
narily gratifying. Hardly more than two months after
the scheme was put into operation, some 1,800,000
broilers and fryers were en route to the markets of the
four states in question from these 52,000 farms, many
of which had never raised a chicken for sale before.

The chickens not only brought the farmers $750,000 in cash, but the pullets were retained for future laying and larger flocks. Instead of squandering this new-found income on useless extravagances, most of the families turned it back into additional chicks, thus helping to guarantee for themselves a much more adequate income in the future and a better-balanced diet than they had ever had before, officials of the Federal agency reported.

Capitalizing to the utmost on this striking evidence of a desire on the part of many small, handicapped farmers of the South to seize upon valid opportunities for bettering themselves, the FSA set out to organize coöperative associations in each of the 339 counties in the four states. It expected to have most of these organizations functioning by the end of 1941. No stores were to be established, and all purchasing was to be done through local sources of supply, thus giving local merchants the benefit of the newly-developed buying power. Participation in these buying and selling associations makes available to members the use of implements and blooded stock, as well as medical, dental, and veterinary service. And so far from competing with, or taking patronage away from, established business or professional men, they seem to provide both with more solid and better-paying customers or clients than either group has ever enjoyed.

A great virtue of this particular form of rural rehabilitation, as well as of those which the FSA developed previously, lies in the relatively low financial outlay. It costs eight or nine times as much to provide a farmer with the money to buy his home as it does to lend him enough for the sort of thoroughgoing rehabilitation which has been outlined above. While home ownership is desirable, tenancy *per se* is not necessarily bad. When a tenant can be provided with intelligent guidance, reasonable stability and comfort, together with hope for the future, his situation calls for no jeremiads. Consequently, given the financial limitations of the Federal treasury, and the tremendous burdens to which it is being subjected, the tenancy rehabilitation program impresses one as better suited to present day needs than the much more costly farm-purchase program. The latter FSA activity has been operating on hardly more than a token basis, owing to the prohibitive expense.

The manner in which the rehabilitation program has been functioning, and the extraordinary results which have been obtained through it, should go far to answer those who say that the Southern tenants and 'croppers are beyond redemption. Spier Whitaker of "Shell Castle," Enfield, North Carolina, made some observations recently on this subject in the Raleigh *News and Observer* which seem to demonstrate unfamiliarity with the record already made by the Southern clients of the FSA. Conceding that the sharecropping system is bad, since it is "worse for the landowners than the workers," Mr. Whitaker went on to say that "the tenants left to their own devices have become with each generation more worthless, until to-day they are ignorant, lazy, trifling, shiftless, improvident, careless, destructive, irresponsible, and totally unreliable." Then he added:

It has been popular of late for the uplifters from the North to come down here to take pictures of the cotton growing up to the cabin doors and to go back shouting about the greed of the landowners. My own experience and observation have been that the tenants are as much, if not more, interested in nothing but cash crops than the landlords, and the reason they don't keep chickens, pigs and cows, and have gardens is because they don't know how and don't want to know how, and wouldn't if they did know. It is too much work, and work is the last thing they are interested in.

Perhaps the key phrase in Mr. Whitaker's arresting series of observations is "the tenants *left to their own devices* have become with each generation more worthless." Much that he says in criticism of them is true, but largely for the very reason that they have been neglected and forced to shift for themselves in the face of wellnigh hopeless and insuperable odds. Almost anybody would become lazy and improvident under similar circumstances. The fact that so many are responding eagerly to the opportunities furnished them by the Federal Government is excellent evidence that what they need, primarily, is a chance, something which has long been denied them.

True, the census indicates that the number of lowincome farmers almost doubled between 1929 and 1939. This calculation takes no account of government payments, and 1939 was not as good a farm year as 1940, but we have here a highly disquieting phenomenon, and one which underscores the growing magnitude of the farm problem. It does not by any means prove, however, that FSA's program has been a failure. That program admittedly reaches only a fraction of the lowincome group, and while it seems obvious that most of those reached have been benefited, the number is too small, as yet, to reverse the downward trend.

It should be said that FSA has made serious mistakes. The most recent was its action in loaning federal funds to farmers in Alabama, Georgia, and South Carolina for the payment of back poll-taxes. This was a bad

blunder, and was compounded when agency officials
explained that they justified the loans on the theory
that "citizenship is the right and that exercise of citizenship is the duty of Americans." In the next breath
they said they were making no poll-tax loans to Negroes,
in deference to local customs, so the argument was un-
convincing. The plan should never have been instituted.[1]

Other farm credit agencies—this time under the Farm
Credit Administration—which make loans to fairly well-
circumstanced farmers are the Production Credit Associations. Administered in the counties by local leaders
who are familiar with local conditions, these federally-
sponsored associations extend credit to farmers who wish
to borrow on their forthcoming crops, at reasonable
rates, especially for the purpose of shifting from the
single crop to more diversified farming. Production
Credit Associations not only provide needed funds for
agriculturalists who are regarded as good risks in their
communities but they facilitate planning in rural areas.

The campaign designed to provide a better chance
for the Southern farmer naturally is bound up closely
with the outlook for cotton and tobacco, particularly
the former. The late W. J. Cash showed convincingly
in his *The Mind of the South* that the Roosevelt Administration is not chiefly responsible for the South's
loss of its foreign market for cotton, since tariffs enacted
under President Hoover, combined with America's failure to handle the war-debt problem intelligently, were
responsible to a greater degree than the New Deal's raising of the price through government subsidies. In considerable measure, the same thing is true of the decline

[1] Enemies of FSA made sweeping, and apparently much exaggerated,
charges against it before a congressional committee in February, 1942,
and demanded an investigation of its operations.

in the foreign market for tobacco. Of course, both were hit hard by the war, which shut them out of important markets both in Europe and the Far East.

With some 12,000,000 persons in the Southern and border states directly or indirectly dependent upon cotton, it is obvious that this crop is of immense importance to the region, despite all the current emphasis upon the need for breaking the bonds which tie so much of the South to this single staple. With foreign markets evaporating, special efforts have been put forth to increase domestic consumption, and these efforts have brought results. All records for the domestic consumption of cotton were broken during 1941. Dr. Claudius T. Murchison, president of the Cotton-Textile Institute, predicted an annual domestic cotton consumption after the war of 10,000,000 to 12,000,000 bales. Many new uses for cotton have been devised by researchers. Cotton houses, cotton insulation, cotton plastics, cotton hosiery, and so on, together with addition uses for cotton seeds, hulls, and linters make the outlook seem relatively propitious, particularly since the price of cotton in 1941 was around 16 cents, or nearly double that of the previous year, and the total cash income of the farmers for the season of 1941-42 was expected to be the highest in a dozen years. The Federal cotton stamp program also helped, as did the export subsidies on cotton goods shipped to Latin-America. During 1941 a long-term research and consumption promotion program was set in motion by the American Cotton Manufacturers' Association, in coöperation with the National Council and the Cotton-Textile Institute at an estimated ultimate cost of $500,000.

Since the South is cursed with vast areas of badly

eroded land, the statement has been made that some of it won't raise anything but spiders. Other Southern soil has been described as "so sterile, you can almost hear the cotton grunting in an effort to grow." The boll weevil also is a continuing problem. They erected a monument to the insect at Enterprise, Alabama, years ago, in appreciation of its having forced a certain amount of agricultural diversification in the South, but the Georgia farmers who saw from 40 to 50 per cent of the state's 1941 cotton crop succumb to its depredations probably are in no mood to subscribe to a similar memorial. In Arkansas and Louisiana, infestation was said to be the heaviest in fifteen years, while 100 per cent infestation was reported in many areas of Northern Mississippi. President Patterson of Tuskegee, in his annual appeal to Southerners for contributions toward Christmas stockings for underprivileged Negro children of the rural South, stated that the weevil had brought "a new low in cotton production" in some areas, and that despite the increase in the price of cotton, tenants, sharecroppers, and day laborers on farms in many sections of the southeastern states "are still without adequate security against suffering and privation during the coming winter."

Cotton growing in the South to-day is gradually falling beneath the sway of the machine, at least in the flat plains of Texas and adjacent states. The threat to the whole Southern economy inherent in the Rust cotton picker never has materialized, since the picker is still quite expensive, and most cotton farmers are unable to afford one. When these machines are reduced in cost, and the manufacturer swings into large scale production, it is estimated that each robot picker will replace about

FSA *photo by Delano*

Erosion in Heard County, Georgia, a landscape which is unfortunately duplicated in many parts of the South.

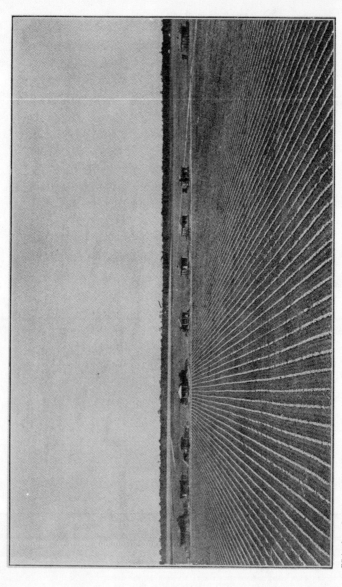

FSA photo by Marion Post Wolcott

Tenant houses on a cotton plantation near Rolling Fork in the rich Mississippi Delta.

seventy-five hand pickers. Much less complex mechanical harvesters are in use on the plains of Western Texas, but these are said to be unsuited to any other cotton state. The introduction of these machines, and of tractors for plowing, harrowing, and cultivating the plant in the entire cotton belt, has greatly reduced the labor required for cotton production. Here we have another reason why thousands of Southern tenants, sharecroppers, and migratory workers have been thrown on relief. (The migrant farm labor problem in the South is most severe in Texas and Florida, where special Federally operated camps have been established.)

The impact of wholesale replacement of men with machines, particularly upon the Southwest, has been softened by some of the Federally instituted and supported measures already outlined. In addition, newspapers in the region have been important corrective influences. The Memphis *Commercial Appeal,* for example, launched a "plant to prosper" movement in 1934 for the states of Tennessee, Arkansas, Mississippi, and Missouri, with emphasis upon diversification of crops, soil conservation, and home improvements, and prizes for the farmers providing the best records. Interest grew rapidly, with the result that Southern farm families with hundreds of thousands of members now are participating each year. A large number of newspapers are coöperating with the *Commercial Appeal,* and it is estimated that over $50,000,000 in additional income has been channeled into the pockets of farmers in the four above-mentioned states, as a direct consequence of the "plant to prosper" movement. Annual contests, similar in conception, were inaugurated in 1940 for Louisiana and South Mississippi by the New Orleans

Times-Picayune, with the agricultural extension services of the two states and the New Orleans Association of Commerce as co-sponsors. Prize-winning farmers are those who have done most to improve their farms, farm homes, and farm life.

Such efforts as the foregoing, combined with those of Federal, state, and county agricultural services, have done a vast deal to bring improved levels of living to the Southern farmer. The news that in 1939 the cash income from cotton and cotton-seed in fourteen Southeastern and Southwestern states totaled only $598,000,-000, as against $666,000,000 from live stock and livestock products, was among the most significant of recent decades, and showed that the shackles of the one-crop system were being rent asunder. Since then, the trend away from cotton has been accelerated, with widespread benefits to the Southern population as a whole. The United States Department of Agriculture announced in 1941 that during the preceding ten years, the number of milk cows increased 25 per cent in the cotton states, the largest increase for any region of America. Much of the increase was said to have been on new farms, or farms which did not have cows at the beginning of the period. Establishment of the beef and dairy industry in the Black Prairie Belt of Alabama and Mississippi is one of the most significant developments of the past decade in the Deep South. Once King Cotton's exclusive domain, this rich soil now produces lush grass for cattle, and they graze by the thousands along a belt 300 miles long and 30 miles wide. The cattle-tick problem does not appear serious. There seems to be no need for a slogan such as the one framed by Huey Long in his early days, when he made his political début by serving as campaign manager for an aspirant to the imposing position of tick inspector for Winn Parish. Huey's rousing assurance to the voters, as he sought support for his candidate in the great battle against the tick, was: "Them that's got 'em will get rid of 'em, and them that ain't got none won't get none."

In the tobacco states—chiefly North Carolina, Kentucky, Virginia, Tennessee, South Carolina, and Georgia —there are likewise some thriving cattle and dairy sections. Conditions in these states have been better, on the whole, than those in the bulk of the cotton belt, and there has been less dependence upon a single money crop. Yet the furnishing merchants, the wasteful mining of the soil, and the lack of stability which characterize the cotton states are excessively prevalent in the tobacco states, two or three of which also grow considerable cotton. The same Federal measures which have aided the tenants of the cotton belt in breaking out of the crushing one-crop cycle have been applied on a smaller scale in the tobacco belt—on a smaller scale because the need is less. It should be noted in this connection, too, that since the opening of the second World War in 1939, the tobacco market has been kept from near collapse by the Federal Government's large purchases of the leaf for the British companies.

An important Southern crop which has fared less happily at the hands of the Roosevelt Administration is Louisiana and Florida sugar-cane. Curtailment of these states' sugar quotas by the New Dealers at a time when producers of competing cane in Cuba, Hawaii, and the Philippines were being generously treated did little to create enthusiasm for the national administration in the sugar-growing sections of the Deep South.

In 1939, nearly one-half of the Louisiana sugar land was idle because of quota reductions. Arguments from Secretary of Agriculture Henry A. Wallace that Southern sugar is an "inefficient industry," which should be eliminated gradually by exposing it "to the winds of world competition," naturally failed to assuage the feelings of sugar planters whose liquidation was thus envisioned. Nor were those planters reconciled to their fate by the argument that the "good neighbor" policy was adequate justification for allowing Cuban sugar men to export from four to six times as much of their product to the United States as Louisiana and Florida combined were allowed to grow. Beet-sugar producers of the West and Middle West were likewise given quotas four to six times as large as those of the South's cane growers. However, the Pacific war has reduced shipments of Philippine and Hawaiian sugar to such a degree that marked expansion of the Louisiana and Florida crops is anticipated.

The producers of Southern sugar-cane seem to be the only substantial bloc of agriculturalists in Dixie who feel that the New Deal has been more harmful to them than otherwise. The much larger groups of cotton and tobacco growers take the opposite view, despite the fact that the New Deal has brought little appreciable benefit to many of the least fortunate tenants, 'croppers, and migrant laborers among them. Southern farming as a whole also owes a debt of gratitude to the monumental work of agricultural planning which the Roosevelt administration launched with the establishment of the Tennessee Valley Authority. The much debated and fiercely fought TVA seems at last to have emerged from the stage of controversy and contention and to be making not only a vital and indispensable contribution to national defense but also to be providing parts of seven Southern states having an area nearly equal to that of Great Britain with the best large-scale agricultural planning being done anywhere in America. The Tennessee and its tributaries flow through portions of Virginia, Kentucky, North Carolina, Tennessee, Georgia, Alabama, and Mississippi, a region presenting some of the worst examples of eroded soil and handicapped humanity in the United States. There can be no question that better levels of living for thousands have been provided in this valley under the ægis of able Federal experts. Doubters should read the joint report made in 1941 by the seven land-grant colleges in the area. These institutions affirm that the experiments which TVA is conducting in all phases of rural life are not only providing data of great practical value to the people of the valley but are also benefiting other regions, and affording the prospect of still more momentous advances in the future. TVA is, in truth, a laboratory in which solutions for the problems of the Tennessee Valley's, and America's, rural population are being studied scientifically and hammered out in the crucible of experience. The spectacular and resounding controversies over the hydro-electric power developments of TVA, which now seem to be at an end, served largely to obscure from the public view the Authority's highly significant and far-reaching program of rural rehabilitation. The development of cheap and efficient fertilizers, systematic education of farmers in the need for soil conservation, and the planting of cover crops to prevent further washing away of the topsoil, reforestation, and cheap electricity for performing manifold tasks on the farm are among the noteworthy contributions made by TVA in this sphere. Not only so, but its industrial technicians in coöperation with universities in the area have perfected or invented various devices and processes, such as a method of quick freezing which will provide new opportunities for local, decentralized industry; a reasonably priced electric hay drier, which likewise opens new vistas to the farmer, since it makes possible much larger profits from hay and thus encourages the growing of this soil-conserving crop; a new high-pressure cooker for cottonseed meal which is being manufactured by private industry and installed in cottonseed crushing plants in various parts of the South, and so on.

In view of the absolutely essential rôle which TVA is playing in building the country's defenses at one of the greatest crises in its history, some may argue that its utility and worth are not even debatable. Yet it must be conceded that when the Tennessee Valley Authority was created in 1933, no world war seemed imminent, and the arguments pro and con centered largely upon whether this new departure in government represented an unwarranted infringement upon private enterprise, and whether there was justification for spending hundreds of millions from the national treasury in the development of one limited area. Chief opponents were, of course, the privately owned electric light and power companies then functioning in the region. These corporations, through their able spokesman, Wendell L. Willkie, pointed to what they termed inconsistencies in the professions of TVA officials, and Mr. Willkie was fond of saying that "the Tennessee River flows through seven states and drains the nation." He asserted that whereas its officials claimed in the courts that their agency "is really not a power enterprise, but primarily a conservation activity...a project to prevent floods, promote navigation on the Tennessee River, and check soil erosion," when addressing a more sympathetic audience, they frankly described TVA as "an instrument for the electrification of America." The companies also questioned the validity of TVA's method of allocating the expense of power-plant and dam construction between "power," on the one hand, and "navigation and flood control" on the other, arguing that far too few millions were allotted to the former. Mr. Willkie declared, moreover, that the power "yardstick," to which so much importance was attached by public power advocates, was "rubber from the first inch to the last," since TVA was exempt from "practically all taxes" and had to concern itself with neither depreciation nor interest charges. Since such items bulk large in the budgetary calculations of the private power companies, he argued that they could not possibly compete with subsidized power on an equal basis, and that the methods by which the private companies operating in the TVA area were forced to sell some, or all, of their properties to the government were almost tantamount to confiscation.

Admittedly, TVA's record is not unassailable, and the Authority has made various mistakes. At times, it has been extravagant in its expenditures, as in the high cost of the town of Norris. Some of its spokesmen have been excessively critical of the private utilities. While the latter have much to answer for, and stringent regulatory legislation to abolish pyramiding of holding companies and other abuses was necessary, there have been times when the attitude of certain TVA officials seemed to imply that there was no such thing as an honest utility corporation or utility executive.

Yet despite his profound distrust of TVA, Wendell Willkie wrote in the *Atlantic* at the height of the controversy: "There is nothing sacred about private operation of business. The utilities have no God-given charter for existing. Provided that the government compensates for what it destroys (a provision which, unfortunately, we can not take for granted), there is no reason why the government should not put the utility companies out of business if the people want the government to do so." He also wrote at the same time: "Utility men, when they are sure no one will overhear them, will occasionally admit that the punitive legislation by the government has spurred them to renewed efforts to lower their rates and put their houses in order."

Is TVA in devastating and destructive competition with private business, as has so often been claimed? While it is obvious that the privately-owned utilities in the valley which were forced to sell out to the government, are *hors de combat* in consequence, the degree to which this much-denounced agency has stimulated private enterprise is remarkable. Skeptics will find a comprehensive article on the point in *Business Week* (May 25, 1940). Entitled "News: TVA Aids Private Business," this discussion adduces many impressive facts. It shows how farming machinery, invented and developed by TVA to meet special conditions in the area, has been manufactured on a large scale and sold by private industry; how TVA researchers invented a new process for refining clays in the manufacture of fine china, and launched a substantial industry which is shipping the kaolin to ceramic plants all over the United

States; how the extension of power lines to rural sections caused sales of electric appliances by private manufacturers and dealers to soar; how farmers participating in the Authority's program buy "more from the hardware store, the lumber yard and the department store than they did before they agreed to follow a new farming practice"; how sales of phosphate fertilizer, mostly produced by private manufacturers, were eleven times as large in ten Alabama counties in which the program was being demonstrated as in ten countries where it was not; how private navigation lines on the Tennessee enjoy prospects for large traffic, in view of TVA's near-completion of its canalization projects, with shipments of petroleum products and grain already moving in substantial volume. *Business Week* sums up in the following words: "What TVA has done to further navigation, electric power, flood control and soil conservation is aiding not only the region, but private business."

An obvious aid to private business is to be found in the flood-control program of the Authority. Army engineers have placed the average annual loss from floods on the Tennessee River alone at nearly $1,000,000, and this takes no account of damage done on the Ohio, into which the Tennessee flows, and on the Mississippi. During the winter of 1936-37, for example, Norris Dam alone held back sufficient water to lower the flood crest at Chattanooga by four feet, according to TVA officials, and the crest at Cairo, Illinois, where the Ohio flows into the Mississippi by nearly half a foot. Those six inches "were critical for Cairo, for at this time waters of the Ohio were above the top of the Cairo flood wall, and the city was protected only by the emergency construction of a mud box on top of the levee." As these results were achieved by a single dam out of a projected series of dams, it can readily be seen that tremendous property damage will be saved when the whole flood-control program is completed. Kentucky Dam, near the mouth of the Tennessee, is designed to store enough water to reduce major floods on the lower Mississippi by two feet. Operation of this vast system is certain to save millions annually in damage to crops, railroads, highways, telephone lines, and power lines. Conversely, in dry seasons, enough water can be released from the reservoirs to augment the flow of water in the rivers substantially, thereby greatly aiding shippers and carriers. Moreover, the lakes created by the building of the dams have proved ideal for boating, fishing, and hunting, and have attracted thousands of tourists and much new business to the area.

All this is aside from the indispensable rôle of TVA in arming America. Without the power developments of the valley, emergency production of aluminum, airplanes, and powder would have been very severely crippled. Moreover, the intensive research done in the laboratories of the Authority is responsible for processes whereby alumina is made from common clay, magnesium from olivine, and a substitute cork from vermiculite. In addition, Nitrate Plant No. 2 at Muscle Shoals has been equipped to turn out ammonium nitrate in large quantities for the duration of the emergency, and to be shifted to the production of the same commodity for plant food after peace returns.

There was also the meaningful burying of the hatchet between the Aluminum Company of America and TVA, when the company signed a contract in 1941 turning over to the Authority operation of its five-dam hydro-electric system. Termed by TVA Chairman Lilienthal "one of the most important developments in the relations between government and business in our time," this arrangement will facilitate the production of aluminum at the company's Alcoa plant, the biggest center of aluminum manufacture in the world. Under the contract, TVA does not assume ownership of the company's plants, but merely directs and controls their operations, integrating them with its own system of dams. Studies had demonstrated that under this plan for unified operation of the two systems, maximum production of power and maximum flood control could be secured. Mr. Lilienthal described the contract as providing "a new kind of relationship between public and private enterprises, and the first such arrangement to be entered into in this country."

The pattern developed by TVA for integrating the resources of an entire region is being followed on a smaller scale in the $57,000,000 Santee-Cooper power development in South Carolina, which went into operation early in 1942. (The Cooper is, of course, the celebrated stream which, in apocryphal Carolinian geographies, unites with the Ashley at Charleston to form the Atlantic Ocean). Cheap electricity, available all the way from Raleigh to Jacksonville, flood control and navigation, as well as recreational facilities, are listed as parts of the Santee-Cooper program, as in the Tennessee Valley. Time will show how well-founded these claims are. The Santee-Cooper development, which includes the world's longest dam (over the Santee), has been pronounced vital to national defense, particularly in the manufacture of aluminum and ferro-alloys. Like the federally constructed dams in the Far

West at Bonneville, Grand Coulee, and Boulder, the Santee-Cooper and TVA dams have fitted into the defense picture. Even though it may be argued that similar dams would have been built by private power interests if the government had not built them (and the argument seems far fetched), that is a supposition, whereas these great Federal dams and power plants are going concerns without which the manufacture of adequate essential materials and finished products for the arming of America would have been seriously delayed.

Another Federal agency created by the Roosevelt Administration which has provided cheap electricity for the country districts both in the South and the United States as a whole is the Rural Electrification Administration. Just as TVA makes cheap power available to remote rural areas within its sphere of operation, so REA provides areas of like character in 45 states with similar service through REA-financed power systems, most of which are built in regions so sparsely settled that private utilities could not enter them profitably. Moreover, privately owned and operated plants frequently furnish the power for supplying these areas after REA builds the lines. Between 1935 and 1941, REA lines carried current to more than 500,000 farms which were without electricity. While farm homes comprise some 80 per cent of REA's customers, the agency also serves rural business establishments and industrial plants, Army camps, airways facilities, Naval and Coast Guard stations, and rural and community institutions of various kinds. By electrifying hundreds of thousands of farms, REA has contributed importantly to the development of diversified farming, has aided tangibly in furthering the "food for defense" program, has made possible the establishment of more small industries in rural areas, and given greater variety and appeal to rural living. Since its establishment in 1935, REA has loaned hundreds of millions, more than 90 per cent of it to farmers' coöperatives established for that specific purpose. Officials in charge report that repayment of the loans is proceeding well ahead of schedule.

The measures inaugurated by the Roosevelt Administration which have been discussed hitherto in this chapter are addressed almost exclusively to the well-being of the rural South. But while the major part of the South is rural, the urban South is extremely important, and the NRA codes in the early days of the New Deal, followed by the Fair Labor Standards Act, have been far-reaching in their effect upon living standards in the cities and towns of the region. Indirectly they have affected the rural areas, as well, since greater urban buying power means more demand for farm products.

In view of the invalidation of the NRA by the Supreme Court in 1935, detailed discussion of its *modus operandi* and the results obtained under it, are hardly called for. Despite the fact that the objectives it sought were unexceptionable, the NRA had failed in most respects before it was adjudged unconstitutional. For example, Charles F. Roos, for a time its director of research, states in his book, *NRA Economic Planning*, that some 500,000 Negroes were thrown on relief in 1934 because NRA failed to establish racial differentials. This agency also fell short of its goal in other respects.

The Fair Labor Standards Act became effective in the autumn of 1938. Almost simultaneously the magazine *Fortune* published a comprehensive examination of

Southern manufactures which asserted that "to industry the South appears as the nation's No. 1 economic opportunity." This was comforting to those who had been annoyed by seeing their native section termed "the nation's No. 1 economic problem," but since *Fortune* pronounced the latter problem "all too dismally clear," their satisfaction was necessarily restrained. The magazine discussed the South's undoubted position as a land of industrial promise, but, while recognizing its great potentialities, did not hesitate to say that the per-capita income of the South in 1935 was only $240, or exactly half that of the rest of the country, and that if the South's income could be raised to the national level, it would mean a $6,500,000,000 addition to the national income, and give a great lift to the entire national economy.

The Fair Labor Standards Act stipulated a minimum wage of 25 cents an hour for all industries doing business in interstate commerce, and a maximum week of 44 hours. The 25-cent minimum affected hardly any workers outside the South, but it raised the pay of a good many inside it. A year later, in October, 1939, the universal minimum became 30 cents an hour (Southern wage-earners again were the chief beneficiaries), and the work week was dropped to 42 hours. There will be no further change in the minimum under the law, until 1945, except in cases where committees for specific industries decide that a raise is possible without "substantially curtailing employment." After 1945, the lowest legal wage is to be 40 cents an hour throughout all industry engaged in interstate commerce, both North and South. Hours of work, which dropped to 42 in 1939, were stabilized a year later at 40, where they will remain.

What need was there for this legislation? The invalidation of NRA created a definite need on both sides of Mason and Dixon's line, especially below it. The breakdown of standards for wages and hours led to a southward rush on the part of Northern industries in search of cheap Southern labor. There were sweatshops in the North, too, but the weaker state labor laws, less formidable unions, and low-wage tradition of the South served as irresistible attractions, especially to chiseling little factories which had swindled everybody in sight up North, and now were seeking new victims. The results were portrayed graphically by Thomas L. Stokes in a series of articles published by the Scripps-Howard newspapers early in 1937. Garment, hosiery, and shoe factories were among the worst offenders, he pointed out, but there were others. These "carpetbaggers of industry" were offered fantastic inducements by Southern states and localities eager for plants and not particularly careful to discriminate between those which offered decent wages and those which did not. In many cases, the factory buildings were paid for by means of five- or six-per-cent deductions from the already low weekly pay of the employees. Wages of $4.00 to $5.00 a week were not unknown, but Southern communities sought such fly-by-night concerns, partly because of the South's heavy relief load and large labor surplus. Mississippi's plan for attracting industry was especially noteworthy, since it contained no stipulations concerning wages, hours, or working conditions. There was even a scheme in that state to use Federal funds to build plants and train workers for the incoming low-wage garment factories from the North and Middle West. In Alabama, the salted fat-back which poorly paid workers had to live on was known as "lam chops," because, as one consumer explained, "you had to lam it against the wall to get the salt off."

Mr. Stokes found a definite need for some sort of protective Federal law as insurance against gross exploitation. Enlightened businessmen agreed, saying that plants paying starvation wages were not only bad in principle but of no value to a community.

The advent of the Fair Labor Standards Act in 1938 eliminated a large percentage of the foregoing evils. Neither the 25- nor the 30-cent minimum seems to have posed many real problems for honest Southern industry. It was when the various industry committees created under the act began raising the minimum well above 30 cents, and these committees insisted also at this level in denying the validity of the minimum wage differentials of long standing, that doubts began to arise in the minds of conscientious Southerners. By November, 1941, thirty-six such committees had eliminated the differential, and not one committee had retained it.

There can be little doubt that the enthusiasm shown in the North and West for the Federal wage and hour law proceeded in no small measure from the fact that it provided machinery for wiping out these lower Southern wage minima, thereby putting the South at a competitive disadvantage. Moreover, if the huge defense and war boom had not absorbed practically all criticism and enabled many shaky Southern firms to stay in business, despite the liquidation of their minimum wage differentials, Southern industry might have been struck a shattering blow. England, a far smaller and more homogeneous country, found it desirable, after thirty years' experience with wage and hour legislation, to have regional differentials.

As matters stand to-day, no one can predict with any certainty what the competitive position of the South will be when peace returns and the Southern economy no longer is bolstered by billions upon billions of Federal spending. Thus far there can be little doubt that the Southern worker has benefited substantially from the law. The higher wages much more than offset the loss of jobs due to the replacement of men with machines and the substitution of able-bodied workers for the unfortunate marginal employees, both white and black, who formerly were given part-time or easy work at low pay. Business has profited through increased purchasing power in the ranks of Southern labor, and industry has not suffered severely from heavier labor costs, owing to the plethora of orders brought about by the armament program. An official of the Wage and Hour Division estimated in 1941 that the Fair Labor Standards Act had increased the wages of Southern labor by $100,000,000 annually. Southern business has learned that wages barely sufficient to keep body and soul together are of little benefit to a community or a region. Southern industry has been taught much also about the value of higher purchasing power, not only for its effect upon the general level of living, but its rôle in creating a wider market for industry's products. It is greatly to be hoped, however, that lessons to Southern industry inculcated by the Federal wage and hour law, particularly in its steady wiping out of minimum wage differentials, will not be comparable in their lethal impact after the war to the effect of hanging upon the Negro in the story: Asked on the scaffold if he had anything to say, he replied: "Naw, sah, nuthin' 'cep' dis sho' is gonna be a lesson to me!"

The freight-rate differentials which operate against the South and Southwest are integral and important parts of the whole Southern industrial picture, since manufacturers who have to pay much higher freight costs than their competitors in getting their products to a given market naturally are under a severe handicap. In 1938 southeastern manufacturers suffered from a 39 per cent disadvantage in freight costs, by comparison with their rivals in the East, while southwestern manufacturers had to contend with an enormous 75 per cent differential. In 1939, responding to directions from Congress for the elimination of inequalities between the sections, the Interstate Commerce Commission abolished the differential with respect to seven commodities. The following year, the railroads were allowed by the I.C.C. to institute a 15 to 30 per cent reduction in class rates on some 3,500 articles moving from the South to the North, in order to meet truck competition. Nevertheless, substantial advantages still are enjoyed by the North. Not only is the rate per mile usually much higher, but the number of miles frequently is greater. Frank L. Barton of TVA told the Southern Political Science Association late in 1941 that discriminatory freight rates had prevented the South from getting its proper proportion of defense contracts.

There is no longer any valid excuse for these freight-rate differentials, a fact which President Roosevelt apparently recognizes. His appointment to the I.C.C. of J. Haden Alldredge of Alabama, a leading exemplar of the movement for elimination of the heavy transportation advantages enjoyed by the North, showed his un-

Springs Cotton Mills, Chester, South Carolina, a unit of the textile industry, the South's largest branch of manufacture.

Negroes planting corn on a large plantation near Moncks Corner, South Carolina.

derstanding of the South's problem in this sphere. Once upon a time, when the greater initial cost of railroad building in the South because of more rugged terrain was a factor, and when the relative lightness of the traffic over Southern roads also played a necessarily weighty rôle in the fixing of the rate base, there was some excuse for the disadvantageous transportation costs applied to the South. But these conditions obtain no longer.

As already noted, it was in 1939 that the I.C.C. was directed by Congress to make an inquiry into these discriminations against the South, and more in the way of tangible relief should have been forthcoming. Not until over a year after the inquiry was formally instituted did the commission hold a pre-hearing conference, and at that conference an effort was made to abandon the investigation. The complainants thwarted that step, but the I.C.C. then lapsed into another long period of inaction, perhaps because the argument was advanced by the North and East that freight rates ought not to be tinkered with during a period of national crisis. The South retorted that at such a time, no section should enjoy unwarranted advantages over any other section, and that it would be especially deplorable if injustices in the transportation field from which the South has suffered for generations, were to be perpetuated as a consequence of a national emergency during which all parts of the United States should be on an equal basis. It remained to be seen what the I.C.C. would do about it, if anything. The South and West joined hands in 1941 with a view to forcing action.

While the freight-rate question is irrevocably intertwined with the wage question, since both are important elements in the cost of producing and marketing, it must be conceded that the higher freight charges against the South are, in themselves, not sufficient justification for much lower Southern wages. The cost of shipping a given commodity is normally only a small fraction of the wage cost which goes into its manufacture. In addition, some Southern industrialists have by-passed the rail-rate problem by using trucks. At the same time, it is not reasonable to expect Southern manufacturers to acquiesce in the elimination of all wage differentials, unless the I.C.C. eliminates freight differentials, too.

This matter of freight charges is only one of the national policies which have operated over a long period to thwart the proper development of the South. The tariffs imposed on the country for more than a century by the industrial East have forced the agricultural South and West to pay higher prices for manufactured products, while those regions were selling their farm commodities on the unprotected world market. Moreover, the South's status since the Civil War often has been described as virtually that of a colonial appanage of the North. The war and its aftermath enabled Northern capital to get such a grip on the South's natural resources and its nascent industrial enterprises that to-day we have the spectacle of absentee ownership below the Potomac on a vast scale. The Roosevelt Administration performed a service in 1938 by directing attention to this condition in its study of the "nation's No. 1 economic problem," as well as to the deleterious effects upon the region of discriminatory freight rates and high tariffs. The study in question pointed to the following facts:

The public utilities in the South are almost completely controlled by outside interests. All the major railroad systems are owned and controlled elsewhere. Most of the great electric holding company systems, whose operating companies furnish the light, heat and power for Southern homes and industries, are directed, managed, and owned by outside interests. Likewise the transmission and distribution of natural gas . . . is almost completely in the hands of remote financial institutions. The richest deposits of the iron ore, coal, and limestone that form the basis for the steel industry in Birmingham are owned or controlled outside of the region. . . .

Other examples were cited in the report, but the foregoing suffice to indicate the trend. A similar state of things prevails in much of the West. Walter Prescott Webb declared in his *Divided We Stand* (1937), that whereas "the South and the West have within their boundaries most of the natural wealth of America," the North has gathered "practically all the economic fruits of a nation's industry and labor." It may even own the thriving business in spoon-billed Mississippi catfish, which passes for caviar at Northern cocktail parties.

Through the good offices of its colonial overlords, coöperating with its own indigenous bankers and businessmen, the South is becoming industrialized at a rapid rate; but industrialization now, as in the past, brings serious problems in its train. One of those problems is child labor. In view of the fact that the child-labor laws of the Southern states are, in general, among the weakest in the Union, passage of the Fair Labor Standards Act in 1938 had a significant impact upon the employment of juveniles in Southern industry. Non-agricultural industries shipping products in interstate commerce were forbidden by this Federal law to employ workers under

16 years of age, or under 18 in hazardous occupations. However, the National Child Labor Committee estimates that this legislation covers only about one-fourth of the non-agricultural child labor in the country. It mentions hundreds of thousands of newsboys and others under 16 who are engaged in street trades, and who are not covered by the act, together with young people working in local industries, such as garages, repair shops, laundries, hotels, mercantile establishments, and so on, as well as in domestic service. It would be fantastic to suggest that all those on this list are being injured by the employment mentioned, but certainly some of them are, both North and South. Incredibly enough, the newspapers of Indiana succeeded in 1941 in having the state legislature abolish all controls over newsboys, so that a boy of any age can now deliver papers there at any hour of the day or night, as long as he is not required at that particular time to be in school. Almost equally pernicious legislation was passed in California, but was vetoed by Governor Olson. No recent Southern legislature has been guilty of anything comparable to this.

Industrialized agriculture has come to be recognized in recent years as a zone wherein some of the most harmful child labor of all occurs. The National Child Labor Committee emphasizes its seriousness, and the Federal Council of the Churches of Christ in America terms it "the next big problem to be tackled." These warning declarations, it should be stressed, have no relationship to the performance of casual chores around the farm. They refer exclusively to what the census defines as "an occupation by which the person who pursues it earns money or a money equivalent, or in which he assists in the production of marketable goods." The census of 1940 found hundreds of thousands of boys and girls under 16 engaged in this commercialized agriculture, a type of employment which is not regulated by Federal law, or by state law, except in a handful of states. Wartime England, and even wartime Germany, despite their urgent need for farm hands, have far more adequate regulation of this form of child labor than we in the United States have ever had. Examples of the sort of harmful work now going on are to be noted in the Colorado beet sugar fields, the vineyards of California, the hop fields of Washington, the strawberry farms of Louisiana, Arkansas, and Kentucky, and the cotton fields of the South. The hours of labor often are too long for immature boys and girls, and in addition, the work interferes with school attendance. A National Child Labor Committee study of 81 families picking strawberries in Arkansas and Kentucky in 1939, showed that 36 per cent of the migratory children of school age had not attended school a single day in the previous calendar year. It is unfortunately true, however, that as matters stand to-day in the South, schooling could not be provided for all the children, even if the compulsory education laws were enforced and strict child-labor legislation was enacted. This is because the school facilities currently available are inadequate, the buildings are not large or numerous enough, and there are insufficient teachers. Nevertheless, rehabilitation loans advanced by the Farm Security Administration to tenant and sharecropper families during 1939 are said by that agency to have made it possible for 210,000 children to attend school who otherwise could not have done so. Many of them were in the South.

Legislatures of the former Confederacy always have

been predominantly opposed to the Federal Child Labor Amendment, and only those of Arkansas and Kentucky are among the twenty-eight which have ratified it since 1924, when it was first proposed. Eight more must ratify before the amendment can become law, but none has done so since 1937, owing, it would seem, to a widespread feeling that the Fair Labor Standards Act of 1938 made the amendment unnecessary. But if the abuses in industrialized agriculture and other spheres where juveniles are employed, continue to be flagrant, and the individual states refuse to act effectively to stop these uncivilized practices, sufficient pressure may be generated to secure the constitutional amendment's adoption. However, as matters stood early in 1942, the outlook for its adoption was not propitious.

The unionization of Southern industry also has been a vital and explosive issue in the South both before and during the Roosevelt Administration. The epidemic of strikes and other labor disorders which gripped the region in the late 1920's flared up anew when NRA and the Wagner Act provided unprecedented federal protection for organized labor. In view of the section's long and grim antipathy to unions, resistance to the militant efforts of the A.F. of L. and the C.I.O. was particularly determined. There were no such spectacular holdouts below the Potomac as those of Ford, Bethlehem, and Little Steel in the North and Middle West, but the vast majority of Southern industrialists were strongly hostile to the organization of their workers. From 1933 to 1942 there were flagrant examples of brutality and violence on the part of Southern foes of unionization. This is not to say that they were always without provocation. While beatings, kidnapings, and tar-and-feather parties are never justifiable, there is little to choose between them and "flying squadrons" or "goon squads." Southern labor has needed the leadership and example of men like the late Steve Nance, a brawny, square-shooting, level-headed man who served as president of the Georgia State Federation of Labor and was in charge of the drive to organize the textile industry in the lower South until his death in 1938. Nance had been warned by his physician that the pace at which he was working would kill him, but his devotion to the cause was so complete that he refused to apply the brakes. His unselfish life brings to mind the words attributed to the poet Heine, whose books are not acceptable to the Galahads who reign over Nazi Germany: "Place a sword upon my coffin, for I have ever been a fighter for humanity."

If there had been more union leaders like Nance, industrial disorders in Dixie would have been held to a minimum, and employer-employee relations would have been more amicable. The advent of the Roosevelt Administration found many Southern employers implacably determined not to allow organization of their plants, while many labor leaders, under encouragement from Washington, were equally determined to break this resistance. It is not surprising that both parties to the struggle committed inexcusable blunders and used inexcusable methods. There were beatings and floggings of labor organizers, sometimes with the connivance of the authorities. On the other hand, there was intimidation by union men of non-union men who felt no need for a union card, and there were wholly unreasonable demands upon management. Moreover, both employers and employees were caught in the cross-fire between A.F. of L. and C.I.O, for the two major labor organizations persisted in carrying on their feud, irrespective of its effect on the South or the country. And when the United States became deeply and irrevocably involved in the second World War, certain elements of labor continued striking, or threatening to strike, in order to secure unreasonable wage increases. John L. Lewis and his United Mine Workers were the most conspicuous example. They demanded elimination of the long-standing basic wage differential between the Northern and the Southern bituminous mines, with an increase of 25 per cent in the basic Southern wage, and of slightly less than 17 per cent in the Northern. If these demands were not met in every single particular, officers of the U.M.W. announced that they would shut down all the soft-coal mines in the Appalachian region and stall the whole defense program. They got what they wanted. One can concede that some of the Southern coal operators are among the most anti-social industrialists of modern times, and still feel that the attitude of John L. Lewis and his mine workers was arbitrary and high-handed, if not unpatriotic. It must be admitted that the coal operators had put themselves in a vulnerable position by refusing Mr. Lewis' original offer, which was to keep the mines running if they would agree to make any wage increase agreed upon retroactive to April 1. Since they declined to entertain this proposal, their loud wails when the miners' ultimatum came some weeks later seemed slightly out of place. In the late autumn of 1941, Mr. Lewis won another victory by threatening again to paralyze the defense program if he was not granted the union shop in the "captive" mines owned by the steel companies. Although the National Defense Mediation Board, a body eminently fair to labor, voted 9 to 2 against him, he refused to accept the verdict and got what he wanted from an arbitration board appointed by President Roosevelt in a desperate effort to avoid a devastating strike throughout the coal industry.

It should be emphasized, however, that not all the demands of labor in defense industries have been unreasonable, by any means. In some cases, grasping employers have profiteered at the expense of their workers, and have refused to share any of their profits, despite the mounting cost of living.

The New Deal's influence in the sphere of labor has, of course, been distinctly on the side of the unions. The Wagner Act and the National Labor Relations Board, not to mention the revamped Supreme Court, have given labor protection which it never enjoyed before. Much of that protection was needed, but it can scarcely be gainsaid that the original N.L.R.B. was composed of extremists whose biased attitude infuriated even reasonable employers. When the board was given a more moderate cast with the appointment of three new members, at least two of whom were fair and judicially minded men of large experience in the adjustment of labor disputes, the outlook for satisfactory employer-employee relations in the South, as well as in the rest of the country, promptly took a turn for the better.

Unionization of some of the major mass-production industries of the South was proceeding apace early in 1942, and both the major labor organizations enjoyed the largest Southern memberships in their history. Tremendous union gains had been made in such fields as textiles, steel, coal mining, and tobacco, which previously had been unorganized to a much greater degree, and President Murray of the C.I.O. declared that the slogan for 1942 must be "organize the South." Already labor's progress gave needed mass purchasing power to Southern laboring men who often had been underpaid. The extent to which Southern industry could operate profitably under such an extra load of labor costs, in competition with Northern industry, which long has been adjusted to such costs, remained a matter to be determined after the defense boom had run its course and the anticipated postwar deflation had set in.

The WPA, and its alphabetical predecessors, also have been important bulwarks of Southern purchasing power, although the "W. P. and A.," as its beneficiaries sometimes term it, always has maintained a lower scale of pay in the South than in the North, thereby buttressing the position of those who contend that Southern industry ought to enjoy a wage differential over its Northern competitors. Similarly, the old-age and unemployment insurance and old-age assistance programs, operating under the social-security system established by the Roosevelt Administration, provide thousands of low-income Southerners with regular checks which formerly they never received. It must be conceded that the relief rolls include the inevitable percentage of chiselers, albeit not as many as the foes of the relief program contend, but the need for some such adequately financed system, affording useful work to the South's and the nation's jobless thousands, is indisputable. There were serious, even fantastic abuses, in the early stages, but more recently the program has been well thought out and well-managed, on the whole, with scandals distinctly rare and large numbers of destitute Southerners enabled thereby to preserve their morale and self-respect. More-

over, WPA has conducted classes for illiterates throughout the South and substantially lowered the illiteracy
rate in various states. An enormous number of school-
houses, jails, sewer systems, and highways have been
built or repaired by WPA, while PWA with its larger
and heavier construction projects, has added even more
permanent values in the form of libraries, bridges, university and college dormitories, hospitals, and so on.
Those who say that the billions spent by WPA and
PWA have been wasted are disregarding obvious facts.
A certain percentage of this money has, indeed, been
wasted, but the better part of it has added lasting values
to the South and the nation, values in rebuilt human
lives, as well as in badly needed material resources.

The CCC camps have been as popular and as useful
in the South as elsewhere, and the United States Housing Authority's slum-clearance projects have been particularly important there. Hundreds of these projects
have been allotted to the South, roughly half of all
those in the nation. The Negroes have been especial
beneficiaries of the program, approximately one-third
of the dwelling units developed or to be developed by
the USHA in the entire country having been earmarked
for Negro slum-dwellers. Many of the slum-clearance
projects are no less ornamental than they are useful. For
instance, the Santa Rita unit in Austin, Texas, was described recently in the *New Republic,* by Professor
Talbot Hamlin of Columbia University, as one of the
"dozen most distinguished buildings completed in the
last five years in America." In Memphis, the Real Estate
Board is loud in its praise of the slum-clearance program,
and declares that "probably no more constructive work
has been done in the City of Memphis in the last fifty

years." The vast preponderance of the slums cleared to
date are in urban areas, but a beginning has been made
in attacking the colossal problem of the South's sub-
standard rural housing. More than $1,100,000 has been
earmarked for modest farm homes in eleven counties
in the cotton, peanut, and sweet-potato belt of Southwest Georgia. Similarly, a total of $2,100,000 has been
set aside for twenty-nine counties in Arkansas and thirty-
three counties in Mississippi. While this merely scratches
the surface, it constitutes a beginning.

Such, in its major outlines, is the New Deal's program
for rebuilding the South. Some brand it as bureaucratic
and socialistic, others term it wasteful and extravagant,
still others condemn it for destroying the initiative of
thousands, a fourth group complains that it has stirred
the once inarticulate masses to demand far more than
they ever demanded before, and others combine some or
all of these criticisms into one spluttering outburst of
fury and disgust. If there is a certain measure of justification for these objurgations, the fact remains that the
Roosevelt Administration has addressed itself more directly and comprehensively to the welfare of the South
than to any other part of America. Moreover, the steps
it has taken, the imagination it has shown in attacking
problems which had gone almost unconsidered for generations, its genuine concern for the alleviation of the
ills of a long handicapped and retarded section, entitle
it to the gratitude of the Southern people. Some of its
experiments have missed fire; others have been ill-considered and half-baked. But the general trend has been
right, on the whole, for the direction of the New Deal
is the direction of democratic polity in the older democ-
racies—Great Britain and Scandinavia—strongholds of

popular government and free institutions in an increasingly totalitarian world. Federal intervention in, and concern for, the affairs of the individual citizen is destined to grow in future, rather than to diminish, for such is the mandate of the age. The era of *laissez-faire* seems gone forever, and the surest highway to liberty traverses terrain where the average man is protected from exploitation and given a decent chance for the good things of life. Such a future relationship between the citizen and his government is as inevitable for Southerners as it is for all other Americans.

IV

BARRIERS TO THE BALLOT

FROM the crags above Harper's Ferry to the mesas fringing the Rio Grande, a revolt is brewing against the poll-tax. The strength of the movement varies in each of the eight Southern states which retains the levy as a prerequisite to voting, but it is definitely a movement. It was well under way before President Roosevelt, in September, 1938, called for elimination of the tax, and it has since gained much impetus. The opposition seems at last to be definitely on the defensive, in the face of the gathering wave of resentment, and this barrier to the ballot may fall in several states during the next few years.

The poll-tax has an ancient, if not always honorable, history. Aristotle refers to it as a "most ignominious imposition" which "none but slaves paid to their tyrants." It was levied by the conquering Romans upon the peoples they reduced to subjection, and was considered at that period to be an earnest of servitude. A thousand years later Wat Tyler led the peasants of England in a bloody rebellion against the tax, and although the uprising was put down, many of its objectives were achieved. The franchise in England was less hedged about with restrictions thereafter.

To-day in the South the people are not brandishing clubs or pikes, like those which Tyler's sturdy rustics brought into play against the English aristocracy of the fourteenth century, but the tide of revolt is rising. Louisiana and Florida abolished the levy on the franchise in the middle 1930's, and an effort toward repeal in Arkansas received legislative approval in 1937, only to be voted down by the people the following year in a referendum which saw the politicians and the press aligned almost solidly in opposition.

The year 1941 marked the emergence of the Southern Electoral Reform League, with active members in each poll-tax state and machinery for presenting repeal arguments to the voters. In Tennessee, where Jennings Perry, associate editor of the Nashville *Tennessean* and league president, is in a position to push the fight with especial vigor, the outlook is rather propitious. Thirty counties abolished the poll-tax in 1941 as a prerequisite for voting in county elections. In Virginia, where no candidate for governor ever before announced prior to election that he favored even so much as modification of the poll-tax law, three of the four candidates in the Democratic primaries of 1941 urged outright repeal. The fourth, former Representative Colgate W. Darden, Jr., the successful candidate of the Byrd organization, let it be known that he would not recommend any change in the poll-tax requirements.

It is a striking fact that Virginia, the oldest American colony, had universal white manhood suffrage for half a century, beginning soon after the first representative assembly in the new world met at Jamestown in 1619. It is also noteworthy that this same Virginia, supposedly the seat of a preëminently aristocratic society, likewise had universal white manhood suffrage during the decade which ended with the outbreak of the Civil War. In the aforementioned decade, which closed the ante-

bellum era, and is now looked back to by many Southerners as a sort of golden age, 53 per cent of the adult
white male population voted in Virginia elections, as
against from 33 to 35 per cent of the white males and
females in the presidential elections of 1936 and 1940.

What would Thomas Jefferson or Andrew Jackson,
who occupy the foremost niches in the hagiology of the
Democratic party, say of the poll-tax, if they should
come back to earth? Dr. John H. Russell, whose series
of articles in the *Southern Planter* in 1937 and 1938 are
the first important contributions made to poll-tax literature during the past several decades, points to Jefferson's observation upon the franchise in his *Notes on the
State of Virginia*. In that volume, Jefferson said:

The influence over government must be shared among all
the people. If every individual which composes their mass
participates of the ultimate authority, the Government will
be safe; because the corrupting [of] the whole mass will
exceed any private resources of wealth. . . . The Government
of Great Britain has been corrupted, because but one man
in ten has the right to vote for members of Parliament.
[One person in 16 voted for all candidates for Governor of
Virginia in the general election of 1937, and one in 21 in
1941.] Corruption is not restrained by confining the right of
suffrage to a few of the wealthier people; but it would be
more effectively restrained by an extension of that right to
such numbers as would bid defiance to the means of corruption.

Every Government degenerates when trusted to the rulers
of the people alone. The people themselves, therefore, are its
only safe depositories.

Although this was written by the master of Monti-
cello rather early in his career, he expressed himself

similarly later in life, so there is no room for debate as to his attitude. The attitude of Andrew Jackson, under whom the Democratic party became democratic in fact, as well as in name (since Jefferson's day it had been called "Republican" or "Democratic-Republican"), was substantially the same. Hence the poll-tax which Virginia, South Carolina, Georgia, Alabama, Mississippi, Texas, Arkansas, and Tennessee retain to-day, either in their constitutions or on their statute books, flies in the face of some of the most deeply cherished beliefs of the founders of the Democratic party, the very party whose leaders in those states have insisted on retaining the tax.

This admission fee to the ballot-box is, of course, the fruit of the Reconstruction era. Various restrictions upon the voting privilege were imposed in the form of property requirements and other similar limitations during most of the colonial and the ante-bellum periods, but the poll-tax, as we know it, was framed late in the nineteenth century as a device primarily designed to sunder the liberated Negro slaves from the polling booth.

After the orgies of Reconstruction some such device was deemed necessary, for widespread electoral fraud had been resorted to by desperate whites during the post-bellum years, and well-disposed Southerners considered such a situation intolerable. So as the turn of the century neared, the Southern states began enacting franchise requirements which were, in most instances, technically legal. By the early 1900's, every state below the Potomac and the Ohio had fallen into line, except Kentucky, which never enacted a poll-tax. In addition, a variety of residence, property, and educational qualifications were imposed throughout the South. Almost all the Negroes were effectively disfranchised.

But a substantial percentage of the whites also were disfranchised. If such was the intention of the framers of these constitutional provisions and statutes, the writer has been able to discover only a limited amount of evidence to that effect. Dr. H. C. Nixon of Vanderbilt University has pointed out that "it was generally understood and frankly stated that these measures for regulating and restricting registration for voting were designed to take the Negro out of politics but to 'disfranchise no white man.'" In Louisiana, for example, the chairman of the constitutional convention said: "Doesn't it let the white man vote, and doesn't it stop the Negro from voting, and isn't that what we came here for?" Similarly, the chairman in Alabama "assumed that it was within the limits of the Federal Constitution to 'establish white supremacy in this state,'" while a member of the Alabama convention "was quoted as saying that he would disfranchise Booker T. Washington if he could." In North Carolina, too, there was emphasis upon "literacy qualifications and white supremacy."

Over against such manifestations as these, however, one must place the fact that in some states, as pointed out by C. Vann Woodward, the biographer of Thomas E. Watson, certain influential whites were anxious to disfranchise the Populist vote, while the upstate masses of whites were openly skeptical, at times, concerning the white-supremacy rationalization of the disfranchisers. It must be recognized, too, that all-inclusive and categorical assertions with respect to this involved question

are apt to be unsound. Mr. Woodward shows where
some of the pitfalls lie:

The motives behind the poll-tax and disfranchising conventions were extremely complex, and certainly one could
not make the bald statement that the poll-tax was a weapon
against Populism, without much qualification. The
Mississippi convention of 1890 preceded the outbreak of
Populism. The South Carolina convention of 1895 was
dominated by the Democratic Populistic Tillmanites, and
of course the Georgia disfranchisement of 1908 was egged
on by the state's most prominent Populist, Tom Watson.
Even in the other states holding conventions around the
late nineties, the Populist elements were usually persuaded
to lend support, on the argument that the elimination of
the Negro would enable the white man to divide politically.
As a further paradox, in Alabama the old Bourbon black
belt element proved a champion of the Negro in the convention, while such men as Heflin and the hillbilly spokesmen were his bitterest enemies.

But whatever the intentions of the men who erected
these barriers to the Southern ballot-box, the fact is
that to-day, from a third to a half-century later, the
number of persons of both races who are prevented by
them from voting is enormous. That is particularly
true in the poll-taxed states, where the number of whites
participating in the business of electing candidates to
office is by far the lowest in the Union.

In the Presidential election of 1936, for example, the
nine states which then had the poll-tax sent only 24
per cent of their adult citizens to the polls, whereas in
the thirty-nine other states, 72 per cent voted. In 1940,
the South made an even more deplorable showing,
for the percentage of its adults who exercised their
sovereign right dropped to 21.1 in the eight states with

poll-taxes. The fact that in the rest of the country, there was a slight decrease to 70.6 per cent is relatively unimportant, since a popular participation in excess of 70 per cent is reasonably adequate. It is the bulk of the South, with its drop from the already low figure of 24 per cent to the even lower figure of 21.1, which must explain, if it can, how such limited functioning of the democratic process can be termed "democracy."

To what extent is the low percentage in the eight above-mentioned states attributable to the fact that so few Negroes vote? That is part of the answer, of course, but by no means all. The whites outnumber the Negroes by large majorities in all but one Southern state to-day, and in that one, Mississippi, the whites enjoy a slight numerical superiority. In other words, the proportion of whites who vote in these eight states is but a fraction of those who do so in the rest of the country. Estimates which seem reliable place the proportion of adult whites voting in these states at a low of 18 per cent for South Carolina and a high of 33 per cent for Tennessee. This is partly accounted for by the comparative lack of competition from the Republicans in the South, with a corresponding lack of interest, and by the other franchise restrictions, in addition to the poll-tax. However, it cannot be doubted that this levy, which ranges from one to two dollars a year, bears a large share of the responsibility.

It is argued, occasionally, that the white voters of the poll-taxed states do, in fact, exercise the franchise freely in the Democratic primaries, and that aspersions based upon the small number of voters in elections are therefore unjustified (Negroes are banned from those primaries in nearly all Southern states). But the late

Representative Geyer of California torpedoed that argument with an analysis of the 78 Democratic primaries held in the poll-taxed states during 1940 for the choice of Representatives in Congress. More than half of them —42 to be exact—were uncontested, while in the 30 where primary elections were held, fewer than one-third as many voters took part as in the general elections for members of Congress in other parts of the country.

Let us also compare the number of voters in Virginia, which has a poll-tax, with the number in North Carolina, which repealed its tax in 1920. In 1936 the number of Virginians who voted for the various Presidential candidates was 334,000, whereas no fewer than 839,000 North Carolinians participated in the same election. In 1940, the Virginia total was roughly 345,000, as compared with 823,000 for North Carolina. The population of the Old North State is only about one-third greater than that of the Old Dominion, and conditions in the two Commonwealths are similar. Yet the number of voters is always vastly greater in the former than in the latter. The same thing is true in West Virginia, Kentucky, and Maryland, each of which borders on Virginia, each of which has no poll-tax, and each of which casts from nearly two to nearly three times Virginia's vote.

Why has the poll-tax persisted in the South? There are various reasons. In the first place, the conviction persists in many parts of the region that this device is still necessary to the maintenance of "white supremacy." In the second place, the political leaders often favor retention of the levy, since those who have been chosen to office by a limited electorate naturally prefer not to risk the uncertainty of a contest in which thousands of new voters take part. Again, those interests which prefer to see political power remain in the hands of the "upper crust" of propertied voters, rather than in those of the masses, likewise back the *status quo*. Lastly, the attitude of the disfranchised whites has been, in the main, either indifferent or inarticulate, until recent years.

What have been the political and social consequences of the levy? It has tended to encourage corruption, for the wholesale payment of taxes by political organizations is a common practice. Another result has been the partial atrophy of the democratic process, owing to limited participation by the people in that process. Another is that it has placed obstacles in the way of securing needed social and labor legislation in states where so many beneficiaries of this legislation cannot vote.

Mississippi still has no workmen's compensation law, while Arkansas, Florida, and South Carolina passed such legislation only in recent years. Virginia, North Carolina, and Louisiana are the only Southern states which limit women's work to 48 hours per week. Child labor legislation and state labor departments are considerably less effective in the South than elsewhere, and the only Southern states with minimum-wage laws are Kentucky, Louisiana, and Arkansas. The first two have no poll-tax, and the $1.25 a day minimum in Arkansas makes the law there largely meaningless.

This tax also makes movements for reform in state or local government more difficult than in regions where it is not levied. Political machines see that their followers' capitation taxes are paid up, with the result that when the ordinary independent voter becomes aroused a short time before election, it is apt to be past the deadline for making the payment, or he may have to pay several years' back taxes before he can vote. In Virginia, for example, he must pay up for three years, if his tax for that period is in arrears, or approximately $5.00, including penalties. In Georgia the levy is cumulative for seven years, making a maximum of $15.50 in tax and interest which can be assessed, while in Alabama a man under forty years of age can be required to pay his back tax of $1.50 for every year since he reached the age of twenty-one.

Those who favor abolition of the capitation levy contend that the tax might be justified if anybody could show that the states which have it enjoy an obviously better brand of state and local government than those which do not. But they ask whether it can be seriously argued that South Carolina, Mississippi, or Georgia is better governed than, say, Connecticut, Kansas, or Colorado. They point out, further, that nearly every notorious political mountebank who has arisen in the twentieth century has been chosen by a poll-taxed electorate, so that the tax is obviously no protection against such exhibitionists. In the case of Huey Long, the most notorious of all, a poll-taxed electorate made him the czar of Louisiana, but his machine was finally smashed by voters who no longer had to pay such an admission fee to the ballot-box. The fee was abolished, after the establishment of the dictatorship. Thus a corrupt, authoritarian régime was established under the ægis of the very tax which is supposed to prevent such eventualities, while the rascals were turned out by the type of enlarged and relatively unrestricted electorate which many believe to be conducive to graft and demagoguery.

As for the maintenance of "white supremacy," advocates of poll-tax repeal deny that this issue has any particular significance to-day. George C. Stoney, who has done a number of incisive articles on the Southern franchise, points out that fewer than one per cent of the Negroes in Louisiana vote, although there is no poll-tax, and that only a few more go to the polls in North Carolina. Moreover, an inquiry into the voting habits of Negroes in two adjacent counties of Virginia and North Carolina, based upon the presidential election of 1936, showed that more than one per cent of the Negroes voted in Mecklenburg County, Virginia, as against one-third of one per cent in Warren County, North Carolina, although there is a poll-tax in the former and none in the latter. By way of contrast, however, fewer than 17 per cent of the whites voted in the Virginia county, as against 40 per cent in the North Carolina county. The Tar Heel State has a literacy test which requires every registrant for voting to "read and write any section of the constitution in the English language." Under this arrangement, hundreds of thousands of formerly disfranchised whites are voting, while the proportion of Negro participants in the elections is no larger than in the average poll-taxed state. While the above-mentioned literacy test evidently is being used at times as a subterfuge for the disqualification of eligible colored citizens, its advocates point out that it at least allows most of the whites to reach the ballot-box. No election law is entirely proof against abuse.

Those who favor retention of the poll-tax frequently say that "if a man isn't willing to pay a dollar or two a year to vote, he isn't much of a citizen," an argument which ignores the fact that in times of economic stress, and even in boom times, there are thousands whose meager incomes will not permit even so small a cash outlay. Another argument on behalf of the levy is that since in the eight poll-taxed states the proceeds from these payments go wholly or partly to public education, abolition of the capitation tax would cause the schools to suffer. But the poll-taxed states do not enforce collection of this so-called tax, which is really a voluntary payment. The consequence is that receipts are far below what they would be if it were a regularly collected head tax on every adult, proceeds from which would be devoted to public education.

Official figures on state-suffrage tax receipts for 1940 give the following totals—which do not vary greatly, in most states, from year to year: Alabama, $467,392; Arkansas, $278,367; Texas, $1,712,315; Georgia, $304,-769; and Virginia, $821,609. In Tennessee, South Carolina, and Mississippi, where the tax is collected locally, it is impossible to secure recent statistics. Collections in 1936 for Tennessee totaled $655,470, and for South Carolina, $255,419, while the Mississippi figure for 1932 was $1,369,000.

It is clear from the foregoing that if a head-tax were levied and collected annually on every adult in these eight states, without relationship to the franchise, receipts would be two or three times as large as at present, with corresponding benefits to education. Massachusetts and Connecticut, for example, each raise between $2,-000,000 and $3,000,000 a year in this way for education, welfare, and other local purposes.

Those who favor the *status quo* in the realm of the poll-tax likewise argue that in these days, when millions are on relief and other millions are crying for largess of one sort or another from the public treasury, it is unwise to throw the polls open to urban laborers, rural sharecroppers, and other underprivileged elements with possibly prehensile tendencies.

Whatever the validity of this argument in other spheres, it certainly has little in so far as old-age pension schemes are concerned. This is because six of the eight poll-taxed states exempt from payment persons who have arrived at a certain age. In one, the exemption begins at age 45, in one at age 50, and in four at age 60. Hence, in the words of the Richmond *Times-Dispatch,* "the limited electorate of younger voters who have paid the levy will be swamped by the older ones who don't have to pay it, and who are apt to vote for weekly 'ham and egg' outlays to the aged—mere scrip-tease devices which are sure to break down in the end."

The poll-tax is, of course, a well-known vehicle of corruption, for despite laws forbidding the payment of such levies *en bloc* by political machines, such payments are made with great regularity in many parts of the South. The defeated machine in San Antonio, a notorious and reactionary organization, tried to use the Texas law which forbids loans or gifts of money for the payment of poll-taxes, against former Mayor Maury Maverick, one of the South's most aggressive advocates of poll-tax reform and cleaner elections. Mayor Maverick was acquitted of lending money to members of a labor union so they could qualify to vote for him, but plenty of this sort of thing goes on. Usually the payments are made by entrenched and sinister politicians, bent on sandbagging the public.

It has developed of late that the poll-tax has not only been used as a device to limit the electorate, but that payment has become a prerequisite to jury service in some areas. In at least one Virginia county it has been definitely established that the list of qualified voters was being used as the sole source of names of prospective petit jurors—and in order to get on this list one must pay one's poll-tax. It is noteworthy, too, that every prospective grand juror in Virginia must swear that he is "entitled to vote and to hold office under the Constitution of this State," which apparently means that he must have paid his poll-tax, although the section has never been construed by the courts. While in the average case, this may not have any special significance, it can readily be seen that in a case involving economic and social conflict between, let us say, a landlord and a sharecropper, the exclusion from both grand and petit juries of all who have not paid their poll-taxes probably would be definitely unfair to the sharecropper.

Opponents of suffrage reform in the South are wont to argue, at times, that poll-tax repeal wouldn't affect appreciably the size of the electorate, and that therefore one of the major objectives of the repealists would not be achieved. It is impossible to understand the basis of their contention, since practically all the figures are against them. The fact that the vote is far larger in the Southern states which have no poll-tax than in those which have it, has been mentioned. Moreover the effects of the poll-tax upon the size of the electorate were manifest from the time it was applied. In Tennessee, for example, 90 per cent of the adult male population voted in the presidential contest of 1888. By 1892, after the poll-tax became effective, the percentage dropped to 70. By 1904, it was 58 per cent, by 1920 it was 46 per cent, by 1928 it was 34 per cent, and by 1940, it had fallen to 28 per cent. These figures are for both white and colored. In Virginia, following the application of the poll-tax to the electorate, the white vote was cut almost exactly in half, to say nothing of the colored vote. More recently, repeal of the tax in Louisiana and Florida was followed by huge increases in the number of white voters. In the latter state, the total vote in the first regular Democratic primary, following repeal, underwent an increase of 100 per cent.

Is it argued that these new voters are merely riff-raff, who are not sufficiently interested in their government to pay a dollar or two a year to exercise the franchise? Then what of the thousands who are disqualified by the requirement that the tax be paid so long in advance of the election as to render voting impossible to those who become interested in a given contest after the deadline? (Payment of the tax must be made from six to ten months in advance of the election in Georgia, Mississippi, Texas, and Virginia.) Consider also the results of a survey made at Alabama Polytechnic Institute in 1940 to determine the effect of the tax upon the eligibility of the faculty to vote. No fewer than 78 teachers and 35 other staff members were found to be ineligible because they had not registered and paid their poll-taxes. All could have voted if they had fulfilled these requirements. The 78 teachers comprised 37 per cent of the teaching staff at the Institute.

The statistics as to this center of learning at Auburn undoubtedly could be duplicated, or nearly duplicated, in many other similar places. Thousands of the South's best-fitted citizens are not voting, because they have not found it possible to thread the maze of barriers to the ballot-box which the Southern politicians have erected. As already noted, these barriers play directly

into the hands of politicians, by enabling them to purchase the venal vote through poll-tax payments *en bloc.*
The question arises, therefore, whether the levy isn't
lowering the general level of public morality, and glori-
fying venality and ignorance at the expense of honesty
and intelligence.

George C. Stoney makes the amazing statement that
in this land of the so-called "secret ballot," the politicians of Texas, Arkansas, Georgia, and Alabama, as
well as Missouri and Illinois, actually can tell how a
citizen votes by checking the number which appears on
each ballot against the corresponding number opposite
his name in the registration book. Similar shenanigans
are possible in South Carolina. The fact that it is against
the law, is not an effective deterrent, as some of the
politicians in these states admit. To illustrate how the
system works, Mr. Stoney mentioned a small Alabama
community where the polling place is the store of the
big local supply merchant, who supervises all elections.
It seemed only too true that this worthy did not reject
the temptation to pry into the electoral preferences of
the few citizens of the community who were able to
meet the state's elaborate franchise requirements.

A different sort of abuse of the electoral process exists in Tennessee, where the boss-controlled vote of
Memphis is large enough to swing almost any state election. The result is that the Memphis machine, ruled
by Edward H. Crump, otherwise yclept the "Red Snapper," controls Tennessee, to all intents and purposes.
Here, again, the poll-tax makes that control easier than
it would otherwise be, for we have noted that the tax
plays into the hands of machines everywhere. Not only
does the levy enable the Crump machine to control the

vote more readily, through block payments, but it keeps the total vote of all parties in Tennessee down to around 400,000. With the Memphis organization able to throw 100,000 Democratic votes in any direction it sees fit, Tennessee has virtually become a political fief of "Boss" Crump, who controls not only the governor, but also the state legislature. Silliman Evans, the liberal publisher of the Nashville *Tennessean,* who has declared war on this political prestidigitator, delivered a memorable attack on him in an address to the Tennessee Press Association in 1941. Discussing the legislative session of that year, Mr. Evans described a situation not wholly unlike Louisiana under the rule of Huey Long:

> Mr. Crump . . . has controlled this legislature lock, stock and barrel. Through his underlings, Gerber, Joyner and Cooper, he has been in daily and minute direction of this legislature. No bill has been passed without his consent; every bill he has desired has been enacted. There have been no public hearings on bills by our committees. Bill after bill has been passed when hardly a dozen members of the enacting body knew what a line of the bill meant nor what it would do when it became a law. Legislative clerks have read captions of bills in a sing song, less understandable than that of a tobacco auctioneer, and then, without the sound of a gavel heard, announced the vote "99 to 1" for passage. . . .
> No man nor woman can hold office under [Governor] Prentice Cooper who is distasteful to Mr. Crump. I not only refer to cabinet members, but to clerks and stenographers.

It was this same "Boss" Crump who knifed the move to repeal the poll-tax in Tennessee, after both he and Cooper, his gubernatorial stooge, had openly advocated repeal. Mr. Cooper did so in 1938, prior to his first election to the governorship. But when the legislature met the following year, all poll-tax-repeal bills were smothered, despite the fact that the Governor seemed to be able to get through any bills he really wanted. Up for reëlection in 1939, Cooper reiterated his advocacy of repeal, and Crump echoed his sentiments. Advocates of lowering the voting requirements took heart, and a concerted drive was organized. Jennings Perry of the Nashville *Tennessean* wrote a series of articles in support of repeal, which was published simultaneously in that paper and in the Memphis *Press-Scimitar*, Chattanooga *Times*, and Knoxville *News-Sentinel*.

Despite this powerful press support, and the apparent fact that a majority of the members of the legislature, as candidates for the law-making body the previous year, had endorsed repeal, it was chloroformed at the session of 1941. The bill was put to sleep by the very pair who had urged its passage shortly before—Crump and Cooper. The result was that a battle royal was looked for in 1942, and the progressive elements in Tennessee were girding up their loins for a showdown fight with the Memphis "Red Snapper." They were confident that they had him heavily on the defensive, at last.

The campaign against the poll-tax in the Volunteer State should be facilitated by the presence of the inevitable corruption, which is an integral part of the system there, as elsewhere. Several persons were convicted recently of distributing counterfeit poll-tax receipts in Chattanooga. Such a conviction is a rare achievement, for usually the laws against this sort of thing are so dependent upon machine office-holders for their enforcement that convictions are hardly ever obtained. If an effort should be made to bring any one to book for such an offense in Memphis, under the guns of the most powerful city machine in the South, the results could only be surmised.

The Southern Electoral Reform League's rôle in Tennessee and other Southern states with poll-taxes may be important. This agency holds no fellowship with Communists or fellow-travelers, having fought the issue out at its initial meeting, and banned these brethren from membership. The argument that the Reds should be consolidated with other elements into a "united front," for the purpose of achieving a common goal, was rejected on the excellent ground that their disruptive methodology and their genius for evoking antagonisms would do far more harm than good.

The league adopted a resolution at its first meeting, approving the Geyer bill for congressional repeal of the poll-tax, in so far as it applies to Federal elections, but some of the league's officers and members do not desire to see this legislation passed, and to date the organization has been concentrating largely upon abolishing the levy by state action. Passage of the Geyer bill, or the Pepper bill, its senatorial companion, would cause a frightful uproar in the South. Such action would be regarded by most Southerners as an unwarranted invasion of their affairs, and would contribute greatly to intersectional bitterness. As in the case of Federal prohibition, unsympathetic Southerners would take pleasure in circumventing the law's provisions and nullifying its effectiveness. Far better that the individual states should resolve this knotty question for themselves.

Until late in 1941, there was the possibility that the result sought by the Geyer and Pepper bills would be achieved through court action. Although the United States Supreme Court held in a unanimous opinion in the Breedlove case of 1937 that the Georgia poll-tax was constitutional, a test of the Tennessee tax as a prerequisite to participation in elections of congressional candidates was initiated by the Southern Conference for Human Welfare. The district and circuit courts had ruled in this case that the tax does not contravene the Constitution, but it was felt that the Supreme Court might decide, despite its opinion as to the Georgia tax, that convincing new arguments had been found, since this case, involving one Henry Pirtle, was presented to the court on a different basis from Georgia's Breedlove case of some years before. Nevertheless, the Supreme Court declined even to hear argument, and the effort to outlaw the tax by this means collapsed. The effect of a contrary ruling upon Southern opinion would not have been salutary, although it would doubtless have evoked a less violent response than would follow the adoption of a congressional act by the North and West over the South's reverberating protest. Efforts to secure the passage of such an act were continuing intensively early in 1942, and there was talk of carrying another poll-tax case up to the country's highest legal tribunal.

Whatever the final disposition of the matter in the courts, and the ultimate arbitrament of the Congress, the fact remains that the South is awakening with considerable rapidity to the iniquitous character of this admission fee to the polling booth. More and more Southerners are arriving at the conclusion that there is no proper relationship between the size of one's bank roll, and one's fitness to exercise the franchise in a democracy. Young men are being drafted by the thousands, and trained for the defense of their country, with no questions asked concerning their payment or nonpayment of poll-taxes. Yet these same young men are not considered competent to vote unless they have complied with archaic and outmoded requirements instituted some decades ago, at a time when conditions bore no resemblance to those which prevail to-day. Small wonder then, that the poll-tax is under fire in the South, and that the fire is getting hotter.

V

CIVIL LIBERTIES AMONG US

ARE freedom of speech, assembly, and religion surviving in the South? Is there equality before the law? Is there genuine collective bargaining for labor? Is the right of suffrage enjoyed freely by the people? Is race prejudice at a minimum?

The consensus among informed Southerners is that conditions are better than they were a decade ago. Only one of the ten persons with whom the writer has corresponded in the preparation of this chapter feels that civil liberties in the South are less firmly rooted than they were in 1932. This dissenter believes "that the causes of industrial conflict are becoming more acute, and that in the South especially, organized labor has been accorded a very partial recognition, and that very grudgingly." Eight others, scattered in all sections of the South, and the director of the American Civil Liberties Union in New York are of the opposite opinion, although one or two feel that much of the recent improvement can be traced to the Roosevelt Administration, and that its replacement by a conservative régime in 1941 would inevitably have brought retrogression.

It is apparent that violations of civil rights in the South, as elsewhere in the United States, occur more frequently in areas of employer-employee conflict than in any other sphere. Even the field of race relations appears to yield fewer denials of individual constitutional prerogatives. When the American Civil Liberties Union listed eleven major "centers of repression" in the entire country for the year which ended in June, 1937, six of the eleven were located in the South—a very high percentage for a region which incorporates only a fraction of the national area and population. While the theater of labor conflict in these six centers impinged in some cases upon the province of race relations, the fundamental reason why at least five of the six were rightfully denounced as "centers of repression" lay in the violent resistance which manifested itself there to the unionization of workers. The six which were black-listed were Harlan County, Kentucky, the sharecropper country of Eastern Arkansas, and the cities of Tampa, Atlanta, Birmingham, and New Orleans. It is gratifying to record that during the year which ended in June, 1938, the Civil Liberties Union found sufficient improvement in Arkansas, Atlanta, Birmingham, and New Orleans to take each of them off the list. However, Memphis and San Antonio were added to the list, with the result that the South had four of the country's eight "centers of repression" for that twelvemonth. Just as in the preceding year, all four were cited because of the violence committed within their boundaries against representatives of organized labor. Another survey of 332 cities by the Civil Liberties Union early in 1939, made on a somewhat different basis, concluded that "the worst communities belong to the Middle West, New England, and the South." However, of the four with the lowest ratings in the entire United States, the South had three: Little Rock, Tampa, and New Orleans. A notable event of 1941 was the freeing by Lieutenant-Governor Rodes K. Myers of the four Harlan County miners who were serving life terms in Kentucky for their part in the fatal clash with mine guards at Evarts in 1931. The other three were pardoned in 1935.

The charge that union men are "Communists," "Reds," or "agitators" is a frequent one in cities of the sort mentioned above, and an authentic Communist is apt to be run out of town by the police—as Earl Browder learned in 1936, when he went to Atlanta to make an address. It was in the following year that Mayor Overton of Memphis made his famous announcement that "C.I.O. agitators, Communists, and highly paid professional organizers are not wanted in Memphis." This was followed by a statement from Police Commissioner Davis that "we will not tolerate foreign agitators," and that "we know Norman Smith and his whereabouts, and will take care of that situation very soon." Within forty-eight hours, Smith, a C.I.O. organizer, was badly beaten up by a gang of men. Police Commissioner Davis then announced blandly that "the city government is opposed to violence." A different approach to the problem was made in Macon, Georgia, where an extraordinary city ordinance was passed to forbid the distribution of "any handbill, circular, pamphlet, poster, postcard, or literature of any kind"—a measure frankly designed, according to the mayor, to give the city council control over labor propaganda. A still more amazing ordinance in Birmingham, which permits the authorities to hold a person indefinitely without placing any charge against him, was invoked at least thrice during 1940. The victims in each case were suspected of Communism.

Sometimes, of course, the charge of Communism is justified, as in the sharecropper region of Arkansas, where the Southern Tenant Farmers' Union became affiliated with the United Cannery, Agricultural, Packing, and Allied Workers of America, a C.I.O. union, and later severed relations with it, after becoming convinced that the organization was under Communist leadership. While there is still resistance to unionization of the sharecroppers, officials of the S.T.F.U. state that violations of civil rights in Arkansas are far less frequent than they were in 1934, when their union was established, and that union meetings can now be held openly almost everywhere in the state. But the organization is moribund, and perhaps the chief benefit derived by the sharecroppers from this activity is the publicity which the sharecropper situation has received.

Too little emphasis has been given throughout this controversy to the serious economic situation of the cotton planters, who were, in many cases, on the brink of ruin, prior to the price boom of 1941. These victims of the severe malaise of King Cotton are often far from being the ruthless exploiters of the poor described by some of our contemporary authorities on the South who have yet to cross the Hudson River traveling west. The predicament of thousands of cotton planters is, or has been, not unlike that of numerous Southern employers whose businesses have been set up and operated for many years on the basis of non-union wage scales, and who suddenly find themselves confronted with a demand for the much higher union scale, which may mean bankruptcy. Violence against the union, under such circumstances, is never justified—and unions which indulge in sit-down strikes and other forms of lawlessness cannot afford to be too derisive, in any event—but the objections of such an open-shop employer to union organization are at least comprehensible. Furthermore, the vicious exploitation of workers in certain New England states, the widespread prevalence of sweatshops in those same states, and the arrogant attitude of certain employers there toward unions and the Federal government itself, should demonstrate that the South has no monopoly on such practices.

It is interesting to note, on the basis of material gathered by Dr. Arthur Raper of Atlanta, that far more strikers and labor organizers were killed in the South in the period immediately preceding the birth of the C.I.O. than subsequently. In 1929 and 1930, when Gastonia and Marion were in the headlines and the first great textile strike was on, seven strikers and one police chief were slain. In 1934 and 1935, no fewer than forty-two Southern laborers and organizers were killed in strikes. In 1936 and 1937, with the coming of the C.I.O., only five workers and organizers were killed in Southern labor disorders; the total for 1938 and 1939 was 14, while the figure for 1940 and 1941 is six. But while slayings have become less numerous, beatings have increased, and organizers are all too frequently set upon by company deputies, sometimes accompanied by irate citizens, or by non-union workers who have been persuaded, whether rightly or wrongly, that unionization will bankrupt their employers.

The sit-down has never been widely used in the South, but transgressions by union labor against the rights of employers or non-union labor occur here as elsewhere. Sometimes these transgressions are flagrant, as they were when "flying squadrons" of textile workers closed many mills in the Southeast by terrorization and other violent means in the A. F. of L. textile strike of 1934. More recently, union pickets have used threats of physical force to prevent non-union men from going to work in various parts of the South, and at times of labor tension, there is too often coercion or intimidation of workers who do not wish to affiliate with the union. Fortunately, the South has been afflicted relatively little by the extremes of labor violence and racketeering which have provoked such a reaction in certain Northern and Western states.

Because of the small number of Negroes in Southern unions, there has been comparatively little invocation of the race issue in labor clashes. At the same time, the Negro question casts its dark shadow over every phase of Southern civilization. There is reason to believe that the Negro is getting a better break than ever before, in most respects, although such legislation as the AAA and the Federal wage-and-hour law may have been more harmful to him than otherwise. Restrictions in acreage have thrown thousands of Negro tenants and sharecroppers on relief, while the fixing of minimum wages has caused thousands more to be replaced by machinery, or by white workers, of whom there is such a large surplus. Many Negroes have, of course, benefited from this same legislation.

But if the Negro is frequently losing his means of livelihood through the operation of laws designed to promote his economic security, and if he is excluded from most labor unions, it can also be said that he is less apt to be lynched than at any time since the Civil War, that he is more apt to obtain justice in the courts, and that his educational opportunities are far better. This last can be attributed not only to the fact that Southern schools and colleges for Negroes have been undergoing a gradual improvement for decades, but also to the recent decision of the Supreme Court in the

Gaines case, which directed the State of Missouri to provide Negroes with facilities for the study of law equal
to those provided for the whites at the University of
Missouri, or to admit them to the latter institution.

The South seems to have reached a point where lynch
law is approaching extinction in several Southern states.
In others—such as Mississippi, Georgia, Louisiana, and
Florida—these barbarities keep recurring, and there appears to be no hope of effective action by state or local
authorities. The answer would be a Federal anti-lynching
law with teeth in it, were it not for the violent feeling
aroused in the South against such legislation by the filibuster of certain Southern senators early in 1938. Prior
to that filibuster—in which the terms of the Federal bill
were distorted, its purposes misrepresented, and a synthetic uproar created—the South appeared to be willing
to accept such a law, and its passage seemed desirable.
But after the statesmen from Dixie had shaken the
Capitol rafters for weeks with apostrophes to the fair
name of Southern womanhood, and had thunderously
bellowed that the Wagner-Van Nuys bill was the greatest threat to "white supremacy" since Reconstruction,
there were alarums from Harper's Ferry to Eagle Pass,
and the excitement hasn't fully subsided yet.

Another violation of civil rights occurs in those areas
of the South where peonage is still practiced, usually
with Negroes as the victims. There was a dramatic example of this in Warren County, Georgia, during 1937,
when a mob organized by local planters forced Negro
workers at the point of guns to go into the cotton fields
and pick cotton for wages well below those prevailing
in nearby counties. A Southern economist and student
of interracial matters who investigated this episode re-

ported that the same thing happened "in a less dramatic and brutal manner in many other cotton belt counties." At about this time it was revealed that a somewhat different method was employed by certain turpentine camp operators in Florida. They were taking truckloads of newly arrived Negro laborers to the commissary, issuing them supplies, sometimes at exorbitant prices, and then invoking a section of the Florida code under which implied legislative consent is given to wholesale peonage. In Arkansas, the legislature has recently struck so hard at the fee system that constables apparently will no longer be able to arrest impecunious persons, mostly Negroes, on misdemeanor charges, have them fined one hundred dollars, and then hustle them off to certain privately owned plantations to work out the fine in chains.

The disfranchisement of millions of Southerners, both white and colored, by means of restrictions upon the franchise, is a practice which must be considered in any appraisal of the current state of civil liberties in the region. Chief among these restrictions is the poll tax, a levy which has been held to be technically within the law by the Supreme Court, but which reduces the number of voters in eight Southern states to a mere fraction of what it would otherwise be, and hence affects directly the ability of Southerners to fight at the ballot box for their civil and other rights.

While the small number of voters in most Southern states serves to deaden the political capacity of the Southern electorate, the existence of anti-evolution laws in Tennessee, Mississippi, and Arkansas constricts the intellectual horizons of wide areas, and at the same time basically affects religious freedom in those areas. Several ineffectual efforts have been made to repeal the Tennessee law under which John T. Scopes was tried in the "monkey trial" in 1925, but the state stands firm for Genesis, secure in the touching faith of the statesman who sponsored the anti-evolution bill in its legislature, expressing the conviction that the Bible was dictated by God in the English of the King James version.

However, the most recent attack on religious freedom in America came when the sect known as Jehovah's Witnesses was the victim of an epidemic of persecution for the refusal of its votaries to salute the flag. Members of this church were set upon violently in many states, both inside and outside the South. Rhode Island, which Roger Williams made the cradle of religious liberty, was the only state to consider legislation outlawing the refusal of any religious group to salute the flag. Fortunately, this effort to desecrate Williams' memory was defeated.

One of the agencies responsible for foisting anti-evolution legislation upon the former Confederacy is the Ku Klux Klan, happily now moribund, but a formidable force in the middle 1920's. Efforts are currently being made to revive it, and a new Imperial Wizard has lately been installed in Atlanta for the purpose of pumping new life into the organization. Published reports have it that the retiring Wizard, Hiram W. Evans, was not sufficiently anti-Semitic and anti-Catholic, and that J. A. Colescott, his successor, will fill this requirement more adequately. Exhorting the kludds, klaverns, and klonvocations to greater heights of prejudice and bigotry, Imperial Wizard Colescott declared at the time of his election that the Klan would represent the "native-born, white, Protestant, Gentile" population of America. More recently, he declared that if it should become necessary to drive Communists, Nazis, and Fascists out of the country, he could call together "4,000,000 of my people on a moment's notice and tell them to grab axes, clubs, anything they can find, and report at once for duty at the nearest police station or army headquarters"!

If one can judge the future by the recent past, the C.I.O. will be a major object of the Klan's hostility. In Florida, where the K.K.K. is especially strong, and where it influences the government of Tampa heavily, a strike of C.I.O. citrus workers was broken by Klan intimidation. The Klan has also been demonstrating actively in South Carolina and Georgia against the C.I.O. Moreover, it has been guilty of numerous flogging outrages in both states, chiefly on "moral" grounds. Nevertheless, it has experienced difficulty in finding a formula sufficiently arresting to captivate the populace, and the racket is clearly showing signs of bogging down.

The South, in the past, has been more anti-Catholic than anti-Semitic, but the publicity given European anti-Semitism may cause the K.K.K. to devote special attention to Dixie's infinitesimal minority of Jews. All the thaumaturgy it can summon will be turned against the Southern "non-Aryans," if impecunious Southerners seem sufficiently gullible to blame the Jews for their woes. Fortunately there is reason to believe that most Southerners are unreceptive to such balderdash. *Fortune's* survey of anti-Semitism made in the spring of 1939 indicated that anti-Jewish feeling is on the increase in the large cities of the country, but not in the towns, villages, and rural regions—which comprise the great bulk of the South. Another evidence of the sentiment in the cotton states is seen in the overwhelmingly enthusiastic reception accorded the late Grover C. Hall's four thousand word signed editorial in the Montgomery *Advertiser,* entitled "The Egregious Gentile Called to Account." George W. Christians, the Chattanoogan who trains his hair and mustache to resemble Hitler's as closely as possible, seems more of an eccentric than a serious menace. Moreover, vast quantities of pro-Fascist and anti-Semitic propaganda no longer emanate from Asheville, North Carolina, for some years headquarters of William Dudley Pelley and his Silver Shirts. Pelley, a New Englander, moved to Noblesville, Indiana, but early in 1942 was brought back to North Carolina and sentenced in the Superior Court at Asheville to from two to three years on a conviction obtained there in 1935 of violating the North Carolina Security Laws, sentence having been suspended on condition of good behavior. The court held that Pelley had violated other laws during the probationary period.[1] There is also the distinct encouragement for Southerners contained in the second successive unanimous reëlection of Sol Blatt as speaker of the South Carolina House of Representatives.

What of anti-Catholic sentiment in the South to-day? Would the nomination of a member of the Catholic Church for the presidency revive the frenzies of 1928, when Al Smith's nomination threw four states into the Republican column for the first time since Reconstruction? The consensus is that the effects of such a nomination would be much less devastating than they were then, because of the weakness of the Klan and the general lessening of anti-Catholic prejudice. It is significant in this connection to consider the results of a Gallup poll

[1] Pelley appealed to the North Carolina Supreme Court from this sentence in February, 1942.

taken in the spring of 1940 to ascertain the relative strength of Postmaster James A. Farley, a Catholic, and of Thomas E. Dewey. Farley ran far behind Dewey everywhere except in the South, where he was just as far ahead, with 63 per cent of the total vote. In the same Southern states, Governor Smith polled 48.5 per cent of the vote in 1928.

To sum up, there is reason for believing that the civil liberties of Southerners enjoy better protection to-day than they have ever done before. The road has been hard and difficult, and many more obstacles must be surmounted, before the end of it is reached. But indisputable progress must be recorded.

VI

IN GROVES OF ACADEME

VIEWED in relation to such arbitrary and mathematically measurable criteria as endowment, enrollment, library, and plant, the Southern institutions of higher learning are overshadowed by the foremost universities of the North and West. Yet their substantial contributions to education and to knowledge are not calculable by stereotyped rules of thumb. The traditions of a college or a university cannot be pictured in a graph, the inspirational influence of its great teachers cannot be adumbrated in a table of statistics.

It is undeniable that higher education in the South suffers from various infirmities, chief among which is a lack of funds, but there are impecunious institutions in the region with a genuine reverence for the truth, and a veritable passion for tending its flickering flame. Scores of well-equipped and intellectually curious graduates go forth from their halls each year. It is equally undeniable, however, that other Southern educational centers with more adequate financial resources fail to realize their opportunities, and flounder along in mediocrity.

Prior to the Civil War, the colleges and universities below the Potomac compared favorably with those beyond that stream. There were scholars of towering stature on various Southern faculties. But the South's defeat struck such a shattering blow to the whole educational structure of the region, especially to its financial underpinning, that its forward surge was interrupted for a considerable period.

No one contends seriously to-day that members of Southern faculties are any less able or industrious, or any less productive, under a given set of circumstances, than those of other regions, but every one knows that they are constantly being drained away from Southern campuses to the wealthy institutions of the North and West. At those institutions they are provided with considerably higher salaries, as well as considerably lighter teaching loads. Small wonder, then, that many of them accept the offers which come to them, or that their contributions to knowledge in their non-Southern environments often are more substantial than they could possibly have been under the more difficult circumstances which previously confronted them.

The average Southern scholar customarily carries a teaching load 30 per cent greater than his Northern or Western contemporary, and works for a salary one-third less. Such, at least, were the average differentials between the sections in 1932, when Dr. Wilson Gee of the University of Virginia explored the problem and published his valuable little book, *Research Barriers in the South*. More up-to-date statistics do not seem to have been compiled by any individual or agency, and the assumption here is that the relative positions of the sections with respect to the foregoing matters are roughly the same to-day as in the early 1930's.

The inadequacy of nearly all Southern college and university endowments and appropriations is a matter of common knowledge. The four American universities which are generally ranked first in the country as centers of advanced scholarship and research, are Harvard,

Chicago, Columbia, and Yale. They are the four with the largest endowments. Harvard, with nearly $142,-000,000; Yale with nearly $107,000,000; Columbia, with $87,000,000, and Chicago, with $71,000,000, all have far larger endowments than any Southern institution.

The University of Texas, with $43,000,000; Duke, with $34,000,000, Vanderbilt, with $25,000,000, Rice Institute, with $15,000,000, the University of Virginia, with $11,000,000, Berea College, in the Kentucky Mountains, with $10,200,000, and Hampton Institute, with $10,000,000, are the only Southern institutions with endowments of as much as $10,000,000. Emory University, which has $5,200,000 and is about to share $10,000,000 more with Agnes Scott College, may also be said to deserve a place on this select list.

Texas and Virginia, as state universities, also have annual appropriations from their respective legislatures, of course. Yet, as centers of graduate research, they are hardly to be classed with half a dozen state universities in other regions, some of which have much smaller endowments. Take the University of California, which has $24,000,000, and comes close to first rank among the state universities of America. Or take the universities of Minnesota, Wisconsin, Michigan, Illinois, and Iowa, each of which must be placed ahead of either of the two Southern universities mentioned in its facilities for conferring the doctorate.

Obviously, one cannot always appraise the value of a university simply by measuring the size of its endowment. For example, one would scarcely compare Duke University to Princeton. Yet Duke has slightly the larger endowment. And while the University of North Carolina has an endowment of only $2,000,000, its relatively adequate support from the state treasury, combined with extremely able and progressive leadership and administration, have caused it to take rank far above some wealthier institutions. Roughly the same thing is true of the University of Wisconsin which, like the university at Chapel Hill, has practically no endowment, but has influenced profoundly the thinking of an entire region.

Since the average Southern state is considerably poorer in taxable values and income than the average state in other areas, and since all Southern states have separate educational systems for the white and colored races, they should have been extremely careful in past years not to establish duplicate state-supported colleges and universities, thus dissipating their limited resources among many more such institutions than they require. Yet precisely the opposite is the case. When it is realized that there are Southern states with eight, ten, or even sixteen colleges of one sort or another, all drawing funds from the state treasury, and offering courses which are duplicated in several other units of the system, it is easy to understand why none of the units receives proper support. Virginia is a notorious example. Like certain other Southern states, it has no fewer than four state teachers' colleges, and a Department of Education at the state university. It also has three engineering schools, two medical schools, and two law schools—all draining funds from the treasury of the Commonwealth. There is a grand total of nine state-supported institutions of higher learning for whites, with another for Negroes, but the job of abolishing even one of the schools in question is tremendous, owing to the vested interests which have arisen

The beautiful chapel at Duke University, one of the
South's principal centers of learning.

A vista on the campus of Tuskegee Institute, Alabama, the famous educational center for Negroes, founded by Booker T. Washington.

in all of them, the loud outcries from alumni as soon as abolition is suggested, and the political and commercial factors involved. The consequence is that in Virginia, as in most other Southern states, already limited appropriations are spread so thin over such a wide area as to be relatively ineffective. Florida, on the contrary, supports only two institutions of higher learning for whites and one for Negroes. However, its case is decidedly exceptional, and nearly all Southern states waste huge sums annually in overlapping services. Yet it should not be imagined that such duplications are found exclusively below Mason and Dixon's line, for similar situations exist in numerous Northern states.

Still another handicap which afflicts too many Southern colleges and universities is their overemphasis upon athletics, particularly football. While some of the most important educationally of these institutions also manage to hold their own in the annual gladiatorial orgies staged in Rose, Cotton, Orange, or Sugar Bowls, it may or may not be significant that the University of Alabama, which has the best long-time record of any American institution at the Pasadena Rose Bowl, is not equipped to award the Ph.D. degree in a single subject. The University of Tennessee with almost equally impressive performance on the gridiron, did not give the Ph.D. until recent years, and then only in a very few subjects. Both institutions are useful to their respective states, and it would be unfair, of course, to dismiss them as educationally inconsequential. Yet the contrast between their almost invariable preëminence in football, and their comparatively low rank in the world of scholarship cannot be overlooked. There is also Louisiana State University which "recently aired its athletic budgetary 'difficulties' in figures running well over one hundred thousand dollars," whereas "a query elicited the response that approximately one-twentieth as much had been benevolently assigned its graduate school." Then, too, a sports writer for the Associated Press declared in 1941 that Coach Dana X. Bible of the University of Texas was getting $15,600 a year, or $100 more than the president of the university. (*Life* magazine stated some months later that when Bible went to Texas at $15,000, he received nearly twice as much as the president.) In his last report to the Duke trustees, dealing with developments during the preceding session, the late President W. P. Few devoted twice as much space to athletics, especially football, as he gave to the graduate school. The University of Georgia conferred its first two Ph.D. degrees at the 1940 commencement. During the years when it was trouncing Yale time and again on Yale's own gridiron, a University of Georgia doctorate was unobtainable. And there was the coach at a Southern university who instructed his charges to carry the pigskin with them to all classes, lest they should thoughtlessly allow their minds to wander to the lecture.

Whether all this adds up to a worse case of overemphasis than obtains in the North and West is, however, debatable. Football is grossly overemphasized in every section.

The serious distortion of values which this state of things has occasioned is bad enough. Even worse is the hypocrisy and lying which too often accompany the building of a championship team. A Virginia newspaper launched a campaign in 1940, directed toward the elimination of the Southern Conference eligibility requirement that every athlete swear on his honor that he

has never "been paid for athletic skill or knowledge."
Five out of six Virginia campus newspapers which discussed the problem agreed that existing methods were
undermining honor systems. At one institution, a var-
sity player stated that hardly a man on the football field
could "answer the question truthfully," and this was the
prevailing view among the non-playing students. Yet, in
the face of this overwhelming evidence, when the Southern Conference held its annual meeting late in the year,
the matter of eliminating this eligibility oath was not
even discussed.

The Southeastern Conference (which, curiously
enough, is Southwest of the Southern Conference), and
is composed mainly of states in the Deep South, has
plenty to answer for in the way of high-powered recruit-
ing and high-pressure subsidization, but at least it has
abolished the requirement that the boys swear that they
haven't been paid, when they have. The mere elimination of such an oath is far from cleaning up the mess
which commercialized football has created in the Deep
South, not to mention the rest of the country, but it is
a step in the right direction.

Since, however, we are here concerned primarily with
scholarship and research, rather than with the vagaries
of triple-threat forward-passers and all-American tackles,
let us examine the intellectual accomplishments and pre-
tensions of the Southern colleges and universities in
greater detail. When Dr. Edwin R. Embree, president
of the Rosenwald Fund and formerly with the Rockefeller Foundation, contributed an article on American
higher education to the June, 1935, issue of the *Atlantic*,
he painted a dismal picture of the Southern universities
as research centers. Not one of them at that time came

within hailing distance of landing a place among the first dozen centers of higher learning in the United States, he declared, after an exhaustive survey. Moreover, in the twenty-four fundamental branches of learning which he used as a basis for ranking the universities of the country, he found that 206 departments were rated "distinguished" by authorities in the respective fields. Of this number, exactly one, the Institute for Research in Social Science at the University of North Carolina, was in the South. In 1934, the American Council on Education had surveyed the facilities for granting the Ph.D. degree in the leading universities of the country, and had asked specialists to designate those departments deemed to be "adequately" staffed and equipped to grant the doctorate, and those of the "highest rank, roughly the highest 20 per cent." The Institute for Research in Social Science at Chapel Hill received "highest" rating in the responses to this questionnaire, as did the Department of Genetics at the University of Texas. Departments deemed "adequate" in Southern universities by the savants who compiled this tabulation showed the following totals: University of Texas, twelve; University of North Carolina, eleven; Duke University, eight; University of Virginia, four; Rice Institute, three; George Peabody College for Teachers, two—or forty "adequate" departments in the South as against 623 in the rest of the country. Because the American Council on Education was concerned here solely with facilities for granting the Ph.D., the professional schools of the South were not taken into account. Moreover, the methods used by the council in making its compilation were criticized as inaccurate and unscientific, and as working an injustice upon the South and some of its institutions. When Dr.

Embree, in 1935, prepared the magazine article referred to, wherein he ranked the foremost universities, he took the council's findings into account, while introducing other factors.

In that article, he said that "a great university in the South is the insistent need in American scholarship to-day." He added that "even one university of the first rank would rally. the intellectual forces of the region, would provide a center at which Southern scholars could make their careers, and to which a fair share of the best minds of other sections could be drawn." No such institution has appeared on the South's intellectual horizon since Dr. Embree wrote those words in 1935. That is, none which can meet the rather mechanical and arbitrary standards of excellence which he uses in appraising the relative merits of the institutions under scrutiny, standards which always result in a low rating for the South, and which seem to leave out of account some of the more intangible criteria.

In calling for a Southern university of the "first rank," which would "rally the intellectual forces of the region," Dr. Embree spoke of the great and salutary influence of the University of Chicago upon the entire Middle West. But Dr. Jackson Davis, Associate Director of Southern Education for the General Education Board, points to the improbability that any one Southern university can ever influence the intellectual atmosphere of the South to the extent that Chicago has influenced that of the North Central states. The Southern states are much older, they have far more deeply grounded local traditions, their people are predominantly Anglo-Saxon and agrarian in background, and there is no Southern commercial center corresponding in regional prestige to

Chicago. Consequently Dr. Davis does not believe the South can have a University of Chicago, and he probably is right.

Of the thirty-three centers of learning whose graduate facilities are deemed sufficiently comprehensive to permit membership in the Association of American Universities, the South has four—Virginia, North Carolina, Texas, and Duke. Each of these universities has made important forward strides since the above-mentioned appraisals were published in 1934 and 1935, as have other Southern institutions. Yet the South's relative rank in the educational scheme of things has changed but little during the period under discussion. It is still impossible to get a Ph.D. degree at any university situated in Alabama, Arkansas, Mississippi, or South Carolina, and in some other Southern states this degree is given in only a few subjects. In Georgia, for example, the doctorate is granted at the University of Georgia, but it is obtainable there only in "Southern civilization," education, and biology. The sad truth that in the entire Deep South there is not a single institution of higher learning which has been admitted to the Association of American Universities, is rendered more poignant by the fact that none seems likely to be admitted at any time in the near future. Moreover, it is depressing to reflect that of all the graduate degrees awarded in the South, less than three per cent are in technology, and slightly more than one per cent in the medical sciences. In a vast and relatively undeveloped region, technological advance is of particular moment, while in a land which is below national standards medically, research in medicine would prove particularly productive. In contrast to the infinitesimal output of graduate students in these fields, nearly 40 per cent of the South's advanced degrees are awarded in Schools of Education.

The late Dean Charles W. Pipkin of Louisiana State's Graduate School stressed the importance of building research in Southern institutions which will address itself to the special problems of the region. He pointed to "the paradox which finds almost half the farms of America, farms with the longest growing reason and extremely rich soil, without a single department fully equipped to administer the Ph.D. in soil science—untold natural resources, without departments and library resources for the training of expert engineers to conserve and develop them for the use of society." Establishment at Duke University of the first forestry school of graduate rank in the South, and one of three in the United States, is an important forward step of this character, since approximately 40 per cent of all the forest land in the United States is below the Potomac and the Ohio. Duke also has conducted valuable researches into the causes and cure of pellagra, and Duke and Virginia Polytechnic Institute have made significant discoveries with respect to the control of blue mold in tobacco. Important for similar reasons is the Bureau of Industrial Chemistry at the University of Texas, which conducts advanced research projects having to do with the three major mineral and agricultural products of the Southwest, namely, petroleum, natural gas, and cotton, with a view to inventing new uses and markets for them, and preventing waste. The University of Virginia's Blandy Experimental Farm and Mountain Lake Biological Station are significant not only for the facilities they afford for graduate work in the plant life of the region, but also for the opportunity made available by the institution to biologists from other Southern colleges and universities to pursue their specialties there, particularly during the summer months. At Louisiana State is the Audubon Sugar School, where the latest sugar refining techniques are taught to persons from many lands. Moreover, through intensive research carried out by the Louisiana Experiment Station, in collaboration with the United States Department of Agriculture and the American Sugar Cane League, improved varieties of cane were developed which vastly increased the yield, and brought the industry back from collapse.

The General Education Board, which has rendered such invaluable assistance to education in the South during its four decades of highly useful existence, has done much to stimulate research in Southern problems, especially in the economic sphere. Many grants have been made by that agency to Southern colleges and universities for projects of this character. Agricultural economics and rural sociology are among the board's favorite subjects. For example, in 1940 the University of Arkansas received a grant for a study of the farm tenancy problem in the state. Another sum went during the year to Vanderbilt toward support of its newly established Institute of Research and Training in the Social Sciences, conducted jointly with George Peabody College. Louisiana State University and the Agricultural and Mechanical College were the recipients of a grant for an enlarged program of teaching and research in agricultural economics and rural sociology, and L.S.U. was awarded another toward special instruction in its new Research Institute in Southern Population Problems. The board also gave substantial aid to the Virginia Polytechnic Institute and the University of Virginia for land use, population and industrial studies, made in collaboration with the Virginia State Planning Board. Duke University is carrying on a five-year program of important research, with the assistance of the General Education Board, in the development of new textile fibers, the growth of Turkish tobacco in North Carolina, and the working out of plans for a better-articulated forest industry.

Such research projects as the foregoing are cause for encouragement. They indicate that Southern colleges and universities are attacking regional problems with intelligence and verve. It should also be emphasized that criticisms of these institutions are chiefly apropos of their lack of facilities for graduate work, particularly for the awarding of the doctorate. It must be borne in mind that only a small fraction of those who enter college ever aspire to the doctorate, and that the type of instruction provided at undergraduate levels has, in some respects, a much wider impact upon Southern life than the opportunities available for research in the upper academic strata. Similarly, the brand of education offered in the professions touches the means of livelihood of a far larger number than do the facilities for awarding a limited number of Ph.D.'s. This is not to minimize the great importance of research, both as a stimulus to intellectual ferment throughout an entire section, and as a means of raising regional levels of living. But sight should not be lost of the fact that undergraduate and professional instruction also have prime importance in the preparation of thousands for leading useful and satisfying lives.

How adequate are the South's facilities in these last-named fields? Again it must be stated that they are not up to the standards set in the North and West, although some Southern institutions are, of course, much superior to some Northern or Western ones. The reason for the prevailing inferiority below Mason and Dixon's line is largely the same as that already mentioned in our examination of the region's graduate facilities, namely, a lack of funds. Moreover, this lack of funds has a doubly detrimental effect, since it is reflected in an inferior public school system, and hence in imperfectly prepared college material. This leads, in turn, in the state-supported colleges and universities, to lower academic standards for entrance and graduation, since a publicly supported institution cannot justify to the state legislature more stringent standards than the public school system will sustain. The Southern states devote a larger share of their limited incomes to the public schools, and also toward support of the higher learning, than the states of any other comparable area, but having elected to operate two separate systems, one for the white and the other for the colored, they naturally have trouble making their low revenues stretch the required distance.[1] One reason why certain State universities of the Middle West and Far West are superior to those in the South is that they have no appreciable Negro population, and no dual public school system. This means that a given appropriation will go further there toward providing a universal nine-months school term and adequate pay for teachers, and that even the country high schools in those states usually are well-manned and efficiently operated. In the South, the country high school often has only an eight-month term, and the level of teachers' pay is lower. Yet

[1] For a discussion of the facilities for Negro education in the South, see Chapter VIII.

if many graduates of such a school fail at the state university, the head of that institution may hear from the state legislator in whose district the school is situated.

Endowed or church-supported institutions do not have to struggle with politicians and their semi-literate constituents, so that these colleges and universities are free from such annoyances and pressures. Yet here again the North and West, particularly the former, enjoy a marked advantage over the South, since, as we have seen, greater wealth has produced far larger endowments. The maintenance of high standards there for entrance and graduation is relatively easy, especially in New England, where the state-supported college or university is a comparative rarity, and where the public school systems are especially well-developed.

While the reasons for the South's inferiority in the field of undergraduate work are not far to seek, sound and thorough instruction is obtainable at not a few Southern institutions, both in the academic departments of the universities, and in the colleges. It must be conceded that there is no endowed or church-supported Southern college with academic standards altogether comparable to, say, Swarthmore in Pennsylvania, Carleton in Minnesota, Amherst and Williams in Massachusetts, or Dartmouth in New Hampshire. If, as Dr. Embree wrote, "a great university in the South is the insistent need in American scholarship to-day," a completely first-rate college, with a sufficient endowment to provide the highest type of instruction, likewise is sorely needed, and would go far to stimulate accomplishment in the academic world of what was once the Confederacy. There are colleges and universities with excellent traditions in the South, institutions without Ph.D. facilities which do well in the training of undergraduates, considering their limited resources. Such institutions as Davidson College in North Carolina, the University of the South in Tennessee, William and Mary and Washington and Lee in Virginia, and Emory University in Georgia are in this category. Emory, with an endowment of over $5,000,000, and prospects for added usefulness as a unit in the proposed Georgia "University Center," is in a particularly fortunate position. In Virginia, too, are two small denominational colleges of ancient lineage which make a remarkable showing in the percentage of their living graduates whose names appear in *Who's Who in America*. Hampden-Sydney College, a Presbyterian institution, led the entire country in 1930 when the first of these compilations was made, and stood fourth in 1940, with Randolph-Macon College, of the Methodist persuasion, third, Amherst second, and Harvard first. Less than one-half of one per cent separated these four leaders in the 1940 ranking. Moreover, the University of Virginia was twelfth in the country on a percentage basis, and first in the South in the total number of its graduates listed in *Who's Who*. Washington and Lee's percentage was bettered by only nineteen institutions in the entire country.

It is important to remember that despite the superior financial resources of numerous educational centers in other regions, many able and devoted teachers have elected to remain in the South at smaller salaries, and despite heavier teaching loads and inadequate laboratory and library facilities. Such a man as Hudson Strode, for example, remains as professor of English at the University of Alabama, where his remuneration is far less than he could command in the North. Nationally recognized as an author and as a teacher of the writing craft, Mr. Strode is a world-traveler who is almost as much at home in Scandinavia or the Argentine as he is in Tuscaloosa. Eight members of his class in the novel have had books accepted for publication by Northern publishing houses within a period of three and a half years, by far the most remarkable record of the sort in the United States. He conducted the course in the novel during the summer of 1941 at the University of Colorado Writers' Conference at Boulder. Or consider the case of Dr. Robert Preston Brooks of the University of Georgia. A native of that state, he elected to take his undergraduate degree at Oxford, and his doctorate at Wisconsin. He has served as president of the Southern Economics Association and the American Association of Collegiate Schools of Business, is the author of various historical works, and has been dean of the University of Georgia School of Commerce since 1920, and director of its Institute of Public Affairs since 1929. Moreover, he is an enlightened and forward-looking student of the Southern scene. A third teacher of especial note and usefulness at an institution which is not equipped to do graduate work of the highest grade, is Dr. Robert H. Tucker of Washington and Lee. After studying in Germany and at Wisconsin and Chicago, he entered the teaching profession. Shortly thereafter he was recognized as one of Virginia's most progressive citizens, participating in many movements on behalf of more efficient government and a more enlightened attitude toward the underprivileged. He was the first chairman of the Virginia Industrial Commission, following the enactment of Virginia's workmen's compensation law in 1918, and first chairman of the Virginia Commission on County Government, in which capacities he influenced the thinking of the state in important particulars. His quiet and levelheaded, yet courageously liberal, approach to public questions has made his advice sought for decades by governors and other public figures.

It is such men as these who give the Southern colleges and universities their distinctive cachets, and their strong leverage upon the youth of the South, to say nothing of the many young men and women who come from other sections to study there, despite the relative poverty of most of the educational exchequers. It is fortunate, indeed, that these institutions manage to hold a fair percentage of their most inspiring teachers and most talented researchers and scholars, in the face of the blandishments and temptations from across Mason and Dixon's line. But beside the fact that Southern institutions are able to make this appeal, there are, of course, certain colleges and universities in the region with especially well-equipped departments, in addition to those already mentioned. At the University of Texas, for example, with the South's largest enrollment, endowment, and library, there is the Latin-American Institute, offering a variety of courses in Latin-American culture, courses which are especially pertinent and valuable to-day. At Tulane, also strategically situated for the exploration of this field, the Middle American Research Institute specializes on the ancient Maya civilization, and has sent numerous expeditions to Yucatan and other sections of Central America.

The foregoing are uncommon types of research. There are also departments in these and other institutions which are more directly in the conventional and classical groove, departments in the social sciences and

the humanities, as well as in pure science, where instruction is to be had which not infrequently will bear
comparison with that to be got anywhere in America.
One thinks in this connection of the Department of
Sociology at North Carolina, the Department of History at Texas, the Department of Economics at Duke,
the Department of Physics at Virginia, and the Department of English Literature at Vanderbilt. Various others
might be mentioned.

What of the South's facilities for professional instruction? Are there first-class schools of law, medicine, and
engineering in the region? First let us consider the law
schools. No one would argue that there is a Southern
school of law with a faculty comparable to that of Harvard, for example, or a student body with the average
mental equipment of that shown year in and year out
by the Harvard Law School. Such an institution as
Harvard is able to attract the best legal talent in America
to its faculty, and to admit only the most competent
matriculates. Yet there are excellent law schools in the
South, some of which have long and honorable traditions. First among them in reputation is the fine department at the University of Virginia, which attracts
many Northern students of capacity. Duke has an ex-
traordinarily able faculty, and a low ratio of students
per teacher. Other law schools offering an unusually
high caliber of instruction are those at the University
of North Carolina, Tulane University, the University
of Texas and the University of Richmond. It should
be noted, however, that Duke and Texas, despite their
large endowments and their excellent academic and
professional schools, are not as financially impregnable
as one might suppose, a fact which is reflected in their

professional departments, as well as in other categories of instruction. In addition to the falling yield from all endowments, the endowments of these two universities are so circumscribed that their faculties are not as well paid as one might surmise. And Texas, which vigorously denies that it is a rich institution, points out that its law school, for example, had 713 students at the 1940-41 session, and 14 full-time teachers, whereas Northwestern University's Law School had 168 students and 14 teachers, Columbia had 479 students and 24 teachers, and Duke had 106 students and 13 teachers. (The authorities at Texas add that whereas the institution's 11,000 students in all departments are taught by a staff numbering 584, some of them part-time, "no other major state university attempts to train more than 10,000 students with a staff of fewer than 1,000 members." So the constantly flowing oil gushers on the university's millions of acres have not liquidated its financial problems.)

In the field of medical instruction, the South likewise is able to boast of several well-manned and modernly equipped schools. The great investment of the General Education Board in the Vanderbilt Medical School, combined with previous Vanderbilt and Carnegie contributions, has given it a department which is splendidly appointed for both instruction and research. Duke also boasts fine hospital and research facilities and an able staff, as does Tulane, whose clinical departments are conducted in the modern Hutchinson Memorial Building adjacent to the new $12,000,000 Charity Hospital. The Tulane Department of Tropical Medicine has been designated by the American Foundation for Tropical Medicine as the center for the intensive training of physicians from Latin-America in this subject. The University of Virginia, with a longer medical tradition than any of these, and an unsurpassed reputation in the South, has physical equipment which is inferior to theirs in some respects. One reason is that the state also supports the Medical College of Virginia at Richmond, which has lately acquired, with the aid of PWA funds, a great new hospital, with among the most complete laboratory and clinical facilities in the United States. These five institutions probably would be ranked first in the South by most authorities. Just below them might be listed the medical department of Emory University in Atlanta, which is expected to be strengthened by the $10,000,000 fund about to become available for the Atlanta-Athens University Center. The University of Texas, whose medical branch at Galveston has suffered from a lack of state support, was successful at the legislative session of 1941 in securing a 100 per cent increase in the appropriation for that branch.

In engineering, the South has some institutions which stand well, although none to compare with such a Northern center as the Massachusetts Institute of Technology. The Engineers' Council for Professional Development, the most reliable and comprehensive accrediting agency, lists 125 engineering schools with at least one accredited curriculum, of which 23 are in the South. The University of Kentucky and the Virginia Polytechnic Institute lead the South in the number of accredited curricula, with seven each, followed by Georgia School of Technology, the University of Alabama, and Louisiana State, with six each. Next in line are North Carolina State and the University of Texas, with five. In the field of graduate work, Virginia Polytechnic Institute and the University of Texas are the

only Southern institutions granting enough graduate
degrees in engineering to place among the first eighteen
in the country. V.P.I. was eleventh, with 31 graduate
degrees granted in 1939, and Texas was fifteenth, with
28. V.P.I. also takes high rank with its engineering
experiment station, as does Texas A. & M. These are
the only two Southern engineering schools which rank
among the first twelve of the 38 institutions with experiment stations. Among the other Southern schools
which are particularly noteworthy for one reason or another are Alabama Polytechnic Institute and Texas
College of Technology, while Georgia Tech deserves a
special accolade for the large number of competent
men it turns out, and its great influence upon engineering trends in a region whose engineering schools must
develop rapidly and soundly in this era of unprecedented industrial expansion. It is heartening to report
that the overall outlook is encouraging.

If the South is unable to provide quite the superlative type of professional schooling which is available in
a few of the best-equipped Northern and Western institutions, its extension work compares favorably with
that in any other region. In fact, it is superior to that
being done in the North, in some respects, and it appears to be developing more rapidly. Each Southern
state maintains a state university, and each of these
universities has a Department of University Extension.
While there is disagreement as to which institution
initiated extension work, the University of North Carolina is generally conceded to have been first in extend-
ing this character of activity to the state as a whole, and
supporting it with a fair degree of adequacy.

Chapel Hill not only was the pioneer in providing

extension courses on a considerable scale, but it promoted such noteworthy contributions to the life of the state as the University of North Carolina *News Letter,* library extension, postgraduate medical education, drama extension work, social and economic studies under the School of Rural Economics, and the Institute of Government and Institute of Human Relations. The university press is an invaluable adjunct.

Another institution whose extension service is important is the University of Texas, with a particularly challenging task, in view of the huge area to be covered. Its extension work includes formal instruction through class and correspondence courses, which provide college training for persons unable to obtain it in any other way. It also includes informal services, such as that rendered by the Package Loan Library, and by the Visual Instruction Bureau, which sends out films and slides in large quantities. In addition, there is the Nutrition and Health Education Bureau, still another bureau dealing with extracurricular activities in the public schools, and an educational program by radio.

The University of Virginia has an extension service which is attracting considerable attention. Its *News Letter* distributes informative data gathered by the School of Rural Social Economics. In the field of postgraduate medical education it has functioned in collaboration with the Medical College of Virginia in a manner so impressive as to influence the American Medical Association. It has been a pioneer in the field of workers' education, and has aided various Virginia communities in setting up public forums. The Institute of Public Affairs should be mentioned as, in one sense, a university extension activity.

The foregoing are the major extension services now being provided in the South by state universities. The Richmond Professional Institute of the College of William and Mary differs from all other Southern institutions in the field, since it offers professional and semiprofessional courses exclusively, and in an academic atmosphere. Among the privately endowed universities, Vanderbilt's School of Religion has inaugurated a program of guidance for rural clergymen in all the Southern states, in which it seeks to influence their thinking in social and economic spheres by lending them judiciously selected books. Vanderbilt's Medical School is instituting a plan for bringing in practising physicians for refresher courses and postgraduate instruction. Extension work also is an important phase of the program at the Tulane Medical School.

What of education for women in the South? The most celebrated colleges for women in the North are older and wealthier than the institutions of corresponding rank below the Potomac and the Ohio. The ante-bellum tradition that no well-bred Southern lady ought to concern herself with anything more mentally taxing than music, art, etiquette, French conversation, or English literature, lingered for some decades after Appomattox. Randolph-Macon Woman's College in Virginia was the first of the Southern institutions of higher learning to escape from the category of the "female institute," of fragrant memory, and to win national recognition for the high quality of its work. It was not only the first Southern college for women to be accredited by the national accrediting agencies, but the first to be granted a chapter of Phi Beta Kappa, in itself a high honor, since chapters of Phi Beta Kappa go only to those centers of instruction which meet certain rigid requirements.

Agnes Scott in Atlanta is the only other privately endowed Phi Beta Kappa college for women in the South which is not an integral part of a university. Its important rôle in the developing Atlanta-Athens University Center, gives it potentialities not enjoyed by any other competing Southern institution. Generally ranked with these two colleges is Sophie Newcomb in New Orleans, the excellent woman's branch of Tulane. These three privately endowed colleges seem slightly superior to any similar institutions in the region. Others which have chapters of Phi Beta Kappa include the Woman's College of the University of North Carolina, Florida State College for Women, and Westhampton College, an integral part of the University of Richmond. Another first-rate Southern college for girls, often ranked with Randolph-Macon, Agnes Scott, and Sophie Newcomb, is Sweet Briar in Virginia, which has high standards and a well-qualified faculty, but has not yet achieved a chapter of Phi Beta Kappa. Hollins College, also in Virginia, dates back to 1842 and has a notable tradition, but its endowment is inadequate, and it suffers from certain other deficiencies, which do not, however, prevent it from doing good work.

Since the best of the Southern colleges for women lack the financial resources of such Northern colleges as Smith, Vassar, Wellesley, and Bryn Mawr, their salary scales are lower, their libraries less adequate, and so on. Yet these institutions are given top recognition in the undergraduate field throughout this country, and in Europe, as well. While the most distinguished of the Northern group provide certain educational refinements which are not obtainable in the women's colleges of the South, it is arguable that as well-rounded a schooling can be obtained in the latter as in the former.

It should be noted that most of the state-supported colleges and universities in the South now are coeducational, so that women may enter these schools, if they prefer not to attend those operated exclusively for their sex. There has been an immense increase in the feminine enrolment of the Southern coeducational institutions in the past five years. As there has been no corresponding drop in the number of matriculates in the women's colleges, the deduction seems warranted that the young women of the contemporary South are exhibiting a greatly augmented desire for collegiate instruction.

Many of those from the Southern mountains attend Berea College in Kentucky, a coeducational institution which not only confers the B.A. and B.S. degrees, but also offers high school and elementary instruction. Ninety per cent of the 2,000 students come from the mountains, and receive at Berea educational opportunity which might not be afforded them elsewhere, for they earn 76 per cent of their expenses, on the average. Berea was founded before the Civil War, and grew out of an anti-slavery church established in the neighborhood. Its first principal was an Oberlin graduate. From the close of the war until 1904, when education of the white and colored races under the same roof was prohibited by law in Kentucky, Berea had both white and colored students. To-day it has one of the largest endowments in the Southern states, and it affords educational advantages to many young people of the Southern highlands, most of whom are of sturdy Anglo-Saxon stock. The college is zealous in the pursuit of the objective set forth in its constitution, namely, "to promote the cause of Christ ... by contributing to the spiritual and material welfare of the mountain region of the South, affording to young people of character and promise a thorough Christian education, with opportunities for manual labor as an assistance in self-support." All students are forbidden to use tobacco, and no Southern college is stricter in banning Leftist agitation on its campus.

A contrasting Southern institution, which has been a center of controversy because of the Leftist orientation of its faculty and students, is the Highlander Folk School in Tennessee. Under attack from various newspapers and industrialists, who charged it unjustly with being a "hotbed of Communism," the school has managed to grow. Highlander is frankly a labor school, and its purpose is to train promising members of trade unions to represent those unions effectively. It also conducts a nursery school for nearby children, an annual camp for children of union workers, and a summer workshop for writers. The last-named was attended in 1941 by students from eight states and the District of Columbia, and offered competent instruction in writing techniques. Highlander seems likely to escape the fate of Commonwealth College, the labor school in Arkansas which was under fire for years, and finally succumbed.

An institution which is unique among American centers of higher learning is Black Mountain College in the North Carolina mountains, founded in 1933 by a small group of teachers and students who left Rollins College in Florida, following a disagreement with the administration. Black Mountain has no fixed entrance requirements, gives no grades and confers no degrees. Yet it has a faculty which includes several former Rhodes Scholars, as well as a number of eminent European refugees. Faculty and students live in the same buildings, work together on their educational problems in informal fashion, do manual labor together on the campus, and constitute a community which has no precise counterpart anywhere else. Classes are usually small, informal discussion groups, and lectures are rare. At the session of 1940-41 there were 19 faculty members and 78 students. Nearly all the students are from the North and West, and applications for entrance exceed the college's present capacity.

An attitude conducive to a more effective absorption of the higher learning is being inculcated in the Atlanta-Athens region of Georgia, where the South's most significant adventure in coöperative education at the college and university level, is being consummated. Facilities of six institutions are being pooled, in accordance with a plan first proposed in 1938, and perfected during the succeeding years, with the aid of the General Education Board. Emory University, Georgia Institute of Technology, Agnes Scott College, Columbia Theological Seminary and the Atlanta Art Association, all of Atlanta, and the University of Georgia at Athens are participating. The greatest measure of coöperation is being arranged between Emory and Agnes Scott, which are near one another, and which are being granted $2,500,000 by the General Education Board, now that they have fulfilled its provisio that they raise $5,-000,000 on their own account. The Atlanta Art Association recently was the recipient of $1,000,000 from

another source, and the institutions which belong to
the center can make use of its collections in offering
courses in the fine arts. Library and laboratory facilities
are being combined, to the extent that this is possible,
and greatly improved apparatus for graduate research
and for offering the Ph.D. is being built up. The experiment is being worked out on the basis of experience
in other similar ventures, notably that at Ithaca, New
York, where Cornell University and three colleges have
pooled their resources.

It is extremely fortunate that the three units of the
Georgia University Center which are providing by far
the major financial contribution to the enterprise are
privately owned and controlled, and hence are not subject to the whims of politicians. The demagogic Governor Talmadge cannot "reach" Emory University,
Agnes Scott College, and the Atlanta Art Association.
The aforesaid Talmadge went berserk on the race issue,
during the summer of 1941, in his effort to create a
political sounding board for his senatorial or gubernatorial candidacy in 1942, and his obedient mouthpieces
on the Georgia University System's Board of Regents
discharged ten educators, including Dean Walter D.
Cocking of the University of Georgia's School of Education, President Marvin Pittman of Georgia Teachers' College, and Vice Chancellor Curtis Dixon of the
University System. Dean Cocking said he was a victim
of "the filthiest sort of concocted evidence," and so were
others. Ralph McGill, executive editor of the Atlanta
Constitution—which joined with the Atlanta *Journal*, most of the smaller papers in Georgia, and
nearly every leading Southern daily in a slam-bang
fight on Talmadge for his unprincipled demagoguery

in ousting these educators—wrote in his paper just before
Dr. Cocking was heard by the regents:

> For two weeks the most vicious campaign of attempted
> bribery, intimidation and falsehood has been carried on by
> various persons interested in the hue and cry against the
> defendant.... It is not a pretty story.... Efforts to bribe a
> Negro to rob a house, efforts to have a picture faked, a
> Negro taken to a place which was said to be the Ku Klux
> Klan headquarters, a pistol put in front of him and a paper
> given him to sign.

This particular "evidence" was not produced against
Dr. Cocking, perhaps because too many facts concerning
the method of its assembling were revealed in advance
by the Atlanta press. But although Cocking had been
retained by an 8-7 vote of the regents, following a previous hearing instigated by Talmadge, he was fired by
10 to 5 vote at the second session, after three regents
had been discharged by Talmadge, and three of his political marionettes had been substituted for them. In
the words of the Atlanta *Journal*, the ousting of Cocking
and the other educators was "a lynching." Trumped-up
evidence that Dean Cocking was in favor of "race
equality," and hysterical charges that he and Vice
Chancellor Dixon were connected with the Rosenwald
Fund, which was violently denounced and depicted as
favoring "race equality," shed a dismal light on the
whole episode.

The *Journal* said concerning the conviction of Dean
Cocking:

> Briefly, the evidence on which Dean Cocking was con-
> victed was a book, *Brown America*, written by Dr. Embree
> of the Rosenwald Foundation, with which Dr. Cocking has
> no official connection; tracts published by the Commission

on Interracial Relations, of which organization Dean Cocking is not a member, and the statement of one witness which
was contrary to the evidence of some thirty others present
at the faculty meeting.

With respect to President Pittman's discharge, the
Journal editorialized:

Dr. Pittman's trial was equally ruthless. Having completely answered the charge that he had personally benefited by sale of products from his farm, or work done there-
on, Dr. Pittman was confronted with a copy of a book, *Calling America*, lifted from the thousands of books in the
college library, a book adopted in 1938 by the Textbook
Commission of the University System. Dr. Pittman asserted
that he had never seen the book, was not aware that it was
in the library, and that it was not used as a textbook at the
Teachers' College. The verdict was the same, 10 to 5.

The atmosphere in which this kangaroo court operated may be glimpsed from the statement of Governor
Talmadge before the hearings began that "we don't
need no Negroes and white folks taught together in
Georgia"—nobody had suggested this, although one person accused Dean Cocking of it—and the declaration
of one of the regents during the cross-questioning of a
witness that "the most uneducated white man is superior to the most educated nigger on earth." Despite
the preposterous unfairness of the whole proceeding,
the regents adopted a resolution unctuously denying
that Talmadge was "trying to inject politics into the
university system," and thanking him, apropos of the
oustings, for the "valuable assistance he has rendered
his alma mater [the state university] and the University
System."

Repercussions from the affair were prompt in coming.

The General Education Board announced that it was severing relations with the University of Georgia. Various academic bodies began investigating the situation, with a view to ascertaining whether the University System should retain its accredited standing with national and regional educational associations. It was recalled that Governor Bilbo of Mississippi had virtually wrecked the educational system of that state a decade previously by similar discharges of three college presidents and numerous professors for political reasons, with the result that the state's four major institutions of higher learning lost their accredited standing with five national or Southern educational associations. Informed that the Southern Association of Colleges and Secondary Schools had named a committee, headed by Chancellor Oliver C. Carmichael of Vanderbilt to investigate the dismissals brought about by him, Talmadge commented: "That ain't in Georgia. We accredit our own schools down here." Later he lost much of his bluster and braggadocio, and sought to dissuade the association from acting adversely, but it voted to drop ten of the university system's sixteen institutions. The Southern University Conference already had dropped the University of Georgia by a unanimous vote, and the Association of American Universities had dropped that institution and Georgia Tech.

The antics of Governor Talmadge, unfortunately only too typical of a certain rather rare species of Southern demagogue, have served as a discouraging factor in the launching of the Atlanta-Athens University Center. A less ambitious example of coördination of educational facilities is to be seen at Nashville, where Vanderbilt University and George Peabody College for

Teachers have worked out a plan for the integration of their facilities. No fewer than 274 duplicating courses have been eliminated, and a great joint library has been built. The process of meshing the curricula and facilities of the two institutions is expected to be carried much further. Fortunately neither institution has to concern itself with the theological taboos of the Tennessee Legislature. The degrees in education which Peabody grants are the South's most highly prized diplomas in that subject. And when the Scopes trial shocked the civilized world, Chancellor James H. Kirkland's comment was: "The answer to the episode at Dayton is the building of new laboratories on the Vanderbilt campus for the teaching of science. The remedy for a narrow sectarianism and a belligerent fundamentalism is the establishment on this campus of a School of Religion, illustrating in its methods and in its organization the strength of a common faith and the glory of a universal worship." The school was established shortly thereafter, and is the only nonsectarian School of Religion in the South.

The developing university centers in Tennessee and Georgia, and the coöperative arrangements in force between the libraries at the University of North Carolina and Duke University—and between the faculties to a limited degree—serve to accent a trend in Southern education which may prove extremely important for the future. This is the tendency toward intensive specialization at certain institutions in a few subjects, and toward leaving specialization in other subjects to other educational centers in the region. Overlapping and duplication can thus be reduced to a minimum, and maximum benefits and usufructs derived from the

South's circumscribed finances and facilities. This process is in its infancy to-day, for its potentialities hardly have been more than glimpsed.[1]

Coöperative arrangements between libraries situated near enough to one another for such arrangements to be productive, should aid the South toward a realization of its educational destiny. We have seen that such plans already have been consummated in Nashville and Atlanta, as well as in the Chapel Hill-Durham area. It is particularly important that this process be carried further, because of the South's inadequate library collections and equipment. Of the forty-four largest college and university libraries in America, the South has only six, and these are all much smaller and less satisfactory as centers of research than the huge repositories at numerous Northern and Western universities. The University of Texas, with 675,000 volumes, is the South's largest, closely followed by Duke, but neither is in the class with nine university libraries in other regions, each of them with more than 1,000,000 volumes. Harvard, in fact, has well over 4,000,000, while Yale has 3,000,000, and Columbia 1,750,000. Even the last-named has nearly three times as many as any Southern library. After those at Texas and Duke, the ranking Southern collections are at North Carolina, Vanderbilt-Peabody, Virginia, and L.S.U., each with from 300,000 to 400,000 books. Since advanced research in any institution necessarily revolves about that institution's library and laboratories, the lagging of the Southern

---

[1] For a discussion of the great possibilities inherent in the establishment of regional institutions offering graduate and professional instruction of the highest grade to white students, and other regional institutions of similar caliber for Negro students, see Chapters VIII and XII.

libraries must be considered in any appraisal of the region's competence in the field of graduate study.

The South's standing in the world of scholarship is enhanced by several university presses, among which the University of North Carolina Press is easily foremost. It is to be doubted, in fact, whether any university press in America is superior to that at Chapel Hill in the quality and significance of its publications, and certainly none has so profound an influence upon the thinking of the region in which it is situated. The University of North Carolina Press has been wise in focussing attention upon the problems of the South, for its able handling of those problems has contributed heavily to the widely accepted judgment that Chapel Hill is preëminent among Southern universities in the sphere of the social sciences. (In the field of pure science, there is no preëminent institution. First place is shared by Duke, North Carolina, Texas, and Virginia. George W. Gray, the well-known writer on scientific subjects, wrote recently in his book, *Education on an International Scale:* "Certainly Virginia stands to-day in an enviable position among Southern institutions as regards scientific research.")

In addition to university presses, the Southern universities have other vehicles of expression which influence public opinion, not only in their immediate vicinities but in the nation. Such quarterly magazines as the *Southern Review* at L.S.U., *Social Forces* at Chapel Hill, and the *Virginia Quarterly Review* at Charlottesville are unsurpassed in their respective fields. The *Sewanee Review* at the University of the South, the *South Atlantic* at Duke and the *Southwest Review* at Southern Methodist are older journals of distinction.

Moreover two new and important publications in the realm of the social sciences have emerged recently at Southern institutions. One is the *Journal of Southern History,* organ of the Southern Historical Association, and probably the best regional historical journal in America. The other is the excellent *Journal of Politics,* which speaks for the Southern Political Science Association. Louisiana State University, now happily free of the Huey Long influence, is the guarantor of the former publication, and furnishes the two chief editors, while the latter journal is issued under the joint auspices of the sponsoring association and the University of Florida, the two principal editors being supplied by that university and L.S.U. The organization of the two associations whose organs the foregoing quarterlies are, plus the similarly recent establishment of Southwide associations for teachers of economics, sociology and other subjects, are indications of a new vitality in social science studies below the Potomac. The fact that separate departments of political science have now been set up at many Southern colleges and universities, in contrast to the former practice of having this subject taught as a sideline by history professors, likewise is significant.

These and other Southern phenomena may be accurately interpreted as signifying that there is greater freedom in discussing controversial and once-forbidden subjects on Southern campuses than ever before. Professor Eduard C. Lindeman, chairman of the American Civil Liberties Union's Committee on Academic Freedom, who has been a close observer of the academic scene for many years, does not feel that "academic freedom in the South is worse than or better than else-

where, with the exception of a section of New England
and a similar one in the Central Northwest, where the
tradition of freedom of expression has been most per-
sistent." He makes the following penetrating observation:

In each region the institutions of higher learning seem
to have, however, a specialized "sacred cow," and the professors soon learn that they may speak freely about all
other cows but not about this one. When I was teaching in
the South this "cow" stood on four sacred legs, one of which
was the race question, the next sex, the next public utilities, and the last trade unionism. At that time the front legs
were race and sex, but the legs you most frequently got
"kicked" with were the two hind ones.

Professor Lindeman is of the opinion that the University of North Carolina is foremost among Southern
universities to-day in its uninhibited approach to such
questions as these, and any informed student of the
South would be apt to agree with him. This is evident
not only in the books and other publications which are
issued there, but in the attitudes of President Frank P.
Graham and his faculty, as well as in the discussions
held annually under the auspices of the university, notably at the Institute of Human Relations. The University of Virginia's Institute of Public Affairs is
generally recognized as the most important university
forum in the country for the discussion of national and
international questions, and in those discussions, the
most unorthodox views are given full opportunity of
expression, but the institute does not concern itself to
any substantial degree with problems peculiar to Virginia or the South. It is in this respect that the University of Virginia differs most sharply from the

University of North Carolina, which has a more dynamic concept of a state university's proper function.

While in these and other Southern institutions, discussion of controversial problems is perhaps freer to-day than ever before, the near future may pose some of these issues in especially acute form—issues having to do with race relations and economic and labor matters, which have been, and still are, centers of violent controversy below the Potomac. It is hoped that if and when these questions arise in Southern academic halls, they will be treated with wisdom, understanding, and tolerance. The South has been for many years a recognized citadel of conservatism on these issues, and the explosive possibilities are great.

Such is the situation which confronts the colleges and universities of the South. Many of those institutions are doing solid, and some are doing brilliant work. A goodly number afford opportunities for sound and thorough training in many branches of learning, including both academic studies and the professions. Certain Southern institutions also have traditions that are distinctive and enduring—as, for example, the University of Virginia, with a century-old honor system which is exclusively the instrument of the students, and probably the most perfectly functioning mechanism of its kind in the United States. By slow degrees, the South is rebuilding on a far greater and more ambitious scale the highly developed college and university system which was shattered by the Civil War. The progress achieved is substantial, and the future holds almost limitless possibilities.

VII

ALONG THE SOUTHERN COLOR LINE

ASK the average American if the Southern Negro is in better case to-day than he was forty years ago, and the answer is apt to be an emphatic affirmative. The conviction will be expressed that the twentieth century has brought many tangible benefits to the Negro below Mason and Dixon's line, and that while there still is much to be done, and gross inequalities and injustices remain, the trend has been steadily for the better.

That is the commonly accepted view. Is it the correct view?

Analysis of prevailing opinions as to the improved status of the colored race will reveal the impact upon the public mind of the Negro's augmented political influence in the North, and his concomitantly greater power in the councils of the Federal Government—a fact that has been reflected in greater fairness toward the race in the Federal courts. Such rulings as those which stipulate that Negroes can no longer be excluded systematically from juries, that they cannot be taxed as other citizens are taxed and then be given vastly inferior educational apparatus, or be charged the same railway fare as the whites only to be shoved into a dingy, cinder-bestrewn coach, with no dining or pullman facilities, naturally have seemed to indicate a substantial and continued improvement in the status of the Southern Negro. Moreover there is his gradual rise in literacy, and the comparative infrequency with which he is lynched, a decline which has been almost steady since the turn of the century, until fewer than half a dozen lynchings occur annually in the region, as against about one hundred a year in the late nineties and early 1900's. All this would seem to testify indisputably to the development below the Potomac of a more conscionable civilization for the Negro.

And yet there are facets of the problem which cannot be fitted into this relatively roseate pattern. For while the Southern Negro enjoys better protection than formerly, in so far as his legal rights are concerned, there is reason to wonder whether his ability to obtain court decisions buttressing his constitutional prerogatives, and his comparative immunity from lynching, should be regarded as counterbalancing certain grave economic disabilities under which he labors. The gains he has made are somewhat spectacular in character, and for that reason they may seem more important than they really are. And while there is no intention here of minimizing in the slightest degree the significance of the sharp drop in the crime of lynching—still the greatest of all blots on the good name of the South—it seems legitimate to ask whether the Southern Negro is more fortunately situated to-day, when he is in far less danger from the mob, but when he also has much more difficulty getting work as a farmer or a skilled mechanic.

It must be borne in mind that although the Negro has benefited hugely from the social security and housing programs, he has been the victim, rather than the beneficiary, of some important New Deal legislation. Take the agricultural benefit payments, which often went to the landlords rather than the sharecroppers, especially in the early days. Take the crop-reduction program, which at first threw tens of thousands of white and Negro sharecroppers off the land and left them no alternative but relief. Take the NRA and the wage-and-hour law, which forced employers to eliminate inefficient and marginal workers, many of them Negroes. (Other Negroes received better wages, under this legislation, of course.) It is reported, too, that whites were substituted for Negroes in some instances by employers who did not desire to pay the stipulated minimum to colored workers.

It should also be noted that the Negro farmer's situation grew progressively worse during the 1930's, in respects other than those already mentioned, despite the benefits received from the New Deal farm program by many individual Negro farm families. Dr. S. H. Hobbs, Jr., wrote in the University of North Carolina *News Letter* recently that "perhaps the most significant thing in Southern agriculture since the Civil War has been the decline of Negro farm operators and especially Negro cropper tenants during the last decade." He pointed out that there had been no compensatory increase in farm ownership among Southern Negroes during these ten years, so that thousands of them obviously had left agriculture entirely and crowded into the cities, both North and South, or they worked on farms as hired laborers.

One of the first informed Southerners to express the view that the current balance sheet for the Negro is perhaps more weighted with liabilities than it was just after the turn of the century, is Jonathan Daniels. The distinguished Raleigh editor summarizes his conclusions as follows:

Sometimes it seems to me that the Negro in America is worse off to-day than he was forty years ago. It has seemed almost that every time the Negro won a legal right he lost an economic chance. We have more Negro Ph.D.'s, but the colored people have been squeezed out of the skilled trades. The result is that the Negro has to be a Ph.D. or a ditch digger with tragically few steps in between. The fire has gone out of both hate and affection. There are fewer lynchings, but also, I fear, fewer warm, human contacts between the races. We have lost—perhaps escaped from—the old master-slave relationship, but we have not established any substitute satisfactory to either race.

Doesn't the treatment of the Negro in the defense program tend to substantiate the view expressed by Mr. Daniels? Instance after instance can be cited of announcements by building contractors that only white carpenters and other skilled craftsmen would be given jobs. Again and again the Negroes protested, and rightly so, only to discover, more often than not, that by the time their protestations were heeded, the contract had been completed.

These discriminations were practiced in the face of repeated appeals from President Roosevelt, Sidney Hillman, and other defense officials on behalf of equitable treatment for qualified colored citizens, not only as a matter of justice and as essential to true democracy, but in order that the country might use all its skilled manpower in erecting its defenses against Hitler. Were the discriminations confined to the South? Far from it. The National Association for the Advancement of Colored People called mass meetings of protest in twenty-three states from coast to coast. Almost the entire automobile and aircraft industries in the North and West excluded Negroes from skilled and assembly-line jobs, as did numerous other concerns with large defense contracts. Summing up the statements of defense officials on the problem, Ernest Lindley, the well-known Washington columnist, wrote in the spring of 1941:

In some respects the Negro seems to be getting less of a break in the North than in the South; and in the South, less of a break from Northern employers than from Southerners ...Labor supply experts say that in many localities the pick of the unemployed, for industrial purposes are to be found among the Negroes. Many of them have decided aptitudes for handling machinery and tools.... An important Southern company making iron products found that it could train a selected group of Negroes in less than half the time it took to train white labor seeking the same kind of work.

By the summer of 1941, the situation had improved considerably, as a result of a Federal requirement that all contractors getting defense contracts agree not to discriminate against any worker because of race, creed, color, or national origin. Mark Ethridge of the Louisville *Courier-Journal* was named chairman of the enforcement committee. Labor unions also relaxed some of their restrictions against Negro members.

But the Southern colored man is losing ground steadily in his effort to hold what formerly approached a Negro monopoly in certain trades. Indeed, he has been largely ousted from some, such as barbering, and he is fighting an uphill battle in others, such as skilled mechanical crafts and waiting on table in hotels and restaurants. All of which means that the Southern Negro of to-day has no substantial middle class upon which to erect a solid and well-balanced civilization. A group of colored college professors and school-teachers at the top of the cultural ladder are training other Negroes, whose employment opportunities are virtually limited to teaching or to work with the Federal Government. A few Negro doctors and lawyers manage to secure degrees and to practice their professions, but the available clientele is limited, since the great mass of Negroes, both North and South, must skimp along on the low-wage scale paid for menial or manual labor, and can seldom afford the services of competent, colored professional men. Yet with all the evils which have accompanied the excessive crowding of Negroes into cities, both North and South, large-scale urbanization has given the Negro professional class opportunities not previously available to it. Negro doctors and lawyers have found it possible to build up larger practices than they could have done otherwise, Negro writers and artists have found wider audiences in the relatively accessible urban centers, and Negro newspapers have been able to operate on broader and more solid foundations.

The Negro often is forbidden to join labor unions, or as a member he is apt to suffer adverse discrimination. While there is less of this in the Congress of Industrial Organizations than in the American Federation of Labor, the cards are stacked against the Negro in nearly all unions. Colored laborers are not being permitted to affiliate in large numbers, except as longshoremen and in steel, coal mining, and tobacco. Moreover the facilities for giving vocational training to colored men and women are far from adequate, albeit in some Southern cities and states these facilities are approximately as good for the Negroes as for the whites.

One of the reasons for the Negro's current disabilities is to be found in the fact that so many whites, viewing the propensity of the N.A.A.C.P. for aggressively seek-

ing every possible Negro right in the courts, have concluded that the colored brother ought to be left to shift
for himself. In earlier days, these same white men and
women would have been much more inclined to lend
a hand, but upon noting of late that the association in
question, with headquarters in New York, is ably staffed
and functioning actively in virtually every field, with
few compunctions against tearing head-on into any situation deemed to affect the Negro adversely, they do not
respond to appeals in his behalf as generously as in
former years. These white Southerners are annoyed by
the pugnacity of the Northern organization, and unfortunately have allowed their annoyance to condition
their attitude toward thousands of Negroes who never
so much as heard of the association.

The Commission on Interracial Coöperation, with
headquarters in Atlanta and with a long experience in
dealing with Southern racial problems, seeks to liquidate
some of the inequities which are under attack from the
N.A.A.C.P., but in more tactful fashion. Under the
guidance of such Southerners as Dr. Howard W. Odum,
Dr. Will W. Alexander, and Mrs. Jessie Daniel Ames, it
endeavors to achieve justice for the Negro in all his
relationships with the dominant race, but without
ruffling Southern sensibilities unduly. Whether its tech-
nic will be more fruitful in the long run than the more
bellicose methods of the N.A.A.C.P. is a matter over
which there are honest differences of opinion. Certainly
the Commission on Interracial Coöperation arouses
fewer antagonisms than the New York agency, and its
judgments are more cordially received in Dixie. Its
quiet, effective work has contributed heavily in every

Southern state to better interracial understanding and coöperation.

The commission recognizes fully the valuable work done by the N.A.A.C.P. in behalf of interracial justice in such a case as that at Scottsboro, for example. It must be said, in all fairness, that the N.A.A.C.P. in this and other instances has performed a national service. Moreover, its approach was far more conservative and conciliatory than that of the International Labor Defense and other extreme Leftist bodies which intervened at Scottsboro with abusive telegrams and other such inflammatory messages to the court and the community. The N.A.A.C.P. also has done much to focus attention upon the need for effective action against lynching. It has been advocating a Federal anti-lynching bill for some years. While the Commission on Interracial Coöperation hesitated for a long while to support such drastic action, it finally endorsed a Federal bill unanimously in 1935. Since that time it has not taken any formal position with respect to this legislation, which has been pending at Washington, in one form or another, for about two decades.

The commission apparently is less enthusiastic for a Federal law than it was in 1935. The fact that it has said nothing further on the subject since that year would indicate as much. Moreover, there are valid reasons why it should have grown less anxious to see such a law enacted. In the first place, there is the almost steady decline in lynchings since 1935. There were twenty in that year, and for the preceding decade the average had been in excess of seventeen, whereas there were only nine in 1936, eight in 1937, six in 1938, three in 1939, five in 1940 and four in 1941. In the second place, there is the rise of a strong opposition in the South to a Federal law which would bring G-men into the region on the trail of any local officer who had failed to act with sufficient vigor in defending his prisoner against a mob. There also is opposition to the provision in the bill which would fine any county or city where a lynching occurred, from $2,000 to $5,000—although more than a score of states have such a law, and South Carolina, which has had one since 1896, actually collected a $2,000 fine from each of seven counties where lynchings took place between 1913 and 1931. (This may explain why South Carolina, with next to the highest percentage of Negroes in its population, had one of the best lynching records of all the Southern states during the decade which ended January 1, 1941. It had four lynchings for the ten-year period, as against 25 for Mississippi, 16 for Georgia, and 14 each for Louisiana and Florida.)

So long as the Southern states give evidence of intention to eradicate lynchings on their own motion, as some of them are doing, it seems obvious that this is the better approach to the problem. In the middle 1930's, a Federal bill appeared both desirable and necessary, for lynchings were far more numerous then than they are now, and the South seemed willing to accept such a Federal bill. Leading newspapers in Birmingham, Columbia, Miami, Louisville, Richmond, Greensboro, Chattanooga, Knoxville, San Antonio, Houston, Fort Worth, and New Orleans were advocating Federal anti-lynching legislation in 1937, and their readers were not protesting that advocacy. Then came the Senate filibuster of 1938, and the situation changed rapidly. Violent opposition to the pending measure was aroused by means of unfair attacks upon it—so violent, indeed, that grave doubts were felt over whether public sentiment would permit enforcement of a Federal law, if one were passed. It appeared only too probable that Southern juries would refuse to convict derelict county officers, and that resentment against the Federal Government's entry into local situations might lead to various kinds of retaliation against the Negroes, thus making their last state worse than their first.

Such is the situation to-day. Some of the most uncompromising enemies of lynching in the South are highly dubious as to the workability of a Federal law, now that so much antagonism to the idea has been openly manifested. While the likelihood of completely wiping out lynching by state action appears infinitesimal in certain states, it also seems hopeless to expect passage or enforcement of a Federal law, unless and until the need for such a severe measure becomes clearer. At the moment, the sharp downward trend in lynchings—due, in part, no doubt, to the threat of Federal legislation—probably renders a Federal statute inadvisable. If, however, the situation grows manifestly worse, and mobs in the Deep South continue to put frequently innocent Negroes to death with blow torches and other such instruments of sadism, while women and children look on, it is difficult to think of any alternative to a Federal bill. Needless to say, it is an open question whether such legislation would be upheld by the Supreme Court.

In sum, a Federal antilynching law ought to be passed only as a last resort. Even such an uncompromising liberal and upholder of civil liberties as Senator George W. Norris of Nebraska announced following the Southern filibuster of 1938, that he would vote against the pending Federal bill, although he was aware that its advocates were counting on his support. He declared that he was opposed to the bill because he believed "it would do more harm than good, even to the colored race." And this revered figure, whose motives are, of course, not open to question, added:

> When I read of the terrible things that happened to the South after the Civil War...I wonder now how the South has done such remarkable work in the way of recovery...I wonder at the great improvement that has come about in the South in the years since the Civil War. The people of the South have done a wonderful job. I confess we could not have improved upon it. With all the hatred, the animosity, and the agony which came to the people, it is amazing to me that the crime of lynching has been gradually dying out. The people of the South have made a record of which they have a right to be proud....We could not improve upon what has been done....Why should we interfere now?

One reason for the steady improvement in the South's lynching record is to be found in the courage with which Southern leaders, over a considerable period, have been willing to denounce this form of savagery. Hardly anybody defends it openly nowadays, but two or three decades ago the situation was otherwise. It is distinctly worthwhile, in this connection, to recall the unselfish and unterrified rôle of the San Antonio *Express,* which unlimbered against the lynchers of Texas in 1918, at a time when mobs in the Lone Star State were burning, torturing, and otherwise mutilating a larger number of Negroes annually than those of any other Southern commonwealth. The *Express* set aside $100,000 with which to pay rewards to any persons responsible for the conviction and punishment of these murderers. The offer stood for five years, and while no eligible claimants appeared during that time, this Texas newspaper deserves an accolade for its pioneer effort, and for the stimulus which its brave example gave to public-spirited organizations and individuals throughout the South.

Valiant in the fight against this evil in more recent years has been the Association of Southern Women for the Prevention of Lynching, with headquarters in Atlanta and a membership of nearly 40,000 white women, all in the Southern states. Founded in 1930, and headed by Mrs. Attwood Martin of Louisville and Mrs. Jessie Daniel Ames of Atlanta, this organization has made itself felt importantly in the struggle to free the former Confederacy of this blight. The association has served its most useful purpose in dramatizing the fact that the lynching bee is not a rite for the protection of Southern womanhood, since of all the Negroes whose lives have been taken in this fiendish fashion during the twentieth century, only about one-sixth were even accused of rape.

So far from defending lynching, the association pronounces it "an indefensible crime, destructive of all principles of government, hateful and hostile to every ideal of religion and humanity, debasing and degrading to every person involved." However, the association's executive committee adopted a resolution in 1940 declaring that the organization "does not support and never has supported Federal legislation to eradicate lynching." It added that "the slow process of educating society . . . is the only sure way to stop lynchings."

The N.A.A.C.P. contends that some of the Tuskegee totals on annual lynchings, which are the totals used in this chapter, are too low, and that even if they weren't, "lynching has gone underground," i.e., "a new and dangerous technique" has been devised, by means of which Negroes are got rid of quietly by small bodies of whites, instead of by huge mobs howling for vengeance. A white Southerner who served as investigator for the association reports that "countless Negroes are lynched yearly, but their disappearance is shrouded in mystery." The chief quarrel one has with this finding is that there is nothing new about these bestial killings, and one hesitates to accept the undocumented statement that "underground" lynchings claim "countless" victims annually. No evidence is adduced by the investigator to prove that this species of barbarism is more prevalent to-day than formerly; it may, in fact, be definitely on the wane— which makes the whole thing sound a little like special pleading designed to refute the argument that lynching has declined drastically, and that therefore a Federal law against it is no longer needed.

The bromidic declaration frequently has been made that when public opinion in the South ceases to countenance lynching, the crime will die out. As a matter of fact, there is an excessively large body of opinion among intelligent and educated Southerners which either condones or defends mob rule and execution by rope and faggot. John Temple Graves, II, the widely read Southern columnist, wrote in 1935 that during a decade as newspaper editor and commentator in the Deep South, he had found that thousands of Southerners who should know better "believe in lynching as a stern necessity under certain circumstances." He quoted a University of Virginia graduate whose "solution" of the race problem was "a general massacre," and a Birmingham physician who said that a certain Negro defendant should be hanged, whether guilty or not. "The important thing," said the physician in a letter to Mr.

Graves, "is that whenever a white woman is raped by a Negro there should be an example and a spectacle of punishment. If possible get the right Negro and string him up. String up one or two of his nearest relatives, at the same time. And if the right one can't be found, take some other Negro." Such doctrine as this from a professional man in the South, or anywhere else, is depressing and disgusting in the extreme. It is gratifying to record that Mr. Graves no longer gets anything like so many letters defending lynching as he did a decade ago, although his column is syndicated much more widely than it was then.

Since the N.A.A.C.P. contends that the Tuskegee lynching figures understate the magnitude of the problem, an effort was made to reconcile these divergent points of view at a conference of representatives of the N.A.A.C.P., the Commission on Interracial Coöperation, Tuskegee, and the press at Tuskegee in December, 1940. The conferees sought a definition of lynching which would be acceptable to all, to the end that lynching totals might be in agreement thereafter. The Southern contingent announced subsequently in the *Southern Frontier,* organ of the Commission on Interracial Coöperation, that the conference agreed to define a lynching as any case where there is "legal evidence that a person has been killed and that he met his death illegally at the hands of a group acting under the pretext of service to justice, race, or tradition." But in its annual report, the N.A.A.C.P. asserted that the definition adopted by the gathering described a lynching as "an activity in which persons in defiance of the law administer punishment by death to an individual for an alleged offense or to an individual with whom some

offense has been associated." Two observations seem
justified with respect to these definitions: (1) They are
so broad that they can be made to cover many gang
killings in Northern cities, although such killings are
never counted as lynchings. (2) It appears certain that
the annual figures on lynchings compiled by the Northern and Southern agencies will continue to diverge.

Less spectacular and less publicized than the increasingly rare practice of lynching, but equally serious in
its implications, is the enormous homicide rate among
Southern Negroes, and the apparent reluctance of Southern courts to address themselves to it effectively. Chicago
during the glorious reign of Al Capone never had a
murder rate even remotely approaching that of a dozen
Southern cities. Moreover, it must be said, in all fairness,
that the white homicide rate in the South also is the
highest in the country, and that during the heyday of
the Chicago gangsters, the white murder rate in such
cities as Fort Worth, Memphis, New Orleans, and Birmingham was higher than the combined rate for both
races in Chicago, although the Negro rate is everywhere
much higher than the white rate. The Negro rate, indeed, is a standing scandal, and the blame must by no
means be placed solely upon the Negroes.

For one thing, the average Southern police department, like many police departments in other sections,
is riddled with politics and operated along traditionally
inefficient lines. If more Southern cities would reorgan-
ize their departments in accordance with the modern
practices introduced by former Mayor Maury Maverick
in San Antonio, vast improvement would result.

For another thing, the overwhelming majority of
Negro killers in the South receive light sentences at the

hands of white jurors—provided their victims are other Negroes. Too often the attitude of white jurors, and even of white judges, is that the killing of a Negro by another Negro is a comparatively trivial crime. When the shiftless, irresponsible, crapshooting, hooch-guzzling Negroes produced by the Southern slums (for which the whites are partly responsible), see that killing other Negroes in brawls over dice, whiskey, or women brings either acquittal or only a few years in prison, they naturally are much more homicidally inclined than they would otherwise be. Pistols, razors, or brass knucks tend to be uniform equipment in the Negro wards of too many Southern cities, and these instruments for the commission of mayhem are used with alarming and devastating frequency.

Take the case of Charlotte, North Carolina, a city of 100,000 population. It had no fewer than 47 murders during 1940, and has been called a leading claimant to the sobriquet of "Murder Capital of America." Sixteen of these killings took place at one street intersection, and of course all sixteen victims were Negroes, as were most of the other persons slain in Charlotte during the year. The combined murder rate for both races in the city for 1940, i.e., 47 per 100,000, is to be compared with the rate of 13.6 for Chicago in 1926, at the height of Al Capone's intramural beer-running and whiskey-hijacking wars. Charlotte, let us not forget, is also "The City of Churches." It has no fewer than 114 inside the corporate limits, and its moral tone is regarded as well-nigh irreproachable.

Let us also consider Chattanooga. With a population of 128,000, it produced no fewer than 61 Negro murders in 1940, a record as bad as Charlotte's. Nobody was electrocuted for any of these killings. Moreover, not a single Negro has been executed for murdering another Negro in Chattanooga in twenty years! The situation in Richmond evidences a like trend. With 200,000 population, it had 39 murders in 1940, nearly all by and of Negroes. Not only was there not a single electrocution, but there has been only one electrocution of a Negro murderer in Richmond in fifteen years, and in that case, the victim was a white police detective. Virginia, North Carolina, and Tennessee all have capital punishment, but, as noted, there is a great reluctance here, as elsewhere in the South, to apply the extreme penalty in the case of homicides involving members of the black race. Moreover, life sentences are rare in such cases. The usual term runs for only a few years. While it can be said in extenuation that many killings of Negroes by other Negroes are not first degree murder, since they take place in fights or brawls, in the heat of anger, and the ultimate penalty is not called for, the tendency of many Southern courts is to run to the other extreme and to impose hardly any penalty at all. This is a direct incitement to crime.

The appalling number of Negro slayings which occur annually in the South make the total of lynchings look like almost nothing. In every Southern city of 100,000 population several times as many Negroes are slain annually by other Negroes as are lynched annually by whites in the entire South. This is not said in extenuation of lynching, but in order to illustrate the magnitude of the problem of Negro homicide, and to emphasize the fact that it is getting far too little attention.

The size of the Southern homicide rate, both white and colored, is due to various factors, in addition to those already listed. The South's dueling tradition, as well as its adherence to the "unwritten law," have tended to inculcate habits of violence. The fact that Negroes were slaves until the Civil War, and were given a status below that of all but the poorest and most despised whites, induced a psychological attitude toward the relative value of a Negro life, as compared to a white life, which seems to have endured. The violence and crime which was so characteristic of Reconstruction, and the rise of such an extra-legal organization as the Ku Klux Klan, which took, and still takes, into its own hands matters deemed to involve political, religious, or racial issues, helped to perpetuate the vigilante tradition below the Potomac. Still another incitement to crime is the relative leniency of Southern laws against pistol-toting.

Until the South is able to rise above the foregoing obstacles, and to develop a new social and psychological attitude toward the slaying of human beings, especially Negroes, present conditions are apt to continue. A step which would go far to reduce the homicide rate among the colored population, but which cannot yet be taken in most Southern cities, because of objections from certain white elements, is the appointment of Negro policemen for service in the Negro wards. At least six Southern cities have such policemen at the present time, and the results are said by white officials there to be uniformly good. Louisville has approximately twenty Negro members on its force, and as in the case of the other five cities under discussion, they are assigned to the Negro sections, where they are said to get better results than white officers could. Other cities which have Negro officers are Houston, Galveston, Knoxville, Daytona

Beach, and Charlotte, which have four, eleven, six, four, and two, respectively. They stay in the Negro districts, and in Houston and Daytona Beach they never arrest white persons. In Galveston and Knoxville they make such arrests occasionally, when whites violate the law in their presence.

If Galveston, with only 4,000 Negroes in its total population of 65,000, finds a need for eleven Negro policemen out of 75, it would seem that Negro officers would be still more useful in cities with populations from one-fourth to one-third colored. Dave Henry, chief of detectives of Galveston, wrote the Charlotte *News,* which made a survey in a successful effort (joined in by the Charlotte *Observer*) to secure colored policemen for Charlotte, that "the Negro officers' work is very satisfactory to the department and the citizens of this city." Uniformly similar reports came from the four other cities mentioned above. Yet there is usually a great uproar when it is suggested to Southerners that Negro policemen ought to be serving their communities and a great pother arises concerning "social equality." Until a more sensible attitude is manifested in the average Southern city, and colored policemen are stationed in colored districts, the colored homicide rate probably will continue at its present unconscionable level. It should not be imagined, however, that this alone will solve the problem. Other important factors in the situation have been pointed out, such as the foul slums in which Negroes have to live, in both North and South, the reluctance of Southern judges and juries to impose reasonably severe penalties upon Negroes who kill other members of their race, and the insufficiently stringent Southern laws against pistol-toting. The problem of

Negro homicides must, therefore, be attacked on a broad front.

Lest the impression be gained from the foregoing that Negroes are inherently addicted to crime, attention is directed to the truly amazing record of Mound Bayou, Mississippi, an all-Negro town of 1,000 souls, which recently tore down its jail, since there was no need for this normally indispensable institution. Founded more than half a century ago, Mound Bayou has had only one murder in its history, and no other serious crime. It is governed entirely by Negroes, and in addition to its superlative record for law-observance, has a better-than-average sanitation record, and a good health record, with no typhoid fever in more than fifteen years, and no smallpox or diphtheria in a decade.

Mound Bayou is, therefore, a remarkable example of what a Negro community can accomplish in the sphere of civic achievement, given an adequate opportunity. Inevitably its success induces the reflection as to how far the members of the black race might go in other directions, if avenues of advancement were open to them. One of the greatest handicaps which the Southern Negro faces is, of course, the fact that he seldom has the vote, and consequently is largely ignored by Southern political leaders. This state of things is changing gradually, but Federal court decisions already rendered, and others in prospect, have not raised the total of Southern Negroes who vote to as much as 50,000 for the whole region, according to one seemingly reliable estimate.

There are various means whereby the Negro is prevented from exercising the franchise below the Potomac, and the poll-tax is only one of them. Complicated registration laws which can be applied with much greater severity against Negroes, also are important factors, as are threats, whether actually uttered or merely implied. Most important of all is the "lily white" primary, under which the Democratic party excludes Negroes entirely in most states from participation in the nomination of its candidates for office. In view of complete Democratic dominance nearly everywhere, the exclusively white primary is the heaviest obstacle of all to the development of strong Negro influence in Southern politics. Except in Kentucky and Tennessee and a few counties and cities of Virginia and North Carolina, the colored voter is excluded entirely from participation in the process of choosing Democratic nominees.

Whether this situation will continue remains to be seen, however, for the Supreme Court held in a Louisiana case during 1941 that state primaries and nominating conventions are subject to the same Federal regulation as are general elections, and a suit testing the validity of the lily-white Texas primary was on its way to the highest tribunal early in 1942. The Louisiana case reversed a Supreme Court decision of two decades before in a Michigan case, and it seemed to mean that the court might also reverse its ruling of 1935 wherein the Democratic party of Texas was held to have the right to bar Negroes from primaries, provided the primaries were conducted as private party elections, and provided also the party itself is organized as a voluntary organization whose rules are not based upon statutory enactments. All these possibilities seemed to open up political vistas to the Negro while engendering headaches for those who have sought to hold the colored vote to a minimum.

The future will tell, however, whether other subterfuges will be devised for use against the Negro, even if the above-mentioned court decisions are in his favor. Southern whites have exhibited great ingenuity hitherto in circumventing both the statutes and the interpretation of those statutes by the courts. It should be noted too, that elimination of the poll-tax might not have a marked effect upon the total Negro vote, if the situation in Virginia is any criterion. Dr. Luther P. Jackson, professor of history at the Virginia State College for Negroes, made a careful survey of the voting of Virginia Negroes in the presidential contest of 1940, when the Old Dominion cast the largest total vote in its entire history. Dr. Jackson discovered that whereas eight per cent of the colored adults in the state had paid the levy and were eligible to participate in the election, in so far as the poll-tax was concerned, two-thirds of these either had not registered or didn't bother to go to the polls. Among the non-voters in November, 1940, were two-thirds of the state's Negro school teachers, one-third of whom had never voted in their lives. At the same time, it is noteworthy that while the percentage of colored voters obviously was quite low, Dr. Jackson pointed out that it was still lower ten years previously.

Several thousand Negroes exercise the franchise in each of a number of leading Southern cities—such as Birmingham, Atlanta and Memphis—but in no other is there a situation comparable to that which prevails in San Antonio, where, according to George C. Stoney, the percentage of Negroes voting is larger than the percentage of whites. San Antonio even had a Negro gambler named Bellinger as its most potent political figure for the twenty years prior to 1939. Louisville also is in a class by itself, for it has elected and twice re-

elected one of its Negro citizens to the Kentucky Legislature, representing a 95 per cent colored section of the
city. He is 35-year-old Charles W. Anderson, Jr., a graduate of Howard University and attorney, whose service
as an assemblyman is highly praised. As the first Negro
to be elected to a Southern legislature since the Reconstruction era, his successive reëlections and his excellent
record are necessarily considered significant. During his
three terms, Mr. Anderson has been instrumental in
securing better educational facilities for Kentucky Negroes, better accommodations for them on trains and
busses, and other reforms. Although he is a Republican,
leading white Democrats of the state speak of his public
service as extremely impressive and constructive.

The fact that a Negro is able to win the respect of his
white colleagues in a Southern legislature evidences the
progress of interracial understanding in the region. Another encouraging phenomenon in this general sphere
is the liberal attitude manifested on racial issues by
Supreme Court Justice Hugo Black of Alabama, an
admitted one-time member of the Ku Klux Klan, who
has since risen above this affiliation, and has demonstrated his ability and his liberalism as a member of the
highest tribunal in the land.

It should be stressed that many of the racial problems
which confront the South are likewise acute in Northern
cities. Some Americans do not realize that New York,
Chicago, Philadelphia, Baltimore, and Washington all
have more Negroes than any Southern city, and that
New York has approximately three times as many as
New Orleans, which last has the highest total of any
urban community below Mason and Dixon's line. Moreover, there are no slums anywhere in the South worse

than those of Harlem, where Negroes are more densely packed than in any other American city, and where crime and disease flourish. The block bounded by Seventh and Lenox Avenues and 142nd and 143rd Streets, has more than 3,800 persons living on it, a population density which, if applied to New York City as a whole would make possible the placing of all the inhabitants of the United States within about half the city's area.

And if it is argued that the South is the region where the Negro is exploited economically, and refused permission to make a respectable livelihood, what are we to say of Massachusetts, where the legislature recently refused to approve a bill permitting Negro girls to enroll in hospital nurses' training schools? The bill passed one branch of the assembly, but was tabled in the other, when trustees and superintendents of hospitals began protesting. In the words of the Norfolk *Journal and Guide,* the South's leading Negro newspaper and one of the very best in the nation: "As far as these descendants of the abolitionists are concerned, matters just do not work out when Negroes want to work in order to have economic security in Boston and in other parts of Massachusetts."

Consider also the "slave markets" in the Bronx where, to quote the N.A.A.C.P., "for more than a decade housewives bid outrageously small sums for the services of domestic workers." There were something like thirty of these places in the Bronx, and others in Brooklyn, Brighton Beach, and Brownsville. Finally in 1941, the N.A.A.C.P. succeeded in obtaining the substitution of an employment bureau, under New York City auspices, for some of these Bronx "slave markets."

So much for economic discrimination against Negroes in the North. Countless other examples could be cited, and those having to do with the defense program already have been mentioned. What of the prevailing attitude outside the South toward the Negro in his social contacts with the white? It is well known that the average Northern or Western white family does not mingle on terms of social intimacy with any Negro family. Is there a different state of things in the armed forces? By no means. There is segregation in both of them. The N.A.A.C.P. constantly protests against the Navy's ruling that Negroes are accepted by the Navy only in the rôle of mess attendants, and an article was published in its organ, the *Crisis,* for December, 1940, by "a Negro volunteer now serving in a Northern Army post," the title of which was "Jim Crow in the Army Camps." The author pronounced segregation "rampant," even in the theater at the post, which had a section reserved for colored soldiers.

The foregoing would seem completely to refute the notion that it is only in the South that the Negro is a victim of adverse discrimination. What of the equally prevalent belief that no colored person in the Deep South can behave with dignity in the presence of a white person, and that the only conduct which is tolerated there is the cringing, servile attitude so vividly and imaginatively described by zealous denizens of other regions? The Deep South's predilection for lynching has been analyzed and deplored in these pages, and it cannot be defended. Yet the visitor who goes South with certain preconceived ideas as to what he will see in the sphere of ordinary, casual interracial relationships and contacts, is in for some surprises, even if he goes to

Mississippi, with the worst lynching record in the Union. Despite that record, he will find that there are many self-respecting and well-poised Negroes in the state, and that one can travel or visit there for weeks without witnessing anything in the way of interracial attitudes which might not just as readily be encountered in Pennsylvania or Ohio. The author of this volume kept a keen look-out on a recent trip to Mississippi for evidences of rudeness, arrogance, or brutality on the part of white Mississippians toward black Mississippians. He saw none. He wondered, for example, whether he might not find an occasional bus driver who was inconsiderate to his colored passengers, but they were all just the reverse. Despite the fact that on more than one occasion a colored youth gave a driver provocation for a just rebuke, the driver took no notice. Drivers were tolerant of slow-moving Negro passengers, even of those who kept the bus waiting unduly when they got off and lingered overlong at local stops. In general it can be said that the atmosphere of "terror" which is widely supposed to hang over relations between whites and blacks in the lower South, is hard to discern with the naked eye. Jackson, the modern and bustling capital of Mississippi, even has a mob-proof jail, situated on the top floor of the new Hinds County Courthouse, and accessible by only one elevator, which can readily be rendered inoperative.

Obviously the Negroes of Mississippi suffer under serious disabilities, but how much worse is their condition than that of their racial kinsmen in Harlem or the Chicago Black Belt? If they are more apt to be lynched in Mississippi they are less apt to die of tuberculosis, and the number lynched is only an infinitesimal fraction of the number carried off by consumption in the densely packed slums of Northern cities. For example, the death rate from tuberculosis in 1938 was higher for Negroes in New York, Chicago, Detroit, Cleveland, and Cincinnati than it was in New Orleans, Atlanta, or Dallas. A recent bulletin of the United States Public Health Service declares that "in the South the ratio of colored to white mortality at all ages is 1.7, while in the North it is 1.9."

"But," the Northerner is apt to argue, "the Negro is afforded a decent opportunity to make a livelihood in the North, whereas in Mississippi and other such states he begins life as a menial and stays a menial. He has no chance of rising to the status of a reasonably prosperous business or professional man."

That is interesting, but it happens not to be true. The statement is too partial to the North and too critical of the South. Consider Natchez, where the incomparably lovely ante-bellum mansions are more celebrated, but hardly less remarkable, than the prosperous Negro community in the town. This community includes various well-managed commercial establishments which enjoy nearly all the Negro business in Natchez, but which are not segregated from the stores of the whites, any more than the Negro residences are segregated from the white residences. The leading Negroes of Natchez are relatively prosperous, highly regarded by their white fellow-citizens, and able financially to send their children to states with better educational facilities for members of the black race. To a lesser degree, the Negroes of Vicksburg also enjoy advantages which persons unfamiliar with Mississippi and its *mores* probably would consider surprising. While neither city is equal in every respect to Durham, North Carolina, with its large and successful all-Negro life and fire insurance companies operating in many states, the fact that such opportunities as have been mentioned are afforded to Negroes in Mississippi deserves more than passing attention.

Thus it will be seen that when the facts as to the status of the Southern Negro are studied, one finds that whereas some deplorable and some fiendish practices remain, and whereas the Negro appears to be having increasing difficulty earning a livelihood, both North and South, there are nonetheless certain encouraging phenomena. We have noted that his civil liberties are more carefully protected below the Potomac than ever before, that he is constantly winning cases in the Federal courts which bear upon the maintenance of his civil and political rights, and that gradual, but significant, improvement in interracial relationships is being recorded, under the leadership of Southern organizations which believe in moving forward quietly and diplomatically to new frontiers.

The picture has its bright and its dark sides, but for a race less than three generations removed from slavery, the Southern Negro has much to which he can point with justifiable gratification. We have, on the one hand, the ingenuity and resourcefulness with which he has made his way slowly upward against manifold obstacles, and we have, on the other, his friends and collaborators among the whites who have perceived the importance of aiding him, of understanding his problems, and of seeking to make of him a useful, competent, literate, and happy citizen. Like many other aspects of life in this troubled world, his progress in the direction of these desiderata has its satisfying, as well as its discouraging, aspects.

VIII

THE NEGRO AND HIS SCHOOLING

NEGRO education has made tremendous strides below Mason and Dixon's line during the past several decades, not only in the primary and secondary schools, but in the publicly and privately supported institutions of higher learning. If the amount of money appropriated by the various states to Negro education at all levels is still low, by comparison with the allotments to the dominant race for the same purpose, the great improvement is obvious. Just as the number and quality of the Negro elementary and high schools have increased enormously since the early years of the century, the facilities for collegiate instruction have multiplied many times over. As recently as 1916 the Negro colleges of the country, nearly all of which are in the South, showed a total enrolment of only 2,637. Six years later the figure had doubled, and by 1927 it had more than doubled again. By 1932 it had leaped to over 22,000, by 1938 to nearly 34,000, and by 1941 to over 45,000. In other words, the enrolment in these institutions increased more than seventeen times in two and a half decades. It is still going up.

Moreover there is a growing disposition on the part of Southerners to facilitate this process, instead of to hinder it. The words of the late Chancellor Kirkland of Vanderbilt are finding a responsive chord. Kirkland said that "the intellectual freedom and efficiency of the white race will be promoted by generous treatment of the Negro," and that "oppression of every kind will work a double woe." He added: "In whatever form slavery may be perpetuated, just so far it will put shackles on the minds of the Southern whites. If we treat the Negro unjustly, we shall practice fraud and injustice toward each other.... The South will be free only as it grants freedom."

The constantly improving attitude of the whites toward the desirability of providing decent educational facilities and standards for the blacks is manifest. There always has been a minority of Southerners who believed that education offers the nearest thing to a "solution" of the Negro problem, and a poll taken by the Gallup organization in the spring of 1941 for the National Education Association showed the white people of the South to be divided almost exactly half and half on the question of providing equal public school advantages for Negro children. A statement from R. B. Eleazer, educational director of the Commission on Interracial Coöperation, apropos of this survey, declared that these results "are believed to be much more favorable to the Negro child than would have been the case ten years ago." That is unquestionably true. Moreover, the 50 per cent who still object to making equal public school facilities available to the Negroes, are being brought into line gradually by decisions of the Supreme Court which leave them few, if any, alternatives to compliance.

These court decisions have been secured, in most instances, by the National Association for the Advancement of Colored People, and that aggressive agency undoubtedly should be credited with achieving certain

substantial benefits for the Negroes of the South, benefits to which they are entitled in both law and morals.
The results are particularly patent in the sphere of
colored school teachers' salaries. There is little reason
to believe that these salaries would have been brought
up to the level of those paid the white teachers, despite
the fact that work and requirements are identical in
many instances, without the imperatives of the Federal
courts. To-day those salaries have been equalized in
certain areas, and the process is going forward in many
others. There is a certain amount of hedging and dodg-
ing, of course, but ultimate equalization is inevitable,
as it should be.

North Carolina was the first state to move toward
equalization of salaries for teachers. At the legislative
session of 1939, before the Supreme Court handed down
its salary equalization decision, a total of $258,000 was
appropriated for the purpose. The legislature of 1941
arranged to disburse $250,000 a year during the ensuing
biennium for the same cause. This placed North Carolina far in advance of any other Southern state, in its
efforts to solve the problem. At the end of five years,
it is hoped that full equalization will be obtained.

Alabama took a significant step toward the same objective at its legislative session of 1941, when an identical salary scale was announced for both races, and some
$200,000 was voted for equalization. While salaries
there have not, of course, been equalized by this single
appropriation, the allotment of any substantial amount
to such a purpose in a far Southern state, is important.
Critics of the plan pointed to the declaration of Alabama's superintendent of education that while the new

scale lowered the minimum for white teachers, no reductions were contemplated, and that none of the whites who were getting the previous $50 minimum would be reduced. The N.A.A.C.P. even contended that it would "cost the state of Alabama $2,000,000 to equalize salaries perfectly," so that by allocating $200,000, "Alabama has gone only one-tenth of the way toward equalization." The organization declared that, under the new scale, "there is still a wide difference between a Negro teacher, for example, who has a master's degree and five years of experience, and a white teacher who has a master's degree and five years of experience." It went on to say that the Negro teachers of the state were contemplating "court action at the proper time to secure complete equalization."

At all events, this Gulf state, with its large Negro population and its deeply ingrained racial cleavage, has taken a step which a few years ago would have seemed impossible. Similar steps are being taken in other Southern states and cities, although they have it within their power to force the N.A.A.C.P. to carry each of their cases all the way up to the Supreme Court. But since the decision there would in every instance be inevitably against them, such obstructionist tactics do not seem to be in contemplation. The prevailing sentiment was expressed by Frederick Sullens, editor of the Jackson *Daily News,* when he took to task Mississippi educators who met, as he put it editorially, "to avoid the issue and to keep out of the press all that was said on the subject." His editorial contained the following pungent and incisive comment:

It isn't any use, gentlemen.
Present manner of distributing the common school fund

is a lie and a fraud on its face. It is not equitable and you know it.

Further subterfuge or camouflage will be useless.

The nation's tribunal of last resort has spoken on the subject.

Whether you like the decision or not doesn't matter. It must be obeyed.

Most Southern states have made no definite provision, as yet, for the Negro teachers, but such cities as Louisville, Norfolk, and Chattanooga have put into effect single-salary scales for both white and colored, and suits or petitions on behalf of the Negro group have been filed in several others. While it will be years before complete salary equalization is achieved, the movement is gathering momentum.

Just as there have been, and still are, wide discrepancies between salaries of the white and colored teachers, so the per capita expenditures of the various Southern states for school buildings and equipment, and for transportation, are far higher for the whites. One-room and one-teacher Negro schools are numerous in the rural South, and transportation, when furnished, is usually inadequate. Beulah Amidon wrote in the *Survey Graphic* recently that "in the eleven Southern states which have the highest percentage of Negro citizens, Negro youth receives only 37 per cent of the amount which would be allocated for his education, were school funds equally divided between white and Negro children"; "more than 60 per cent of all Negro schools are one-teacher schools," and "in 230 counties in fifteen Southern states, there are no high schools for Negro youth."

Such a statement leaves a good many things unsaid,

however. Here is a race only a couple of generations removed from slavery whose education became the responsibility of a conquered and looted people. Although that people had wholly inadequate funds with which to finance even one satisfactory system of public schools, it was saddled with the staggering extra burden of a dual system. One finds scant reason for believing that the people of the North or the West would have acquitted themselves any more handsomely, under like circumstances. Moreover, those regions to-day, with a relatively negligible Negro population, do not have the double load of a dual system of education, and they have the added advantage of being wealthier than the South to start with. Recent estimates by the National Bureau of Economic Research of the annual income per child for the various states show an average of $2,481 for the country as a whole, with the Southern states ranging from a low of $930 to a high of $1,528. And although the South spends a larger percentage of its wealth on education than any other region, per pupil expenditures for public education average $74 for the United States, while the Southern states have a low of $25 and a high of $55. There would be a smaller discrepancy between the regions, were it not for the fact that in addition to its other handicaps, the South has much the largest number of children, per adult, in the nation.

Confronted by such basic and well-nigh insurmountable disadvantages as these, the South naturally encounters extreme difficulty in its efforts to offer educational facilities comparable in excellence to those in wealthier states with only one public school system, and proportionately fewer children. It has been widely sug-

gested that the only satisfactory solution lies in Federal
aid, apportioned in accordance with a formula which
would provide some assistance to every state, but would
channel most of this Federal money into the school systems of the predominantly rural South and West. In
justification it is argued that the needs of the Southern
and Western states are greatest and their financial
ability least. Legislation designed to carry out such a
plan has been pending in Congress for some time. Thus
far it has failed of enactment largely because of opposition from those who feel that the Federal treasury and
the Federal tax-payers are being subjected to too great
a strain already, and from those who fear the plan would
lead to Federal control of the schools, or who regret
that it would give no aid to parochial and other non-
public education. There are even persons who profess
to anticipate Federal edicts forcing the South to operate
a unified public school system for white and colored,
if the bill passes, but since the late Pat Harrison of
Mississippi was the Senate patron of the bill, it is impossible to take this apocalyptic vision seriously.

Dean C. H. Bynum of Texas College is one of those
who see no alternative to Federal aid, if the South is
to bring its public schools up to minimum national
standards. He writes in the *Southern Frontier* that in
order for the region to reach the national level, "it
would have to apply practically its total income from all
sources to this objective." Dean Bynum's "South" includes eighteen states, and he says that in a most favorable year, the total taxable resources of those states
"would yield approximately one billion dollars, nine
hundred million of which would have to be allocated

to the support of schools, which would then reach only the minimum average of the nation."

In the light of this summation, it becomes altogether obvious that the unaided South cannot hope to develop public schools for either race which are equal in every respect to those in the rest of the country. Abolition of the dual school system would bring the objective much nearer realization, but it may as well be stated that the South has no intention now, or at any time in the measurable future, of seeking economies by the education of both races in the same public schools. The desire for separate schools is too deeply ingrained for any but an infinitesimal minority of white Southerners to wish for change.

Several large foundations have rendered invaluable assistance in raising the level of Southern Negro schools. Without the philanthropic and altruistic services of these organizations, the schools in question would be considerably less adequate than they are. But the South cannot count on these foundations for unlimited assistance in the future. The two largest and most important, the Julius Rosenwald Fund and the General Education Board, have arranged to expend all their assets and to close out their activities in a comparatively few years. The former has made possible the erection of 5,357 modern school buildings for Negroes in fifteen states, has greatly stimulated better libraries for the colored schools, and has initiated special studies in the field of rural Negro education. The latter has concentrated to a greater degree in the field of the higher learning, but it has given substantial aid to Southern state departments of education, which administer the public school systems of both races.

In addition to these two foundations, there are others with smaller resources which have rendered important aid to the Negro schools over a long period. For example the $1,000,000 Jeanes Foundation, established in 1907 by a Philadelphia Quaker, still helps in the maintenance of Jeanes supervisors for those schools in 430 Southern counties. The $1,000,000 Slater Fund, established in 1882 by a Connecticut manufacturer, still aids in the development of central county training schools in Southern regions where secondary schools are lacking. The $1,000,000 Phelps-Stokes Fund, established in 1911, continues to sponsor studies and surveys of Negro education.

With the demise of the Rosenwald Fund scheduled to take place not later than 1957, in accordance with the stipulation of its founder, and the liquidation of the General Education Board's assets arranged for a much earlier date, it can readily be seen that the substantial aid which Negro education in the South has received from Northern philanthropists, is to be much reduced, ere long. This condition arises just when the Southern states are faced with the necessity of finding millions of dollars for Negro schools and colleges, in order to comply with recent Supreme Court decisions.

So large a sum of additional money probably would not be raised by taxation within the South to-day, even if everybody in the region was desirous of providing both races with completely adequate educational facilities—and there is still strong opposition to placing the public schools of the blacks on a parity with those of the whites. The interracial tension occasioned in Memphis and Dallas during 1941—which is said to have begun in Memphis when leading Negroes defied the instructions of the Crump municipal machine as to how they should vote, and in Dallas brought bombings and threats of bloodshed when Negroes purchased homes in a section partially occupied by whites—is symptomatic of the feeling in some parts of the South. Since the latest Gallup poll shows that only half of the Southern whites are amenable to the idea of equal school facilities for the blacks, the power of the opposition can be readily imagined. Moreover, there are Negrophobes in high places, like Governor Talmadge of Georgia, who can stoop to the lowest forms of demagoguery to make political capital out of the race issue. Talmadge even vetoed an appropriation voted almost unanimously by the Georgia Legislature in 1941 for the operation of a training school for delinquent Negro girls. The building had been paid for with the nickels and dimes of Georgia's Negro women, and had been presented by them to the state four years before. It had never been opened, for lack of funds—and doubtless won't be, as long as Georgia sends Talmadges to the gubernatorial mansion, although Georgia has a training school for delinquent Negro boys. So has every other Southern state except Mississippi, which has practically as many Negroes as whites, but no training school for either delinquent colored boys or delinquent colored girls.

In view of present trends, it seems merely a question of time before such institutions are provided in every Southern state. Meanwhile attention is focused upon the equalization of salaries in the public schools and the efforts of Negroes to secure graduate and professional instruction at Southern universities which hitherto have been reserved exclusively for whites.

These efforts were being pushed with greater vigor by the N.A.A.C.P. in 1939 and 1940, immediately following the Supreme Court's decision in the Gaines case, than they were early in 1942. That organization appears more interested at the moment in the matter of teachers' salaries. However, the sundering issue which revolves about the possible admittance of Negroes to the white universities is the most controversial and challenging of all the interracial questions now pressing for a solution. Although, as stated by Edwin Camp of the Atlanta *Journal*, leaders of both races throughout the South are working together on the problem "with a singleness of purpose and a tolerant understanding and sympathy which would have seemed impossible a decade ago," there are many potential areas of conflict.

The Supreme Court held in the Gaines case, which involved the attempt of a Missouri Negro to enter the University of Missouri Law School, that "the state was bound to furnish him within its borders facilities for legal education substantially equal to those which the state then afforded for persons of the white race." The phrase "within its borders" appeared to preclude the establishment of regional institutions offering graduate and professional instruction exclusively for Negroes, although the number of Negroes desiring such instruction in any single Southern state is so small at this time as to make the maintenance by each state of separate but "equal" law, medical, engineering, and graduate schools prohibitively expensive, if not ridiculously extravagant.

Several possibilities seemed to present themselves. There was, of course, the "solution" to be arrived at by opening all state-supported institutions to members of the Negro race. There was the second possibility, realizable through the establishment of separate institutions which would offer graduate and professional instruction to Negroes, or the enlargement of existing state-supported undergraduate institutions. Another proposal was that separate schools for Negroes be set up within the white universities. A fourth alternative called for making state aid available to strong private Negro colleges, thus enabling them to provide first class graduate and professional training. President Harmon W. Caldwell of the University of Georgia presented these alternatives to the annual Southern University Conference in Atlanta in 1939, without clearly indicating his preference. He made it plain that he did not favor admitting Negroes to the white institutions, and declared that the "fourth possibility should make a particularly strong appeal to states like Georgia, with its Atlanta University Center, and Tennessee with Fisk University." He seemed to regard a fifth plan as the best of all, namely, establishment of regional institutions supported jointly by the various states, but he doubted if such a scheme would be countenanced by the Supreme Court. He did not mention still another alternative, likewise deemed to be in conflict with the Gaines decision, i.e., the granting of tuition subsidies by Southern states to Negroes, so that they might attend Northern professional and graduate schools. This plan still is functioning in a number of Southern states, apparently as a temporary stop-gap.

Dr. Jackson Davis of the General Education Board followed President Caldwell on the program. He warned against settling the question "by hasty action along the line of least resistance," and added:

Most of us who did graduate work in Northern universities attended some classes in which there were a few Negro students. The experience didn't do us any harm. I never heard of a Southern white student objecting to the presence of students of other races. Their presence is assumed in the great centers of learning, which should be open to the elect of all races. These are mature students working in advanced fields.

I have sometimes been asked when Negro students would be admitted into the graduate and professional schools of Southern universities. My answer has been that it might occur when those universities became primarily graduate institutions rather than undergraduate institutions. When the same set of circumstances prevails in some Southern institutions that now prevails in some of the Northern universities, with more mature students, we have no reason to think that they will react differently.

Dr. Davis is, of course, a much more advanced thinker in the sphere of race relations than the average Southerner. Moreover, it will be many years before any Southern university is properly describable as primarily a graduate institution, so that even he does not regard the present as a propitious time for the admission of Negroes to white universities. Certainly the overwhelming majority of white Southerners are opposed to this, and it seems safe to say that if it were tried in any of the former Confederate states, trouble of one sort or another could easily result. This trouble might be relatively mild, or it might be severe. It could take the form of persecution of Negroes on a wide scale throughout the state into whose university one or more Negroes had forced themselves by court action. In other words hundreds, if not thousands, of Negroes might be made to suffer in order that one or two might exercise their undoubted legal right to the same grade of graduate and professional training as is provided for white citizens. The danger probably would lie not so much in the possibility of overt acts on the part of the white students with whom the Negro students would be thrown into contact in the classroom, as in the attitude of the uneducated "poor whites" in the remoter sections, who would be likely to register extreme resentment over "uppity niggers" going to the white university and enjoying schooling which they themselves were utterly incapable of absorbing.

Would a handful of Negro students registered at a Southern university for whites be apt to find themselves in congenial surroundings? It seems highly doubtful. They probably would suffer no violence, but they would almost certainly be happier at an all-Negro institution providing work of equal excellence. Evidence of this is seen in the fact that 42 per cent of the student body at Fisk University, Nashville, comes from the North, and evidently prefers the homogeneity of the Fisk all-Negro student body to the mixed student bodies available to them in their home states. Moreover, about one-fourth of these Northern Negroes remain in the South after graduation.

Consider also the experience of the United States Military Academy and the United States Naval Academy. The former institution has admitted Negroes since 1870, but only nineteen of that race have entered during the nearly three-quarters of a century that the institution has been open to them. Of that number, exactly four had been graduated down to 1941. The experience at Annapolis has been the same, only more so. Three Negroes entered the academy there between 1872 and 1941. Not one completed the course.

The analogy between a military or naval academy,

where cadets or midshipmen are thrown into intimate contact in barracks and mess halls, as well as in the classroom, and a Southern university where the only contact would be in the classroom, is not exact, of course. Yet the opposition in Southern communities and on Southern campuses to mingling the races in the same educational establishment, would be apt to bring similarly unsatisfactory results. While the risk would be less serious in the upper tier of Southern states, it would be substantial in those along the Gulf. In fact, the Gulf states would not be apt to accept a system of mixed education, despite the mandate of the Supreme Court. Ways would be found to circumvent that mandate, or to render the sojourn of any Negro student in a far Southern state university so unpleasant that the arrangement would prove unworkable. In other words, even if a few Negroes were accepted willingly in, say, the University of Kentucky or the University of North Carolina, and no trouble of any sort ensued, the system would not function equally well throughout the region, and some other plan would have to be devised for most of the states and institutions concerned.

As a matter of fact, the University of North Carolina, the most liberal Southern university in the field of race relations, has recognized already that admission of Negroes to its graduate and professional schools would be contrary to the institution's best interests—perhaps contrary to the Negro's best interests. It has opened a separate law school at the State College for Negroes at Durham, an institution which draws, to some extent, upon the Chapel Hill and Duke faculties, and is able to use the libraries of those two institutions. Yet its graduate and professional facilities are limited, and adequate financing of those facilities by appropriation from the state treasury would impose an impossible burden of expense.

How much more economical and effective it would be for North Carolina to join with several other Southern states in maintaining the very best grade of graduate and professional instruction at some centrally-located point, perhaps at a well-established Negro college or university. Such a regional institution would be adequately financed, in contrast to the school now functioning at Durham, and would be large enough to justify the building of a faculty of the highest class. The expensive laboratories, libraries, and other equipment required would be much more readily secured, under such circumstances. The only major obstacle most persons see to such a plan is that the Supreme Court might refuse to sanction it.

There is no question that many of the most enlightened students of the race problem, both North and South, regard the establishment of regional institutions exclusively for Negroes as wiser, under existing circumstances, than the mingling of white and colored students on campuses hitherto reserved for whites. Dr. Edwin R. Embree, whose work as director of the Rosenwald Fund has given him an unexcelled opportunity to judge this problem on the basis of the best solution for all concerned, wrote in 1940:

Graduate and professional education for Negroes is now becoming an increasingly acute question. . . . Southern states must open their regular universities to Negroes (which has been done in certain instances in professional offerings in the border states of Maryland, Missouri, and West Virginia, but which probably will not be done for many years in the states further South) or provide courses in state colleges for Negroes parallel to those provided in the state institutions for the rest of the population.... An interesting suggestion is that several Southern states pool their educational offerings at strong regional centers.... If some plan can be worked out for interstate coöperation, the important universities, especially at Washington, Atlanta, and Nashville, might begin to develop work of highest standard in advanced studies and in preparation for the professions. This would seem a wiser course than dissipating the relatively small funds available to Southern states over a series of "universities"—pretentious but shabby.

Dr. Guy B. Johnson of the University of North Carolina declared in 1937, the year before the Gaines decision was handed down, that a system of regional subsidy probably would best meet the need of Southern Negroes for advanced instruction. He proposed that established Negro universities serve as centers of graduate work. Dr. Walter D. Cocking of the University of Georgia suggested in a formal report a few weeks before the Gaines case was decided, that Georgia Negroes be given graduate and professional schooling in regional centers. Dr. Fred McCuistion, then of George Peabody College for Teachers and now the General Education Board's field agent for Southern education, wrote in 1939, apropos of the Gaines decision: "Since the lack of ability to support adequate programs of graduate and professional instruction is reflected in statements of taxable wealth of the Southern states, and since there is a limited need for advanced work in certain fields, a larger unit of support for centrally located institutions serving a wider area would be justified."

Such opinions as these are held by many detached observers of the Southern scene. What likelihood is there that the Supreme Court would place its imprimatur upon a coöperative arrangement of this character? We have noted the pessimism of various Southern educators on the subject. Is that pessimism justified?

It is difficult to answer with complete assurance until we have a ruling on the point from the Supreme Court itself, but an opinion from one of the country's most distinguished constitutional lawyers, a man whose general point of view coincides with that of the majority of the present court, and who has been mentioned frequently during the Roosevelt Administration as a likely appointee to that tribunal, is highly significant. This opinion as to the legality of regional institutions for Negroes in the South, comes from Dr. Edward S. Corwin of Princeton University, and is here presented for the first time. Dr. Corwin says:

> I base my opinion that a regional university for Negroes in the South would be constitutional on three considerations:
>
> 1. That what a state can do for itself it can—at least there is nothing to the contrary—do in association with other states by means of a compact to which Congress has given its consent.
> 2. In giving its consent to such a compact Congress would not only exercise its powers under Article 1, Section 10, but also its powers under the 5th section of the 14th Amendment.
> 3. That the court, recognizing that the states could provide much better education in the manner suggested than they could individually, would certainly sustain such a compact.

In view of the confidence with which Dr. Corwin expresses himself on this subject, it seems reasonable to assume that if Congress will authorize the procedure, regional institutions can be established constitutionally through joint action of the various states. Would the necessary authorization be granted by the national legislature? Much might depend upon the attitude of the National Association for the Advancement of Colored People, which was instrumental in securing the Gaines decision, and which might seek to block congressional action. The N.A.A.C.P. has given clear indications in the past of wanting to break down the segregation of the races everywhere. For example, Charles H. Houston, its special counsel, told the association's annual convention in 1939 that nothing would satisfy the N.A.A.C.P. but admission of Negroes to the graduate and professional schools of the Southern state universities. "There can be no compromise now upon this question," said Mr. Houston. "It is not a question of wanting to sit in the classroom with white students. It is a question of vindicating one's citizenship." Mr. Houston made it plain that establishment of separate, but equal, graduate and professional facilities in a given state would not be considered satisfactory. Applying this principle all along the line, it seems logical to conclude that in 1939, Mr. Houston and the organization for which he spoke intended, at some opportune time, to press for the admission of Negroes to the undergraduate departments of state-supported colleges and universities in the South, in order to "vindicate" the "citizenship" of the race, and ultimately to seek the abolition of segregation in the public schools. This was charged publicly at the time, and was never denied.

Whether such plans are entertained to-day by the N.A.A.C.P. is unknown, however. We have seen that it has been less aggressive of late in the matter of forcing

Negroes into the Southern universities, and it may have decided that so drastic and radical a course would do more harm than good to the Negroes. If a demonstration could be made that great and lasting interracial bitterness would be aroused through insistence by the association upon its legal rights in this sphere, and it could be shown that most of the Negroes' white defenders and well-wishers in the South would be driven into the opposition by such tactics, the organization might modify its position. Indeed, there are indications that it may have done so already.

Americans must admit candidly that the democratic ideal is at war with the thesis that American citizens can be placed in separate pigeonholes and given varying educational and social advantages, depending upon the color of their skins. Any discrimination among citizens of this country for reasons of race or religion, is undemocratic. Yet sight must not be lost of the fact that the modern South inherited a problem of tremendous complexity and difficulty at the close of the Civil War. Moreover, if the South is to be blamed for the system of slavery upon which it built its economy and its society prior to that war, what are we to say of the eminent New Englanders who made vast sums out of the uniformly barbarous slave trade? How shall we explain away the fact that slavery was not abolished in New England until it was found to be unprofitable there? Is it not obvious that the factors which created a slave system in the South would have created one in New England, if the climate and the agricultural system had been favorable? Let us not forget that William Lloyd Garrison said as late as 1831, following a tour of the country for the purpose of arousing the people against the slave system, that in the free states "and particularly in New England," he found "contempt more bitter, opposition more active, detraction more relentless, prejudice more stubborn, and apathy more frozen, than among the slaveowners themselves." So much for the attitudes of the respective sections only three decades before the Civil War. After that war was over, the beaten and bankrupt South was saddled with the huge problem of caring for millions of emancipated Negroes. Despite all this, and in the face of the interracial prejudice and acrimony which Reconstruction, so-called, aroused, the South laboriously began the task of providing educational and other facilities for the blacks. To-day, remarkable progress has been recorded. In the already quoted words of Senator Norris of Nebraska, "the people of the South have done a wonderful job." Yet they are criticised severely for maintaining separate educational establishments for the two races, and otherwise seeking to prevent ultimate racial amalgamation. Even in the District of Columbia, almost in the shadow of the Lincoln Memorial, there are separate public school systems, and the same situation obtains in parts of New Jersey, Pennsylvania, Indiana, Ohio, and Illinois. The South, with a population one-third Negro, is trying to solve its far more serious problem on the basis of equal, but separate, establishments from the elementary level on through the graduate and professional school. It should be repeated that even advanced Southern thinkers in the realm of race relations are predominantly of the opinion that, given existing sentiment throughout the region, this is the most feasible and satisfactory plan for all concerned.

The extent to which, in recent years, attention has been focused upon the problem of graduate and professional training for Negroes, is evidenced in the following statement made by Dr. Charles S. Johnson of Fisk University in 1939:

Less than a decade ago the major concern was that of meeting the demand for adequate academic standards in liberal arts colleges, and the preceding decade that of developing colleges out of the loosely organized institutions just emerging from the high school level. To-day there are no less than twenty institutions which meet the exacting requirements for accreditation as sound liberal arts colleges, and in the logic of this development, the demand has increased for personnel of more mature academic preparation.

It is unfortunate for the Negro graduate and professional schools that they did not attract much attention until after the era of splendid munificence on the part of our philanthropists had passed. Dr. Fred McCuistion points out in his valuable *Graduate Instruction for Negroes in the United States* that there were 171 gifts of $100,000 or more to American institutions in the year 1928, whereas the number had dropped to 28 by 1935, and to 18 by 1938.

Having begun to develop graduate and professional instruction long after the white institutions, the Negro colleges and universities are, in most instances, unable to compete with them on anything like equal terms. No Negro institution offers the Ph.D. in any subject, and not many give the M.A. or M.S. Practically all were established after 1865, most of them during the last 35 years of the nineteenth century. In 1938, a survey showed that of the 999 members of faculties in the 37 colleges rated by the Southern Association of Colleges and Secondary Schools, only 75 were Ph.D.'s. With the exception of two relatively unimportant institutions in Pennsylvania and one in Ohio, all the Negro colleges and universities are in Southern or border states. Hampton Institute in Virginia is the only one with endowment of as much as $10,000,000, and Tuskegee and the institutions centering in Atlanta and Fisk Universities are the only others with more than $5,000,000.

Ten Negro institutions, nine of them in the South and the tenth in Washington, D. C., give graduate degrees. Howard, in Washington, has been offering these degrees since 1921, and awards considerably more annually than any of the ten. Atlanta is next in the number of such diplomas, with Fisk third. The others are Hampton Institute, Prairie View State College in Texas, Virginia State College, Agricultural and Technical College of North Carolina, North Carolina State College, and Xavier University and Southern University in Louisiana. These institutions should serve as nuclei for regional graduate and professional instruction, if and when a system of regional centers is established. They are well-distributed, with at least one in each major section of the South. Moreover, there are other Negro centers of learning which have excellent standing in the undergraduate field, and may later develop more advanced work. Such, for example, are Dillard University in New Orleans, with a particularly able young faculty; Talladega College and Tuskegee Institute in Alabama, and Virginia Union University, which has just acquired its first Negro president, as well as a fine new library building, formerly the Belgian pavilion at the New York World's Fair.

Education is the favorite subject of study for Negro graduate students, as it is for whites. Far more degrees are awarded in it than in any other discipline. English, history, sociology, mathematics, and chemistry are other fields in which there is a concentration of interest. Howard offers instruction in more subjects than any other institution, and has over twice as many faculty members in graduate work as its nearest rival, Atlanta. In third place comes Fisk.

These three centers of graduate instruction are preeminent—Howard, largely because of its location in Washington and the aid it receives from the Federal Government, and the others because they have been associated with nearby institutions in Atlanta and Nashville, respectively, and have more adequate resources.

In Atlanta, for example, there is a coöperative arrangement involving no fewer than six institutions—Atlanta University, Clark College, Morehouse College, Spelman College, Morris Brown College, and Gammon Theological Seminary. This plan is similar in conception to the Georgia University Center for white institutions, which it antedates—for Atlanta, Morehouse, and Spelman decided to affiliate in 1930. Graduate and professional instruction were reserved for Atlanta University, which the president of the Rosenwald Fund describes as "among the educational leaders of the country regardless of race"; undergraduate teaching of men was allotted to Morehouse, and undergraduate teaching of women to Spelman. Substantial financial aid from the General Education Board and the International Education Board made the venture possible. To-day all six of the institutions have been brought into the plan. Those which are denominational in character retain their autonomy but share their resources.

At Nashville, a similar program has been worked out, with Fisk University, Meharry Medical College, and the Tennessee Agricultural and Industrial State Teachers College as the participating institutions. One or two weaker colleges were liquidated when the arrangement was brought to fruition, and a strong educational center resulted.

Since neither Fisk nor any of the nine other Negro colleges and universities offering graduate degrees confers anything more advanced than the M.A. or M.S., the question arises whether it is likely that any of them will be able to award the doctorate in the near future. Dr. McCuistion wrote in 1939 that they ought not to attempt this, but should concentrate on strengthening existing courses. Roughly the same situation obtains to-day, although if regional institutions could be established, each drawing support from several states, opportunities for conferring the doctorate would brighten at once. It is practically hopeless to expect any single Southern state to finance a separate university for Negroes offering anything remotely approaching adequate instruction at the Ph.D. level. Yet the extent of the progress achieved since the turn of the century can be partially grasped when it is pointed out that as early as 1924 the Virginia State College for Negroes received a larger annual appropriation from the state treasury than the University of Virginia received from the same source in 1900. The colored institution's allotment has been greatly increased since that time, of course. Similar figures could be cited for other Southern states.

In the field of professional instruction eight Negro institutions are offering degrees, but only four are among the ten listed above as providing the master's diploma in academic subjects. The four are Howard, which leads in the variety and scope of its professional instruction, just as it does in graduate work; Atlanta, Hampton, and

Xavier. The others are Gammon Theological Seminary, Atlanta; Meharry Medical College, Nashville, Johnson C. Smith University, Charlotte, and the State College for Negroes at Durham.

Law can be studied at Howard and State College, and the former is the only well-equipped Negro law school in America. Medical education is available nowhere except at Howard and Meharry, both of which have Class A ratings with the American Medical Association. Both also offer high-grade courses in dentistry, and Howard supplements this with a course in dental hygiene, as well as one in pharmacy. The only other Negro institution with a course in pharmacy is Xavier, in New Orleans. Meharry and Hampton provide courses in nursing as does the Medical College of Virginia; Atlanta offers graduate schooling in social work and library training, Gammon Theological and Johnson C. Smith in theology, and Gammon in religious education for women; Howard in religion; Hampton in business and trade school; and Xavier in pre-medical courses and social service. There is no engineering course anywhere exclusively for Negroes.

Should additional centers for training Negroes in such subjects as law, medicine, and engineering be established? A good law school somewhere in the central South would be highly desirable, since Howard is on the fringe of the region, and is not readily accessible to the majority of Southern Negroes. Meharry, established as a medical school at Nashville in 1876, adjoins Fisk University, and their coöperative arrangements and possible formal union in the future, makes this the natural medical center for the Middle South. The two institutions have combined endowments of nearly $4,000,000, a substantial portion of which has been contributed by the General Education Board, and more is in prospect from various sources. Dr. Embree calls Fisk "one of the really important institutions of the South, regardless of race." The two centers of learning complement one another in important particulars, and in view of their high standards and excellent facilities, the setting up of another Negro medical school anywhere else in the South seems undesirable at this time. An engineering school can be established at some central point, as soon as the need for it becomes manifest, but it is difficult to understand how this will be possible, without a joint arrangement under which ten or a dozen states can combine for the purpose of financing regional engineering instruction for Negroes.

Important as graduate and professional training are, the overwhelming mass of Negroes is more directly concerned with undergraduate studies, and still more with the public schools. It goes without saying that rural education is of particular concern to a region which is largely rural, and certain significant advances in this sphere deserve our attention.

At Tuskegee Institute, for instance, the effort to prepare students for better rural living is receiving increased emphasis. This fine old institute is supervising six rural schools in the area, using them as "practice centers for the prospective teacher," and has established a curriculum laboratory. The departments of agriculture, home economics and industrial arts are being coördinated to a similar end. Since its establishment by Booker T. Washington in 1881, as a place where the Negroes of the South could learn the dignity of work, and be taught how to earn their livings with their hands, Tuskegee has filled a great need. To-day, when there is a renewed emphasis on the importance of vocational training for both white and colored, the institute's significance is growing, rather than diminishing. An important departure in 1941 was the establishment there of training facilities for about a hundred Negro aviation cadets to man the 99th Pursuit Squadron, the Army Air Corps' first colored tactical unit.

A renewed vitality also is apparent at Hampton Institute, which provides a limited amount of graduate instruction, but like Tuskegee is primarily agricultural, technical, and vocational in character. Both these institutes have been not only national, but international, in scope and influence. Hampton always has had a white president and Tuskegee always a colored one, and both have made significant advances under their present executive heads. A noteworthy feature at Hampton for more than a decade was the school for librarians, lately transferred to Atlanta University. Its numerous graduates have been leading factors in the rapid development of Negro colleges and universities throughout the South.

Training in special aspects of rural living is being developed at the new Fort Valley State College in Georgia, where courses of value to the rural teacher are being given particular attention. A practical laboratory has been set up, and students who are preparing themselves to be rural teachers live in small cottages, surrounded by plots of land for the raising of foodstuffs, perhaps with hog pens or chicken yards. In this way they experience at first hand some of the problems which later they will wish to aid their pupils in solving. The college supervises the Negro schools of the county in which it is situated, and thus makes its influence felt beyond its own campus.

Prairie View State Normal and Industrial College in Texas is of particular significance, by virtue of the realistic and practical character of the undergraduate instruction offered there, as well as its excursion of late into graduate fields, and the great number of Negroes who look to it as the one institution of its kind in the vast Southwest. The Virginia State College for Negroes also has made notable advances in recent years, and offers a well-rounded and thorough undergraduate course, as well as graduate training in certain disciplines. In Mississippi the opening of Jackson College in 1940 represented an important step taken by that state to provide adequate instruction for teachers in the Negro public schools, supplementing the four-year course offered by the state at Alcorn A. & M. College. As yet, Jackson College offers only a two-year course, but is distinctly significant in a state whose population is practically half colored, and which has neglected its Negro school-teachers for so many years. Of 6,000 such teachers in Mississippi's colored public schools in 1940, one half had had no education beyond the high school level, and many had stopped at the fifth grade.

Education is, of course, one of the major remedies for the Negro's economic plight, and recognition of this was a leading factor in the revival in 1941 of the old Atlanta conferences, which had been discontinued about a quarter of a century before. Representatives of educational institutions in Southern and border states met in Atlanta in April to discuss the Negro's economic problems, with Dr. W. E. B. DuBois presiding. Dr. DuBois, significantly enough, came back to the Atlanta University faculty in 1932, after nearly a quarter of a century spent in the North, where as editor of the *Crisis*, the organ of the N.A.A.C.P., he had been the spearhead of agitation for equal rights, and the intellectual leader of the Negro in America. But although born in Massa-chusetts, the brilliant Dr. DuBois decided to cast his lot again with the Negroes of the South (he took his A.B. at Fisk in 1888, and taught in Atlanta University for the fourteen years which ended in 1910). His decision to close his career on the Atlanta University faculty would appear to indicate that genuine opportunity awaits the Negro scholar in the South. Moreover, if regional institutions for Negroes can be established there with congressional sanction, the opportunities will be far greater.

Another eminent Southern Negro is Dr. George Washington Carver of Tuskegee. Unlike Dr. DuBois, Dr. Carver was born of slave parents, and as an orphan was swapped in his youth for a $300 race horse. He has elected to pass his entire life among the Negroes of his native section, despite tempting offers to go elsewhere. The extraordinary facility with which he has manufactured hundreds of synthetics from such commonplace agricultural products as cotton stalks, corn shucks, sweet potatoes, and peanuts, has won him membership in the Royal Society of Arts, London, and frequent national recognition in this country, the latest evidences of which are the first award of the Catholic Committee of the South and the Humanitarian Award of the Variety Clubs of America. Forced to abandon many of his test tubes in 1941 because of failing health, Dr. Carver designated his able young assistant, Austin W. Curtis, to carry on his work.

Other distinguished younger Negro scholars in the South include Dr. Charles S. Johnson, the Fisk sociologist, who is preëminent in this group; Dr. William H. Dean, Jr. of Atlanta University, one of the most promising American students in the field of economic history, and Dr. St. Elmo Brady, whose conspicuous ability as a chemist is being utilized at Fisk, where he has been devising new industrial uses for the castor bean. An able group of young researchers has been assembled at Howard University, an institution in many ways comparable to the regional centers of learning advocated here, since it is subsidized with public funds and operated exclusively for Negroes.

The achievements of Negro scholars in the South are illustrative of what can be accomplished by members of the race, when opportunities are vouchsafed them. Such opportunities will become ever more numerous, as the Southern centers of elementary, secondary, and higher learning develop into adequacy. Moreover, it is reasonable to predict that when this time arrives, not only Negro literacy and Negro scholarship will show vast improvement, but Negro earning power and Negro citizenship, as well. Various investigators have shown that education is a great antidote to crime among Negroes, that literate Negroes are less criminal than illiterates, and that college graduates are hardly criminal at all.

Joel Chandler Harris said more than half a century ago that if education will not provide the "chief solution" of the Negro problem, "then there is no other conceivable solution, and there is nothing ahead but political chaos and demoralization." That dictum is as true to-day as it was when Harris first uttered it. The difference is that in Harris' time the vision seemed so far away as to be well nigh unrealizable, and only a few Southerners had the wit to grasp its significance, whereas in 1942 there are genuine prospects for its consummation. When one contemplates the remarkable advances made in Negro education during the past two decades, almost anything seems possible during the next two.

IX

THE SOUTH AND TOLERANCE

THE decade of the 1920's witnessed the enthrone-
ment of the "Thou Shalt Not" philosophy in America. The adoption of Federal prohibition signalized the
emergence of a whole new series of *verbotens,* ranging
from the consumption of any beverage with more than
the fabled one-half of one per cent to the teaching of any
theory which hinted at simian progeniture for the human race, and from the sniffing of a faintly alcoholic
cork to the wanton dropping of a fishing line into a pond
on the Sabbath.

The ranting apostles of the unco guid were entrenched
in the South during the 1920's, primarily because the
South is more preponderantly rural than any other cor-
respondingly large section of America, with the exception of the belt of states between the Mississippi and the
Rockies—also a prohibitionist and evangelical stronghold. To-day that belt has two legally "dry" states—
Kansas and Oklahoma—to the South's one—Mississippi—
and during the era when Wayne B. Wheeler was regnant
in Washington, Kansas and Tennessee even slapped a
ban on cigarettes.

The advantages which accrue to rural regions, by
virtue of the fact that they constitute the bulk of every
Southern state, are greatly accentuated by their enjoy-
ment of a far greater political representation than they
are entitled to on any fair and reasonable basis. This is

because the South seems to have been more heavily gerrymandered in favor of the country districts than any other part of America. A survey in 1940 showed that Mississippi and Kentucky had the two most indefensible records in the United States, for they had had no legislative reapportionments since 1890 and 1893, respectively. Alabama and Tennessee had had none since 1901. Even where there has been a more recent reapportionment, the cities nearly always have only a fraction of the representation in the state legislature that they ought to have, while the small, thinly-settled counties have far more than they should. This appears to be true to a greater or lesser degree of every section of the Union.

Georgia is the prime example of a state which is held in a straitjacket by its rural population. C. E. Gregory, chief legislative reporter for the Atlanta *Journal* wrote not long ago:

A total population of 1,757,676 in the thirty-eight largest counties in the state is represented by eighty-four members of the House and a relatively small membership in the Senate.... The remaining 121 counties, with a total population of 1,336,047, have one Representative each, or 121 of the 205 members, eighteen more than a majority... That is why Governor Talmadge was able to say during his campaign eight years ago that he could be elected Governor without carrying a single county that had a street car in it —and he was. That is why the last six Governors of Georgia and most of those who preceded them hailed from small cities and towns.

Moreover, the state has the "county unit system" under which the cities cannot possibly poll their proportionate vote in electing a governor or senator, or obtain the representation due them in the State Democratic Conventions, which dominate Georgia politics. Under this bizarre arrangement, the three smallest counties in the state, with a total combined population of less than 11,000, have the same vote in statewide elections and in state conventions as, and often more influence than, Fulton County (Atlanta), with nearly 400,000.

Georgia is the only state with the "county unit system," but the rural districts of other Southern states are almost as grossly over-represented. Birmingham, for example, has less than half the representation in the Alabama Legislature which its population calls for, and other cities below Mason and Dixon's line are at a similar disadvantage. Kentucky's case is typical. Not only should Jefferson County (Louisville) have one more senator and five more representatives on the basis of census returns, but Meade County, with fewer than 9,000 inhabitants, has one member in the house, the same number as Harlan and Leslie counties, with a combined total of over 90,000. Populous Campbell and Kenton counties in the northern tip of the state, across the Ohio River from Cincinnati, also are grievously under-represented.

This state of things is largely responsible for the enactment of such fantastic legislation as the Alabama law which for seventeen years forbade the possession or sale of anything which "tastes like, foams like, smells like, or looks like beer," whether alcoholic or not, or even the possession of a bottle shaped like a beer bottle or a whiskey flask. Georgia likewise outlawed "near beer," and at the same time forbade any Georgian to have any non-alcoholic "liquor, beverages or drinks made in imitation of or as a substitute for beer, ale, wine or whiskey or other alcoholic or spirited vinous or malt liquors." These two priceless enactments have gone down the drain long since, together with prohibition, but they will be remembered as the apotheosis of the "no" philosophy which burgeoned and flowered in the land of mint juleps and planters' punch during the second and third decades of the twentieth century. Even Southern cities succumbed to prevailing attitudes during the period in question, as did those in some other sections. It was impossible for a time to buy a coca-cola on Sunday in Richmond, and from 1919 to 1927 Atlanta was represented in Congress by William D. Upshaw, than whom there was no more violent and vociferous darling of the Anti-Saloon League.

With the advent of the 1930's, the reaction against prohibition set in, and the incredible happened. Following passage of the repeal resolution by the Congress, the states began ratification. The climax came in the summer of 1933, with the referenda in Arkansas, Alabama, and Tennessee. Each had long been accounted a "dry" stronghold, but each voted for repeal. There was no doubt as to the fate of Federal prohibition, after these three Southern states had spoken. North Carolina and South Carolina subsequently refused to ratify the Twenty-First Amendment, but 37 states, one more than enough, landed in the repeal column before the end of the year.

When prohibition was liquidated, the event was symbolic for the nation, and particularly for the South, which had been sweating under the lash of Ku-Kluxery, legalized Fundamentalism, and kindred blights. Thousands of sincere and intelligent Southerners had supported the Eighteenth Amendment, as well as prohibitory laws in the various states, on the theory that liquor is a curse to millions—as it is—and on the assumption that it could be effectively eliminated by passing laws.

As matters turned out, they finally were confronted with a choice between bootleg liquor in unlimited quantities, paying no tax, and legal liquor in similar quantities pouring a stream of much-needed revenue into local, state, and Federal coffers. They made the only sensible decision.

Yet to-day in several Southern states, as elsewhere in the Union, there is a resurgence of "dry" sentiment. The evils of the prohibition era have not served to obliterate the desire for a return of legislation outlawing all forms of beverage alcohol. Mounting arrests for drunkenness and drunken driving in some areas, and higher commitments for alcoholism, have stimulated the various Anti-Saloon Leagues to action, with the result that parts of the South seem a likely theater for a resuscitation of the prohibitionist formula.

Indicative of the fact that there is a good deal of latent "dry" sentiment below Mason and Dixon's line was the astounding performance of the Virginia Legislature in 1938. Two years previously, that body had requested the University of Virginia and the Medical College of Virginia to provide a scientific study of the effects of alcohol in moderation and excess upon the human system as a substitute for the ancient and outmoded textbook which had been used in the public schools since the turn of the century. This latter volume embodied typical Anti-Saloon League doctrine, and could not have been regarded as scientific by any one except a professional prohibitionist. Dr. J. A. Waddell and Dr. H. B. Haag, reputable members of the two medical faculties in question, accordingly were designated to perform the task outlined by the General Assembly. Late in 1937, they finished their 184-page study, and it promptly received the imprimatur of the State Board of Education which pronounced it a "most valuable contribution . . . scientifically sound and very scholarly." The board recommended that 10,000 copies be struck off and distributed to the schools and libraries of the commonwealth.

Summaries of the study then appeared in the press. These summaries made it clear that while the authors minced no words concerning the dire effects of excessive drinking, they eschewed the extremism which had characterized some previous pronouncements on the subject and sought to formulate an appraisal which would stand the test of competent medical inquiry. Their work contained the statement that small quantities of alcohol "may favor digestive activities," and "small quantities . . . do not directly affect the heart or the blood vessels." There was also this forthright declaration: "It has been proved that we cannot abolish drinking by legislation nor frighten a person into sobriety." These relatively mild declarations were surrounded in the text by far more numerous and emphatic affirmations as to the evils of overindulgence.

But the Anti-Saloon League and the Woman's Christian Temperance Union were profoundly outraged by this "dangerous doctrine of moderation." Approximately two weeks were available in which to arouse the state against the report before the legislature convened, and both organizations unlimbered their blitz battalions. Hardly anybody, except a few privileged individuals, had seen the full text of the report at this stage, but thousands of pastors and church members, especially in the country districts, signed petitions demanding that the document be destroyed. Neither the pastors nor their flocks had read anything but a few fragmentary extracts, and many not even that, but the avalanche of petitions landed in the statesmen's laps as they convened, and the said statesmen were thrown at once into a panic.

Of the forty members of the Senate, exactly one, Senator Hunsdon Cary, had read the text of the Haag-Waddell report, and he agreed with the State Board of Education as to its exceptional value. Yet nearly all his thirty-nine colleagues were stampeded by the petitions into voting to suppress this scientific study which they themselves had ordered made! Senators Cary, Goode, and Holland protested that the least the senators could do was to read the material before acting upon it, but they were howled down. The W.C.T.U. had informed the law-makers that the report failed to pronounce alcohol a poison under every conceivable circumstance, and that was enough. It promptly became unthinkable that such a pernicious document could be allowed to fall into the hands of a single school teacher—so unthinkable, indeed, that the senators voted not to let it fall into their own hands, either. They ordered the study burned, unread.

The House of Delegates concurred in this fearful and wonderful decision. Although the published reports had cost the state nearly a dollar each, the legislature ordered the destruction of the 1,000 copies which had been struck off. So the great pile of books was solemnly shoveled into the capitol furnace to a thunderous obligato of bronx cheers. The text was even formally banned from the official journals of the two houses, with a view to protecting future generations of Virginians from the subversive doctrine that it is possible to consume alcohol in small quantities without filling a drunkard's grave.

The harried authors of the work succeeded in retaining the copyright to their brain-child, and after the frightful dither had subsided, the volume was published by the William Byrd Press of Richmond. Not only so, but the state of Vermont bought 3,000 copies for use in a course on temperance education offered in the Vermont high schools. But the state which produced this scientific examination of the effects of alcohol on the human system would have none of it. The very men who had directed that the study be made, voted to consign it to the flames unread—and this in the face of the unanimous opinion of recognized scientific authorities in all parts of the country that it was one of the few adequate treatments of the subject.

This depressing episode occurred slightly more than four years after the people of Virginia had voted down both state and national prohibition by substantial majorities and had set up a control system which is generally regarded by impartial observers as one of the best, if not the best, in the Union. Such a performance on the part of a general assembly which undoubtedly was composed of men of better-than-average intelligence, and which many had imagined to be largely insusceptible to Anti-Saloon League and W.C.T.U. pressure, set observers to wondering what the significance might be. The prevailing conclusion was that this was a temporary aberration. It was impossible to believe that the Virginia Legislature's record in disposing of this report was clearly indicative of its future attitudes on similar issues. At the same time, a certain amount of uneasiness was unavoidable, for if the assembly could be stampeded once, there was always the possibility that it could be stampeded again.

The prohibitionists, over a period of a good many

years, have demonstrated considerably more puissance in several other Southern states than in Virginia. North Carolina, for example, returned a majority of well over two to one in 1933 for the retention of the Eighteenth Amendment, while South Carolina gave the "drys" a margin of 2,771 votes. Moreover, such states as Georgia and Tennessee were slower to abandon statewide prohibition than Virginia. The natural conclusion was that if such potency was demonstrated by the professional prohibitionists in the Old Dominion in 1938, they must be at least as influential elsewhere below the Potomac.

This conclusion would appear to be borne out by the recent upsurge of prohibitionist sentiment in a few Southern states. In South Carolina, for example, the voters returned a majority of nearly 59,000 against the existing system of legalized sale, and legislation restoring statewide prohibition was introduced in 1941. Confronted by the substantial majority against legal liquor polled by the people the preceding year, the solons demonstrated gratifying ingenuity. They passed a state prohibition law, but stipulated that it should not become effective unless the $3,000,000 realized annually from liquor, beer, and wine was replaced from some other source by July 1, 1942. No effort was made to find the $3,000,000, and one gathers that reliance is being placed in the deity to produce the money. Thus have the statesmen of South Carolina passed their law and kept their liquor.

During the months when that Commonwealth was wrestling with the importunate Anti-Saloon Leaguers, Georgia and North Carolina were doing likewise. Here, too, the revenue question loomed large. Had it not been for the fact that annual profits of from $2,000,000 to

$2,500,000 accrue to these states from the sale of liquor, and neither knows how to replace such an amount, both might have plumped into the "dry" column in 1941. The prohibitionists in these two legislatures were thwarted, but by narrow margins, and it appeared certain that the issue was far from dead. In North Carolina, especially, the "drys" expressed indignation over the means used to block them, and vowed retribution in 1943.

However, it is not only in the South that these brethren are militant. Oklahoma gave a resounding repudiation in 1940 to an effort to repeal its constitutional prohibition law. A majority of more than 84,000 was cast against the proposal, and since a majority of all votes polled in the election was required to eliminate prohibition from the state constitution, the move failed by over 133,000 votes.

No such effort has been made in Mississippi, the sole Southern state which remains legally "dry." Whether such an effort would succeed is doubtful, for, in the immortal words of the late Will Rogers, Mississippi will always be dry "so long as the voters can stagger to the polls." There is also the Mississippi jurist who is quoted as insisting upon "the right to drink my whiskey without the stigma of legality." A major consequence of prohibition there seems to be that one can secure the best brands at lower prices than in surrounding states, since there is no tax on the stuff in this "bone-dry" commonwealth. The philosophy which prevails among Mississippians would seem to be that the combination of a prohibition law and plenty of good liquor, at well nigh unprecedentedly low rates, is almost ideal. A charming citizen of the state, with whom I bent an elbow in

Jackson not long ago, seemed to express something of the Mississippi point of view when he confided: "My grandfather was a bourbon-tippling Baptist."

Admittedly the current effort to restore prohibition to the South finds its principal momentum in abuses which are still current. These abuses are flagrant in some areas. For example, the saloons of New Orleans are sometimes nauseous and foul-smelling affairs, through whose swinging doors drunks reel almost at will. There are no fewer than two hundred saloons in Mobile County, Alabama, a condition which the "drys" of that state may find increasingly intolerable. In Georgia, the Brunswick *News* said not long ago that the state's "liquor dealers, taken as a group, appear to have had little more respect for the law than did the bootleggers."

These phenomena would be improved through the enactment of reasonable and effective legislation. The not wholly defunct Southern passion for "passing a law" may manifest itself in these areas shortly, as was the case in Georgia not long ago, when the ancient ban against fishing on Sunday was reaffirmed by the legislature. However, such "blue laws" are becoming increasingly rare below the Potomac, and perhaps the strongest urban citadel of sabbatarianism in the whole South capitulated in 1941, when the council of Charlotte, North Carolina, "the greatest church-going town in the world, except Edinburgh," a city which has been legally "dry" since 1904, voted eight to three for Sunday baseball, movies, tennis, golf, and swimming. Only those who are familiar with Charlotte's Calvinistic conservatism can appreciate what this victory means. It far outweighs Georgia's reaffirmation of the statute against

Sunday fishing, for one still can legally play poker, golf, or tennis in Georgia on the Sabbath, or attend a motion-picture show. But before we write Georgia or other Southern states down as the last refuges of puritanism and reaction on the American continent, let us remember certain areas in the Middle West, and also Delaware, the state which still flogs prisoners in public, and which did not repeal its 200-year-old blue laws until 1941.

While the adoption of such restrictive legislation in the South and the Middle West is, in part, the result of nothing more sinister than misguided adherence to outmoded theological and behavioristic concepts, and a too-naïve faith in the efficacy of statutory enactments, there is another side of the canvas which must not be ignored. This is the impetus given such measures by the Klan when it was in its heyday during the 1920's, and the sympathetic eye with which the remnants of that organization regard those measures to-day. We have here a definite link between prohibition laws, blue laws, and anti-evolution laws on the one hand, and anti-Semitic, anti-Catholic, and anti-Negro movements on the other. Thousands of supporters of the legislation referred to will protest that they abhor the Klan and all that it stands for. Moreover, they will be speaking the exact truth. But the fact remains that the Klan, and those who are Klan-minded without ever having been formally inducted into the mysteries of the order, constitute a formidable phalanx of support for the type of legislation under notice. The current fondness of the Klan for flogging persons not deemed by it to be behaving in accordance with its "moral" concepts evidences the ideological affinity between the K.K.K. and those who would make everybody behave by statutory compulsion. It seems reasonably clear that legislation outlawing the evolutionary hypothesis could never have been passed in Tennessee, Mississippi, and Arkansas without the aid of the Klan, which was at the height of its power in the 1920's. Its influence with the rural population was especially great, and many rural pastors were members.

To what extent have the curricula in the high schools and state-supported colleges and universities in Tennessee, Mississippi, and Arkansas been changed as a consequence of the passage there of anti-evolution laws? Informed persons seem unanimous in holding that it has made little practical difference. True, the biology textbooks have been bowdlerized in both Tennessee and Mississippi, to conform to the law, but there appears to be no doubt that the theory is taught anyway in both the high schools and the state-supported colleges and universities. The teachers usually tell their pupils about evolution, even where the text omits all reference to it. In Arkansas it would seem that even less attention is paid to the law than in the two other states which have such statutes. Dean Thomas S. Staples of Hendrix College, Conway, Arkansas, asserts that "the anti-evolution law had no effect whatever on the teachers or the teaching in the universities, colleges, and high schools of this state." He adds that "so far as I can learn, there has never been a textbook, a reference book, a manual, an outline or a syllabus changed one iota as a result of the enactment of that law." The enlightened element in Arkansas thinks it is wiser to leave the legislation in its present defunct state than to stir up the animals with efforts at repeal.

Arkansas does not boast an anti-evolutionist institution comparable to two which were established in Tennessee soon after the conclusion of the Scopes trial. The ambitious founders of one of these set out to raise $5,000,-000. Since only a small fraction of this sum was realized, the "university," as it was called, opened in 1930 in an abandoned high school. After functioning there for five years, it moved into a concrete basement, the only structure which had been built with the scanty funds available. Later several rooms were added to the basement, and a dormitory was secured. Other improvements and additions subsequently were made, and the main building now has a couple of floors.

"God Above All" is the motto of this seat of the higher learning which is largely unknown throughout the South and which, curiously enough, has far more students from Pennsylvania than from any other state, including Tennessee. Of the 90 matriculates enrolled for the session of 1939-40, no fewer than 31 came from Pennsylvania, as against 13 from Tennessee and 10 from Ohio. The use of tobacco by any student brings immediate expulsion, although the catalogue states that "the religious attitude of the university is one of Christian love and sufferance." It goes without saying that alcoholic beverages "of any strength or kind" are forbidden. Moreover, no undergraduate "who visits beer parlors, pool halls and other such places of ill repute will be tolerated in the university." Every member of the teaching staff, which is composed of "consecrated Christian men and women," must subscribe annually to a "Statement of Belief," which commits him or her to the dictum that the Bible is "of final and supreme authority in faith and life, and, being inspired by God, is inerrant in the original writings," and to the further thesis that the "origin of man was by fiat of God in the act of creation as related in the Book of Genesis." Allegiance to these principles is solemnly renewed each year by the faculty, lest heresy rear its head.

Among the institutional needs emphasized in the university's fugitive literature is "an enlarged science department, the better to combat false teachings [masquerading] under the name of science." Those who may be desirous of contributing to this objective should consult the catalogue. It says: "The attitude of the Science Department of this university is that the theory of evolution is not supported by scientific evidence. Facts of nature which prove the theory of evolution to be without sound basis are abundant and are brought to the attention of the student. The facts of science are found to be in harmony with the Bible, our foundation and guide." A recent issue of the university's *Newsette,* published monthly, listed the names of seven "recognized scientists who discredited evolution." Five of them had been dead anywhere from thirty-one to forty-two years, the sixth was an unidentifiable Englishman, and the seventh was in reality an evolutionist, although the quotation given from his writings, when hastily read, created the opposite impression.

The other Tennessee institution which rests its appeal primarily upon its belief in the "absolute authority of the Bible" and the "creation of man by the direct act of God," boasts that it is "America's Most Unusual College." The boast seems justified, if for no other reason than the college's announcement in 1941 that "every graduate ... has a good position and is a leader in his profession or business"! All faculty members sign a statement annually which expresses complete faith in every syllable in the Bible. "Whatever the Bible says is true" sums up the attitude. While the college protests that it is "not 'overly-pious,' " the catalogue points out that "every class is opened with prayer, and our social gatherings blend easily and naturally into 'a little prayer before we go.' " Each student is required to take the Bible course every year. The administration makes the statement that "because we limit our student body [to 500 students] and because of the intensely Christian atmosphere of our institution, we are in a better position to do the work in the fields that we cover than any other institution in the country." It also boasts "the most contented group of students on the American continent," and like its Tennessee competitor, grants the B.A. and B.S. degree. "Training in the Department of Science . . . strengthens a student's faith in the Word of God and its divine inspiration," says a prospectus.

Also founded in the 1920's, and emphasizing the inerrancy of the Scriptures, is a Bible College in South Carolina. At the session of 1939-40, it had 228 matriculates from twenty-seven states and seven foreign countries. While South Carolina, with 53, furnished more than any other state, Pennsylvania—seemingly a Fundamentalist stronghold—was next, with 27; North Carolina was third, with 24, and New York fourth, with 20. The institutional keynote seems to be struck in the following paragraph: "It is urged that Christian educators recognize that a course of study in which Christ is central, and in which God's revelation is the determining guide, is the only truly scientific way to educate young people. It is, at least, an ideal toward which we should work. Deuteronomy 6:4-9 is God's plan for educating our children." The college does not offer a separate course in biology, but does give one in "Physiography and Introduction to Science," and the catalogue elucidates the course's methodology as follows: "Reference is made to important theories of modern science, and the proper attitude of Christians toward those which affect one's belief in divine revelation is explained." The college requires its faculty to pledge allegiance to the Bible as "the verbally inspired Word of God, without any errors in the original manuscripts."

A similar attitude toward the biblical story of the creation is inculcated by an Institute and Bible College in Georgia—founded in 1911 "strictly as a matter of faith in God," says a publication of the school. There are 400 students, distributed among the high school, the four-year Bible College course, the Commercial Department specializing in vocational training, and the Music Department. "Possession of firearms and playing cards, the use of profane or improper language, and the use of tobacco and alcoholic beverages, in any and every form is positively forbidden." The founder, who is still president, finds "it much easier to believe the Bible story of the origin of man than to believe the evolutionary hypothesis." The institute does not accept the theory of organic evolution as to the origin and development of man, and is in full accord with the views of the late William Jennings Bryan as to the theory's incredibility.

It should be emphasized that most Southerners have never even heard of this Georgia college, or of the three other obscure Fundamentalist institutions described above. Their influence upon Southern thought is almost nil, and they are eclipsed in the public mind by the many progressively oriented and competently manned

colleges and universities of the region. The processes of
mass education throughout the South are having a continuing effect in nullifying the efforts of those who
would indoctrinate this and all other areas of America
with atavistic Fundamentalist theology, the complete
antithesis of modern scientific inquiry. Religious me-
dievalism is fighting a losing battle below the Potomac,
as elsewhere.

But if a few minor Southern institutions stress Fundamentalist doctrine far too heavily, at the expense of
scientific truth, what is one to say of the Middle Western
colleges and Bible institutes which do likewise? There
are no anti-evolution laws outside the South, of course,
and Northern and Western states never seriously considered passing any, even during the hysteria of the
1920's. But there is a college in Illinois with more than
1,100 students which officially proclaims its belief in the
Scriptures "as verbally inspired by God and inerrant in
the original writing," and it not only forbids all students to use either liquor or tobacco, but also to dance,
play cards, or attend any theatrical performances, including motion picture shows, on pain of expulsion.
Every applicant for admission must answer the following in writing: "Have you ever read through the Gospel
of John consecutively? ... What is your attitude toward
Jesus Christ? (Think carefully before answering this
question)." Of the 1,149 students in 1940-41, a total of
291 came from Illinois, 92 from Pennsylvania, 91 from
New York, 63 from California, and scarcely any from
the South. There is a Bible College in a large Ohio city
with a biology course wherein "life and its origin will
be considered in the light of divine revelation." All
women matriculates are required to wear sleeves which

reach at least to the elbow, and skirts "well below the knees, not higher than 14 inches from the floor." Other important Fundamentalist centers of the Middle West are an internationally famous Bible institute in Illinois, and a large seminary and Bible institute in Minnesota. The latter was founded, and is still headed, by a man who, as executive secretary of the World's Christian Fundamentals Association, said in 1927 that every state would be "thoroughly organized" for state and Federal anti-evolution laws within a year, and that ample funds were in hand. Neither of these celebrated centers of religious learning offers so much as a single course in natural science.

If further evidence is needed that the Middle West is a stronghold of Fundamentalist doctrine, consider a recent editorial in the *American Lutheran,* the monthly organ of the Evangelical Lutheran Synod of Missouri, Ohio, and other states in that region. With a membership of nearly 1,500,000, the Lutheran Church in America belongs to the extreme Fundamentalist wing of American Protestantism, and the *American Lutheran* apparently spoke for the denomination when it pronounced "the rapid and inevitable decline of the momentary heresy known as Modernism... perhaps the most hopeful sign on the immediate horizon of the church militant."

The South produces little or nothing to-day more uncompromisingly Fundamentalist than this. And although three Southern states wear the stigmata of unrepealed anti-evolution laws, convincing evidence is lacking that the evolutionary hypothesis is, on the whole, more greatly in disrepute below the Potomac than in the corn, hog, and wheat belt. Moreover, the ultra-vicious form of Fundamentalism exemplified in quasi-Fascist and anti-Semitic attitudes, is far more virulent in the Middle West. Both regions are threatened by the resurgence of the Klan and the prohibitionists, and the South may be facing another era wherein comstockery, racial and religious bigotry, and clerical kaiserism will reëstablish some slight measure of ascendancy. On the other hand, it appears highly improbable that the hegemony of the Imperial Wizard, or of the ineffable Bishop Cannon and his compatriots, ever will be so complete in the former Confederacy as it was in the decade and a half which ended with the demise of the Eighteenth Amendment.

X

NO NORTH, NO SOUTH

T HE acme of futility, if not stupidity, for any citizen of America, especially in times of international crisis when the country itself is endangered, is the stirring up of intersectional rancor. Most members of the younger generation to-day, both North and South, feel that the Civil War and its aftermath are so far behind us as to be unworthy topics of serious dispute between intelligent men and women. These grandchildren of the men who faced one another at Shiloh and Vicksburg, along the Shenandoah and in front of Richmond, find it a little difficult to condition their intersectional attitudes in the middle years of the twentieth century upon circumstances surrounding a war which ended more than three quarters of a century ago.

Almost the only persons on either side of the Potomac who indulge in recriminations to-day concerning the issues of the sixties and seventies, are a few overzealous members of Union or Confederate organizations, and their auxiliaries or affiliates. An occasional commander-in-chief of the Grand Army of the Republic calls Robert E. Lee a "traitor," and an occasional dignitary of like importance in the hierarchy of the United Confederate Veterans expresses himself with similar acerbity concerning Ulysses S. Grant. But the rank and file of both organizations do not join in these pronunciamentos, nor do the rank and file of ordinary citizens.

The average Southerner is more sensitive to this species of criticism than the average Northerner, simply because the South was the defeated party in the Civil War, and its people were subjected thereafter to ten years of exploitation and degradation. While it would not be accurate to say that this has given most Southerners an inferiority complex, they do tend to be on the defensive when such matters are under discussion. The fact that their much smaller, less populous, and less wealthy section held out for four years in the face of tremendous odds, inflicting defeat after defeat on a more numerous enemy, and producing far more knowledgeable and glamorous leaders than did the North, gives the Southerner great pride in his heritage. At the same time, there is the stubborn fact that the South lost the war, which helps to explain Southern queasiness on the subject.

Wholly aside from the defensive psychological atmosphere engendered by this defeat, the Southerner is genuinely attached to the land of his forefathers. As some one has said, he looks upon its imperfections and infirmities with a tolerance not unlike that felt by a doting parent for a backward child. In his love for his Southern homeland, the dweller below the Potomac may be compared to the Frenchman of old Provence, the German of beer-inhausting Bavaria, or the Italian of the sun-steeped Neapolitan littoral. Moreover, in his fondness for leisure, his appreciation of the fact that the amenities should not be sacrificed on the altar of "success," his easy-going warmheartedness and informality and his drawling speech, the Southerner is often spiritually akin to these representatives of older European cultures.

Yet it must be conceded that just as some Northerners persist in regarding nearly all Southerners as lubberly and semi-literate, there are Southerners who look upon persons from other sections as outlanders and parvenus. There was, in fact, a lively debate in the columns of several Southern newspapers during 1937, and also during 1940, over the attitude of Southerners toward visitors from other regions. By a curious coincidence, both controversies got under way when two Bostonians who had settled in Virginia, wrote a Richmond newspaper protesting that they had not been cordially treated. In both instances this set off a series of responses from other Northerners domiciled in the state. Most of them took issue with the New Englanders who had written the Richmond paper. (The pair which wrote in 1940 from two separate sections of the state were not the same ones who had done so three years previously.) One said that he and his family were moving to another state, where they would be treated as " 'Americans,' not 'Northerners.' " There were comments from editors in both Virginia and North Carolina, and the consensus seemed to be that newcomers who entered into the spirit of a community, whether North or South, were apt to be received hospitably by that community. The net effect of both discussions was a demonstration that a majority of the Northerners living in Virginia who took the trouble to express themselves in epistolary fashion, were much pleased with the manner in which they had been received. An example of the other variety, whose conduct serves to illustrate the desirability of understanding the point of view of one's neighbors, was the lady from New England who wrote a letter to a Richmond "Voice of the People" column in which she referred to Robert E. Lee, quite matter-of-factly, as "that scoundrel." The ensuing explosion from one end of Virginia to the other hit the Massachusetts letter-writer with such staggering force that she uttered no further word for weeks. Finally she followed up her communication with a somewhat bewildered apology.

But if there are New Englanders who regard Robert E. Lee as a "scoundrel," there are Southerners, as I have indicated, who entertain similar notions concerning Ulysses S. Grant. The fact became distressingly evident when it was proposed in the early 1930's to erect a monument at Appomattox. This plan was formulated carefully with a view to sparing Southern sensibilities, and every effort was made to provide a memorial which would be suitable in design, symbolism, and execution. The bill providing for the memorial was introduced in the Senate by the late Senator Claude A. Swanson, and in the House by the late Representative Harry St. George Tucker, both Virginians, and the winning design was chosen by a commission whose chairman was William C. Noland, a Richmond architect. Apropos of the contest held by that commission, the War Department made the following statement:

"As the monument authorized by Congress is to commemorate the termination of the War Between the States, the design should carry out this thought, and should not call to mind the tremendous conflict with all its attendant sorrows. It should symbolize an undivided nation and a lasting peace."

The commission accordingly chose a design which

provided a 57-foot shaft of stone, with two pylons merging near the top into a harmonious whole, banded with laurel, symbolizing a reunited nation. A pavement in blue and gray surrounded the base, the front of the shaft bore the great seal of the United States, and there were plaques of Lee and Grant on the two sides. The inscription was as follows: "North—South; Peace, Unity. Appomattox, the Site of the Termination of the War Between the States, 1861-1865."

Incredible as it may appear, the proposal was promptly assailed by various Confederate organizations. "An insult to General Lee and every Southern soldier who fought and died for the Confederate cause," said one member of the Confederated Southern Memorial Association, composed of women's memorial associations throughout the South. Resolutions vigorously opposing the erection of the monument were adopted by this organization.

The plan for the memorial was suspected in such quarters of Northern parentage. Although prominent citizens of Appomattox explained, as the storm rose, that the Lions Clubs of that town and of nearby Lynchburg were responsible for the original proposal, the suspicion would not down that the War Department had cooked up this nefarious plot for the purpose of humiliating the South. The fact that the Federal Congress had authorized a $100,000 expenditure for the erection of the monument seemed to them suspicious, *per se*, even though the legislation had enjoyed completely Southern sponsorship. It was vociferously contended by a loquacious lady who held membership on a history committee of the United Daughters of the Confederacy, that the bill authorized "an appropriation of $100,000 to commemorate the defeat of Lee and the South, and the putting of her under Negro rule."

This unreconstructed lady, who issued numerous statements to the press, also found her soul greatly troubled by another thought, namely, that the shaft was to bear plaques of both Grant and Lee. There were doubtless Northerners who felt that it would be insulting to the memory of the Union general to place his profile on the monument in juxtaposition to that of the arch-Rebel, but the critic under notice was disturbed for precisely the opposite reason, i.e., she could not bear the thought of her hero's image being on the same monument with "that butcher" who commanded the Army of the Potomac.

But a still more reverberating blast was sounded against the plan when the Sons of Confederate Veterans met in annual conclave in 1933. Dr. William R. Dancy of Savannah, the retiring commander-in-chief, spoke as follows in his address to the gathering: "We should never forget that our superb leader died an alien... because he was deprived of citizenship by Grant, President of the United States. General Lee, generous and magnanimous as he was... would never have permitted his figure to be placed on the same monument with General Grant."

When Dr. Dancy's deliverance drew adverse criticism, he elaborated in this remarkable language: "My critic should, however, be informed that the magnanimous terms of surrender at Appomattox were dictated by General Lee and granted by General Grant."

It would be difficult to compress scrambled history into a few sentences more effectively than Dr. Dancy succeeded in doing in the two foregoing pronouncements. Far from having been "deprived of citizenship by Grant," Lee was aided importantly by Grant, of whom he spoke as "brave and magnanimous," in his effort to secure a pardon from Andrew Johnson, who was then President. Grant urgently recommended the pardon. It was approved by Johnson in 1869, but the Fourteenth Amendment's adoption deprived the President of his pardoning power.

What of the amazing statement that Lee "dictated" the "magnanimous terms" at Appomattox? Such an assertion is, of course, contrary to all the authoritative accounts of the surrender. It is well-known that Grant not only refrained from demanding Lee's sword, but that the terms offered by him were generous in other respects. Colonel Charles C. Marshall, Lee's military secretary, who was present, wrote in his memoirs that the Northern generalissimo "manifested that delicate consideration for his great adversary which marked all his subsequent conduct toward him." Colonel Marshall mentions only one suggestion as having come from Lee when the terms were being arranged at the McLean house, namely that the men in the ranks be allowed to keep the horses and mules which belonged to them. All the others originated with Grant. Aside from everything else, the idea of a defeated general "dictating" terms to his conqueror is slightly naïve, to put it mildly.

In addition to the fact that General Lee and Colonel Marshall both called General Grant "magnanimous," the Northern commander performed an extremely generous act many years after Lee's death which also should entitle him to the gratitude of the South. This was when Grant contributed $500 in the early eighties toward the erection of the Home for Confederate Soldiers at Richmond. Later, in 1884, when a fair was held at Richmond to raise additional funds for the home, the former Northern commander was invited to attend. He found it impossible to do so, but he wrote the following letter to the committee in charge:

I hope your fair may prove a success, and that the object contemplated may receive a support which will give to all the brave men who need it a home and rest from cares. The men who faced each other in deadly conflict can well afford to be the best of friends now, and only strive for rivalry in seeing which can be the best citizens of the grandest country on earth.

In 1933 and 1934 the foregoing facts were called to the attention of the objectors to the $100,000 "peace monument" at Appomattox, but without appreciable effect. The uproar in opposition continued. True, vigorous and influential voices were raised in the South on behalf of the plan, and the vast majority of inarticulate Southerners probably thought the idea appropriate. Yet the vociferous minority, which spoke through Confederate organizations and which, in all likelihood, represented only a minority of those organizations' members, succeeded in thwarting the scheme. The National Park Service finally announced that if there was any opposition in the South, the monument would not be erected. The Virginians who had sponsored it accordingly decided a few months later to ask for the substitution of a national military park. Their request was granted.

It is arguable that such a park at Appomattox is preferable to a shaft. For example, a park seems a more useful and interesting type of memorial than a non-utilitarian stone monument, especially such a park as now has been developed at the scene of the surrender, and which ultimately will include an exact reproduction of the hamlet of Appomattox, as it was in 1865. One regrets that such reasonable arguments as these in opposition to a shaft were drowned during 1932 and 1933 in a welter of bogus history and intersectional bitterness, worthy of the reconstruction era.

It is more pleasant to contemplate the effect upon North-South relations of the meeting held by Union and Confederate veterans at Gettysburg in the summer of 1938, on the seventy-fifth anniversary of the battle. Such a gathering had been held there in 1913, on the fiftieth anniversary, and the success of that affair seemed to justify the belief that a like reunion a quarter of a century later would be equally salutary in its effects. Yet serious obstacles had to be surmounted before the meeting could be held.

This writer is familiar with the preliminaries to the successful staging of the reunion of 1938, since he sought in the spring of 1935 to promote a joint gathering of the surviving veterans in Washington. The Grand Army of the Republic had announced that it would not meet with the United Confederate Veterans, unless the latter body agreed to leave its Confederate flags behind, and the "Rebs" naturally were unwilling to entertain this stupid proposal. Into this churning cauldron of controversy the author of this volume, who had been urging such a joint gathering in a series of newspaper editorials, thrust his unsuspecting head. Thinking that a quiet and unpublicized letter to the adjutant and chief of staff of the U.C.V. at Nashville might help toward the desired end, he dispatched such a communiqué, inquiring concerning the possibility that the G.A.R. might be willing to withdraw its proviso against

the display of the Stars and Bars. Immediately upon
receipt of the suggestion, the adjutant and chief of staff
of the U.C.V. gave it to the newspapers, together with
an emphatic refusal even to consider it. The aged gentleman in question had interpreted the proposal in-
correctly to mean that the U.C.V. should "plead with"
the G.A.R. to permit the unfurling of the starry cross,
and his Confederate blood naturally had boiled up, and
over, at the thought. The idea of one last meeting of
the Blue and the Gray, seemed permanently dead.

Yet the objective was to be realized three years later.
Representatives of a Pennsylvania commission appointed to arrange for ceremonies at Gettysburg in
1938, finally managed by some legerdemain to circumvent the stipulation made by the G.A.R. concerning the
Confederate flag. But not until all manner of vicissitudes
had been successfully endured. Five months after the
above-mentioned unequivocal announcement had been
made from Nashville, the U.C.V. voted unanimously
at its Amarillo, Texas, convention to accept an invitation to the joint ceremonies at Gettysburg. The members had been assured by a spokesman for the
Pennsylvania commission in charge of plans, that they
could wave their flags at will. But two days afterward
the commander-in-chief of the G.A.R. proclaimed that
he would never agree to the display of the Stars and
Bars on such an occasion. A year later, the U.C.V. was
assured again, this time at Jackson, Mississippi, that it
would be free to display its banner at Gettysburg, and
it voted again to accept, despite the protestation of one
venerable "Reb" that "they waited 35 years to invite
us, and I ain't havin' nothin' to do with them Yankees
until they pay us for the property they destroyed in the

war." Once more the G.A.R. met to consider the reunion, and after two full days spent in cogitation behind closed doors, it emerged with the dictum that the sole condition on which it would consent to foregather with the U.C.V. was that "only the flag of the United States of America" should be shown. Again the reunion seemed an impossibility, and since there was no further meeting of the G.A.R. prior to the celebration at Gettysburg, it will always remain a mystery how the Pennsylvanians in charge managed to persuade both "Yanks" and "Rebs" to attend. One formula used with recalcitrants was that it wasn't a "joint reunion" at all, since the survivors of the conflict were merely accepting the invitation of the State of Pennsylvania to the anniversary ceremonies.

Until the Confederate flag was actually put on view there before the eyes of the Union veterans, nobody could be sure that the latter wouldn't organize a posse for the purpose of hauling it down. Indeed, it was feared that the unfurling of the starry cross might set off a second Battle of Gettysburg, comparable in ferocity to the first. Yet nothing even mildly unpleasant occurred during the entire celebration, which was attended by 1,800 Northern and Southern veterans, all of them cared for at the expense of the United States Government.

One of the major problems incident to the reunion was that of keeping the assembled nonagenarians supplied with sufficient whiskey. The Southern contingent was afflicted with a notable thirst, and principally because of this fact, the original consignment of five cases of liquor was exhausted almost immediately. Those who dispensed the drinks proceeded on the assumption, at the outset, that the veterans would be satisfied with small beakers, containing a teaspoon of the stuff. When loud outcries arose from the boys in Blue and Gray, and one of their number snorted "That ain't even a good sniff, much less a drink," the formula had to be revised drastically upward. An airplane accordingly was dispatched for twenty-two more cases. A veteran, aged 104, was picked up subsequently, suffering from acute alcoholism, but most of his compatriots seemed to know how to handle the usquebaugh which had been made available to them. Under its benign ministrations, Northern and Southern soldiers of the sixties sat together beneath the trees, swapping yarns and exchanging friendly gibes, as the bands played *Dixie* and *Yankee Doodle,* and the Stars and Stripes and Stars and Bars floated side by side in the breeze. This went on for eight days, and fifteen more cases of whiskey had to be hurriedly sent for. The old warriors found the effects to be so beneficent that, when the reunion ended, they demanded a small flask apiece to "see them home." The phials were provided.

It is difficult to imagine a more successful reunion than this one turned out to be. John M. Claypool, commander-in-chief of the U.C.V., said, as he left for his home in St. Louis: "I've just been tickled to death. I've been to lots of reunions, but never anything like this. I knew it would be good, but it turned out better than anything I could conceive."

Commander-in-chief Overton H. Mennet of the G.A.R. joined him in saying that they had had "the time of our lives."

It was, indeed, a fitting culmination of many patriotic efforts to bring the Blue and the Gray together for one last bivouac, a deeply symbolic occasion for the people of America. Here the North and South buried the battle-ax. Here, on ground consecrated with the blood of thousands of brave Americans, the survivors of one of the world's decisive battles clasped hands in token that the wounds opened by the war of which it was a part, were healed.

Here, where the Gray wave reached its high tide amid the acrid smoke of the Federal batteries on Cemetery Ridge, the white-haired men who lived through that storm of steel added the final superscription to the seal of intersectional good will fashioned when Northern and Southern boys fought side by side at Santiago and Manila Bay, in Belleau Wood and at St. Mihiel.

Many of the fast-dwindling company which fraternized together in 1938 already have answered the last roll call. Their few remaining comrades in arms will join them soon. The sole surviving inmate of the Home for Confederate Soldiers in Richmond, died in 1941.

Nearly all the modest wooden cottages and dormitories, which once housed hundreds of veterans there, have been torn down, and the large tract, with its great oaks, is being turned into a Confederate Memorial Park. Yet in 1932, when most of the veterans and their widows had been gathered to their fathers, and it was clear that the survivors would follow them ere long, a magnificent $250,000 Home for Confederate Women was erected on the grounds. This establishment, far more sumptuous than anything which had been provided previously for the veterans, or their widows, became available just when there were scarcely any widows left to use it! Sisters and daughters of veterans had to be pressed into service, because the supply of relicts was so inadequate. Granddaughters will be welcomed into the home, when the number of sisters and daughters becomes insufficient.

Is there the slightest justification for such an institution as this, chartered to operate in perpetuity? What has any granddaughter or great-granddaughter of a Confederate soldier done to deserve special care in a home of this character? The fact that the organized Northern veterans got their feet into the Federal trough soon after the war and kept them there for half a century, does not excuse the erection of a $250,000 home whose inmates, ere long, will be mostly granddaughters of Confederate soldiers, born many decades after Appomattox.

While the home's *raison d'être* remains obscure, there are no grounds for believing that its existence will serve to arouse, or keep alive, intersectional antipathies. Its administrative officers are not heard from on public questions from year's end to year's end, and they are never articulate where controversial issues affecting the Civil War are concerned.

Fortunately, the same propensity is increasingly prevalent in the ranks of both Union and Confederate bodies. Despite occasional eruptions from other commanders-in-chief of the G.A.R., the gentleman who occupied that post in 1935 actually expressed the view that Confederate Veterans ought to be placed on the Federal pension rolls! And although his predecessor who served in 1930 pronounced the United Daughters of the Confederacy "America's worst enemy," it is easy to forget such an ill-considered outburst in contemplation of the letter which Mrs. Louise Ward Watkins, president-general of the Daughters of the Union, wrote to Mrs. Charles E. Bolling, president-general of the U.D.C., who had invited her to attend the U.D.C. convention at Montgomery, Alabama. It follows:

Pasadena, Calif.
November 16, 1940

MY DEAR MRS. BOLLING:

You cannot imagine how disappointed I am [that I am] unable to accept your gracious invitation to attend the 47th Convention of the United Daughters of the Confederacy. I can think of nothing which would give me greater pleasure than to be a guest at some of your sessions and witness the unveiling of the statue of Jefferson Davis which the Daughters are presenting to the State of Alabama.

Please accept my warm felicitations for the success of your convention. I trust that it will be harmonious in every detail and that much accomplishment will result.

Although you doubtless will have many flowers as gifts from admirers from all over the country, please wear the corsage which I send with my loving greetings some time during the convention.

Yours sincerely,
LOUISE WARD WATKINS
President-General
Daughters of the Union, 1861-65

When such messages can be exchanged by the heads of official Union and Confederate bodies, one feels justified in saying thankfully that the bloody shirt has become a badly outmoded garment. As a pendant to the foregoing, it should be stated that Mrs. Watkins was an honored and much-fêted guest at the U.D.C. convention in Los Angeles late in 1941. Truly the war is over, at last.

XI

THE SOUTH LOOKS ABROAD

THE active involvement of the United States in the second World War has aroused Americans, both North and South, to a keen realization of their country's peril. Every one now is aware that this conflict will determine the fate of Europe and the British and French empires, and bring a settlement one way or the other of Japan's effort to rivet her hegemony upon the vast riches of eastern and southeastern Asia. It will answer the question as to what philosophy of government is to predominate not only in those regions, but also in Africa and other parts of Asia, and in Central and South America. It will determine the destiny of all North America as well.

As the people of the Southern states look across the Atlantic toward a Europe prostrate under the hobnailed boots of storm troopers, their sympathies from the beginning have been almost solidly against the totalitarians. They are particularly distraught over the brutal bombing of Great Britain, which for so many of them is the European motherland. That country's resolute stand against the combined might of Hitler and Mussolini probably has evoked a more lively and enthusiastic response below the Potomac and the Ohio than in any other section of the United States.

Geographically nearer to Latin America than other sections, and also less isolationist by nature than the

Midwest and Far West, the South is especially concerned over events beyond the seas. Southern agriculture long has been dependent upon exports for its
prosperity. From 50 to 60 per cent of the South's cotton
and 40 per cent of its tobacco have been exported in
normal times. So have more than half of its rosin and
turpentine, as well as substantial percentages of its
fruit and other farm products. Hitler's admission several years ago that Nazi Germany must "export or
die" is equally applicable to the South under existing
conditions. Cotton and tobacco, around which so large
a share of the entire Southern economy is woven, already have lost a considerable part of their foreign
markets, as a consequence of the war. Both of them,
particularly cotton, had suffered severely in the foreign
field before Adolf Hitler sent his steel-shod legions
against Poland in 1939. The Hawley-Smoot tariff initiated the process of limiting American exports of
nearly all kinds, by sharply reducing imports and thus
provoking other nations in the early 1930's to raise
similar barriers against American goods. The AAA,
with its price-pegging policies, gave a fillip to the restrictive tendencies previously under way. Other
countries began raising cotton in large quantities. For
example, between 1931 and 1936 Brazil's exports of
raw cotton increased ten-fold.

The program of reciprocal trade pacts inaugurated
in 1934 under the leadership of that distinguished
Tennessean, Secretary of State Cordell Hull, tended
definitely to expand the foreign markets for Southern
cotton and tobacco, as well as other products. It had
made good progress when the German invasion of
Poland set in motion destructive forces which have

well-nigh nullified its beneficent effects. As matters stand to-day, the trade pacts may still become extremely important elements in the reconstruction of the post-war world; but, as wider and wider areas fall beneath the blight of totalitarianism, they enjoy relatively little current significance.

Some Southern industrialists have desired tariff protection, but the South as a whole always has suffered from high American tariffs. These have forced it to buy in a protected domestic market but to sell most of its products in an unprotected foreign market. Peter Molyneaux of Texas discussed the region's historic attitude on the tariff not long since in the following cogent language:

The leaders of the Old South were right when they concluded, more than a century ago, that the high tariff policy meant the ruin of the cotton states. When sixty-four of the sixty-seven representatives of the Southern states then in Congress voted against the tariff of 1824, and all but two Southern senators did likewise, they acted in recognition of the fact that the measure was "utterly destructive" of the South's interests. It is well-nigh forgotten to-day, but the first talk of secession in the South, the first proposal by a Southerner that the time had come to "calculate the value of the Union," was occasioned by a realization that the high tariff policy, which the Federal Congress had forced upon the South, condemned the cotton states to economic decline and perpetual economic inferiority; and this happened more than thirty years before the Civil War. It is not remarkable that during the more than one hundred years that have elapsed since then the people of the South have stubbornly opposed that policy.

This Southern opposition had little effect, except at rare intervals, until the enactment of the Hull reciprocal trade program in 1934. Four years later, Dr. Gallup found that 92 per cent of the Southern people favored the general principles of trade underlying the Hull program, but that half of them had never even heard of Mr. Hull's efforts to translate those principles into reality. Some who had heard of them didn't understand them. On the whole, as it became understood, the program seems to have met with overwhelming favor in the South. There was a protest from Louisiana and Florida sugar producers against the method of fixing Cuba's quota in the agreement signed with that country; but the fundamental desirability of such agreements was not called into question. If the program had not made all the headway which some hoped for, by the time the present war broke out, it nevertheless had established itself in Southern favor and may yet become a major factor in the South's economic rehabilitation.

The relatively small gains in cotton and tobacco exports brought about by the Hull policies were more than wiped out by the war's wholesale closing of foreign markets. During the season of 1940-41, the United States lost the place it had held so long as the world's premier cotton exporter, and fell behind both British India and Brazil, with their lower-priced product. Record-breaking domestic consumption helped to compensate for the drop in American exports to only 1,100,000 bales, and the defense program, combined with the lease-lend program, apparently was responsible for reducing loan stocks held by the government from 11,-000,000 to 6,000,000 bales, but there was no gainsaying the seriousness of the foreign market's collapse.

Virtually, the whole continent of Europe was cut off by the blockade, and Japan, the best single cotton market of all, reduced its imports year by year from the inception of the "China incident," until late 1941 saw them reach the vanishing point. The normal Japanese importation of 1,650,000 bales annually provided employment for approximately 350,000 Southerners, with some 1,400,000 dependents. The sharp cuts in Japanese importations of cotton after 1937 were due chiefly to Nippon's desire to use her foreign exchange in the purchase of essential war materials; for although huge quantities of cotton were shipped to Japan after that country invaded Manchuria in 1931, nearly all of it was used in the manufacture of textiles, rather than bombs. On the other hand, the immense cargoes of oil and scrap metal which went to the same destination from Southern ports, served much more sanguinary purposes.

The blackout of the Japanese market, coupled with the crisis throughout the Far East and the dearth of shipping, have, it is true, helped to create new uses for cotton at home. Since imports of Japanese silk have been obliterated, cotton must serve, in large measure, as a substitute. Moreover, a substantial share of the available wool is needed by the Army and Navy, while certain chemicals used in making rayon are essential to the manufacture of explosives. In addition, jute, burlap, hemp, linen, and manila are being imported in only small quantities, if at all, owing to the war and shipping stringencies. So cotton substitutes have their chance here, too. The substantial curtailment of the burlap supply is a particular windfall for the cotton growers, since large quantities of their product are

needed for the manufacture of bags now made of
burlap.

It is possible that, in time, a domestic silk industry
in the South will replace the silk formerly imported in
such volume from Japan. Experimental silkworms are
feeding busily on twenty acres of white mulberry trees
at the Alabama State Prison Farm, under the direction
of Colonel W. E. Persons, state chief of correction, who
hopes they will become the nucleus of large-scale domestic silk production. The project is still in the cocoon
stage, however. Machinery for unraveling the silk is
not yet available in this country, and labor costs are far
higher than in Japan. Yet Colonel Persons believes in
the ultimate realization of the dream which various
American colonials had two centuries or more ago,
when the mulberry was widely cultivated, especially in
the Southeast. This eventuated finally in the manufacture of silk waistcoats of domestic material for such
statesmen as Henry Clay and Daniel Webster, but the
industry died, in competition with that of Japan, and
is only now being revived on the limited scale mentioned.

If the collapse of the foreign market for cotton is
being partially compensated for in the use of cotton as
a substitute for various materials whose importation
has been rendered difficult, if not impossible, no similar
circumstance is operating in the case of tobacco. From
two-thirds to three-fourths of the whole American
export market is either lost or threatened, as a result
of the wars in Europe and Asia. The once substantial
shipments to China and Great Britain, to Scandinavia,
the Low Countries and France, have been drastically
affected. Sweeping readjustments have, of course, be-

come necessary. Southern growers of the bright, or
flue-cured, leaf, which constitutes the great bulk of
the American tobacco crop, voted in 1940 by a seven-
to-one majority for a three-year control program designed to salvage as much as possible from the
wreckage. The crisis in the bright-leaf market had
come in the fall of 1939, when the British companies
found it necessary to withdraw from that market, because of British governmental restrictions put into
effect to conserve foreign exchange to meet urgent war
needs. These companies had been buying one-third of
the American crop annually and paying the American
farmer half of all the money he received for the flue-
cured leaf. To the rescue of the Southern growers,
situated mainly in the seaboard states from Virginia to
Florida, came the Commodity Credit Corporation. By
1941, it had purchased 360,000,000 pounds of tobacco
from the British companies, and during that year
large-scale shipments began moving across to England,
under the lease-lend act. Department of Agriculture
officials predicted that probably the entire poundage
bought for the British from the 1939 crop would be
shipped to them during the fall and winter of 1941-42.
Obviously the program of government purchase and
price-pegging was the only thing which kept the tobacco
market from collapse, under the impact of the war.
However, the prices paid for the 1941 crop were the
highest in many years, in some instances almost double
the 19.6-cent minimum fixed by the Federal authorities. Despite acreage curtailments under the control
program, it was estimated that the growers of flue-cured
tobacco might receive as much as $175,000,000 for their
1941 crop, or $48,000,000 more than the previous year.

The bonanza which cotton and tobacco farmers enjoyed during 1941 caused them to look askance at the government's "food for defense" program, for the fancy prices brought by their staple crops naturally turned their thoughts from diversification, and lessened their enthusiasm for the suggested shift to live stock, dairy products, poultry, fruits, and vegetables. Nevertheless, "food for defense" bade fair to hasten trends toward diversification already begun in the South. Secretary of Agriculture Wickard's thesis that "food will win the war and write the peace" is a slogan calculated to aid the former Confederacy in its efforts to achieve a new form of emancipation, and also to free post-war Europe from the specter of famine.

Southern industry's annual output is valued at more than two and one-half times that of Southern agriculture, but Dixie factories are less dependent upon foreign markets, and hence have not been hit as hard by the huge drop in international trade. Accurate and up-to-date statistics on the region's industrial exports are extremely hard to come by, but it would appear that whereas its shipments of such products as steel, textiles, machinery, chemicals, and paper to the countries of Latin America have increased, there has been a net loss in such exports, owing to decreases in shipments to Europe and the Far East. Since the South's lack of industrial diversification in the sphere of finished manufactures is almost as noteworthy as its lack of agricultural variety, the region's industrial exports necessarily fall into a limited number of categories.

The slump in the South's foreign market for manufactured goods has found a large measure of compensation in the fact that Southern heavy industry is enjoying a great defense boom. Steel, powder, and aluminum mills, shipyards, electric power plants, textile mills, airplane factories, and other similar establishments are working night and day in the most gigantic armament program America has known. War contracts totaling high up in the hundreds of millions have been awarded in Virginia, especially in the vital Hampton Roads area, with its huge naval and air bases, its shipyards and coast defenses, standing athwart the path of any transatlantic attack on Washington; and in Texas, with its naval and ship-building developments on the Gulf of Mexico, and its enormous warplane factories and bomber assembly plants at Dallas and Fort Worth. Birmingham steel and Mobile ship-building have brought large contracts to Alabama. Tennessee, with its TVA power, its Chattanooga aluminum and its Nashville and Memphis aircraft, has received substantial defense contracts, as have several other Southern states, particularly those with coastlines on the Atlantic or the Gulf, for the South is taking a major share of the ship-building program. Arkansas, South Carolina and Kentucky obtained the smallest totals of defense business in the region up to the end of 1941, and there was cause for concern over the fact that the South as a whole seemed to be getting less than its proper share of the more important war business—business of the type which would contribute to the upbuilding of the region.

One of the first to call attention publicly to this was Chester C. Davis, a citizen of Montana and a member of the Advisory Commission to the Council of National Defense. Mr. Davis deplored the fashion in which the highly developed industrial areas of the Northeast and

Middle West were getting the cream of the defense contracts, while the South, as in 1917-18, was being given mainly powder plants and cantonments which would be of little or no use after the war.

Various Southern individuals and Southern newspapers joined in the chorus of criticism. It was pointed out that the region with the greatest surplus of manpower, with a labor supply capable of learning how to operate the machines required by the defense program, was being partially ignored. A golden chance to build industries of a permanently valuable character in the small towns of the South, which might thus balance agriculture and create a more stable economy, was being allowed to slip, and manufacturing was being concentrated still further in the heavily industrialized section North of the Potomac and the Ohio, and East of the Mississippi.

Here was an opportunity for the Federal authorities to do something about Economic Problem No. 1 while arming the country at the same time, but it was not being utilized to the fullest. Obviously contracts had to be awarded in the early stages to those areas which were capable of fulfilling them promptly, and the South did not have the factories or the trained workers that the North was able to make available almost overnight. On the other hand, there was the question whether the South's capacity for industrial expansion and for the training of its huge labor surplus, were being harnessed to the defense program in a manner calculated to achieve the best long-term results for either the South or the country. A compensatory factor seemed to be the possibility that many of the tenant farmers who made considerable cash money building cantonments, were putting this money into the purchase of farms.

It would not be accurate, of course, to say that defense below the Potomac has brought only an "ice-cream-and-powder-mill boom." Substantial and permanently valuable industrial developments in the region already have been mentioned, and there are others. In addition to huge naval and air bases and ship-building plants along the coast, and steel, aluminum and warplane factories in the interior, as well as a tremendous upturn in the Piedmont's cotton textile industry, one notes such phenomena as the following:

New plants at Baton Rouge, Louisiana, costing well up in the millions, for making synthetic rubber.

The world's first all-welded passenger ship, the *African Comet*, launched at Pascagoula, Mississippi, in 1941, with two sister ships following a few months later, all for the New York to Cape Town run, on which they were to haul vital chrome and manganese to this country.

A government-built tin smelter under construction at Texas City, Texas, to handle a substantial percentage of our total annual tin consumption, making possible the use of Bolivian tin in the United States, without the long delay involved in shipping it to England for smelting.

A $15,000,000 plant being built at Freeport, Texas, for extracting magnesium from sea water.

To operate such vast and varied industrial establishments, enormous quantities of power were required, and it was here that the rôle of the Tennessee Valley Authority became so vital. Without TVA, much of

Airplane carrier entering drydock at Norfolk Navy Yard, one of the vital military and naval installations around Hampton Roads.

Planting corn in the Shenandoah Valley of Virginia, one of the South's richest farming regions.

the South would have been under an almost insuperable handicap, and the South's share in the arming of
America would have been considerably smaller than
it is. The severe drought of 1941 threatened to reduce
the effectiveness of TVA and all other hydro-electric-
power developments in the region, but there can be no
gainsaying the essential rôle which the much-debated
agency played at this critical moment in history.

Another factor contributing to the South's part in
arming the country is the presence there in large quantities of a number of the "strategic," "critical," and
"essential" raw materials for defense. More than half
of our deposits of bauxite, from which aluminum is
made, are below the Potomac, chiefly in Arkansas, Alabama, and Georgia. The last named also is a leading
state in manganese reserves, essential in the manufacture of armor plate for battleships and hard steel used
in tanks. Tennessee, Virginia, and Alabama likewise
have considerable deposits of this strategic mineral.
Alabama's plant at Anniston for converting low-grade
manganese ore is considered particularly significant, for
whereas the country is deficient in high-grade manganese, the South has large deposits in the lower grades.
North Carolina's great mica supply is important, and
so are the quantities of titanium in Virginia. This is
only a partial list.

Since Georgia and the Gulf states have important
Hispanic elements in their cultural backgrounds, and
since there also is the factor of geographic proximity,
they feel more closely drawn to Latin America than
do other sections of the country. This interest is increased by the activities of the great port of New
Orleans, with its network of shipping to all Latin

America, and by the airplane services which radiate
out to Central and South America from Miami.

A highly constructive contribution to closer relations
between the Americas was made early in 1941 by the
University of North Carolina, which provided a "summer school" for 105 visitors from seven South American
countries. The idea developed from a sojourn of some
sixty Americans during the previous year at the University of San Marcos in Lima, Peru. This group insisted that some North American center of learning
reciprocate the hospitality of the Peruvian university.
The trip to Chapel Hill accordingly was arranged, and
the visitors spent six weeks there, improving their
knowledge of English in special courses provided for
their benefit, attending the regular university lectures,
and visiting points of interest in North Carolina, as
well as across the border in Virginia. Before they returned to South America, this group of literary and
professional men and advanced students in the fields
of medicine, law, engineering, economics, architecture,
and the humanities also had an opportunity to see
some of the important cities of the Eastern seaboard,
and to arrive at the conclusion that Latin American
long-range impressions of the United States are "wholly
erroneous." The prevailing reaction, reached in the
light of this bouleversement of popular misconceptions
entertained below the Rio Grande, was: "We do not
believe that there can be anywhere greater courtesy,
friendliness, and generosity than we have found here
in the United States."

Another link which has bound the South to Latin
America is its long-time interest in the project for a
Nicaraguan canal. Numerous prominent Southerners

were directors of the company which first undertook work on the canal in the 1880's. Southern business concerns were active champions of this canal, as opposed to the Panama route. Interest in it still is alive in the South, not only for the general reason that it would give the country the safeguard of an alternate route for the fleet, in case the Panama Canal were put out of commission, but also because it would supply a shorter passage from Gulf ports to our Pacific Coast and the Orient. The distance from New Orleans to San Francisco would be nearly 600 miles less via Nicaragua than it is via Panama.

Isolationist sentiment is weaker in the South than in any other section of the United States. The leading public opinion polls demonstrate that on every issue, from extension of the draft and passage of the lease-lend bill, to American entry into the war on a basis of full belligerency, the South has led the way. Although prolongation of the draft in 1941 passed the House by a margin of only one, the House delegations from Alabama, Georgia, Louisiana, Mississippi, North Carolina, Texas, and Virginia were all solidly for it, while only one negative vote was cast from South Carolina, Arkansas, Kentucky, and Florida, and only two from Tennessee. This is to be contrasted with the fact that in the delegations of eleven Middle Western states, the count was 100 against extension, to 18 for it. The only isolationist senator from the South is the depressing North Carolina exhibitionist, Robert R. Reynolds. Senator Walter F. George of Georgia, presidential purgee-designate No. 1 in 1938, developed subsequently into a staunch wheelhorse of the administration in the field of foreign policy. As chairman of the Senate Foreign Relations Committee, he rendered Mr. Roosevelt such valuable service at crucial periods that the latter must have rejoiced secretly that the Georgian's political liquidation did not materialize.

Why is the South so much more belligerently pro-Ally than any other region of the United States? The fact that it was settled so preponderantly by the English, Scotch, and Scotch-Irish doubtless accounts, in part, for the strongly pro-British trend of thought among its people. Then, too, it has a much smaller percentage of foreign born, with no large concentrations of Germans, Italians, or Irish, such as form pro-Axis or anti-British nuclei in other sections. Except in Louisiana, where the French influence is dominant, and in all the Gulf states, where faint Spanish overtones are discernible, the South tends to be overwhelmingly Anglo-Saxon in its political and cultural attitudes. Then, too, there are the ties which bind cotton and tobacco farmers to Britain, a well-nigh unrivaled foreign outlet for their product, and there is the dependence of these farmers upon foreign markets, in general, which gives the region a more than ordinary stake in the preservation of a sane, orderly, and solvent civilization abroad. Many Southerners also remember gratefully that an influential segment of British opinion favored the Confederacy in the sixties. There is likewise the South's martial tradition. Throughout its history, most of the great Southern heroes have been soldiers. To-day, of eight military colleges in the entire country which belong to the Officers' Reserve Corps, six are in the South. These are the internationally famous Virginia Military Institute, The Citadel at Charleston, South Carolina, Texas A. and M., North Georgia Col-

lege, Clemson College in South Carolina, and Virginia
Polytechnic Institute. Lastly, there is the fact that
despite the Old South's development of a slave society,
the New South is conscious of the Virginia parentage
of George Mason's immortal Bill of Rights, a document
completely incompatible with totalitarianism.

Although Erskine Caldwell made the strange assertion in 1941 that the South's interventionist attitude is
just another sign of the South's ignorance, the fact is
that the region grasped the true significance of this
world struggle more quickly than any other part of
America. The South, as a whole, is much better informed with respect to the issues involved in this war
than it was in 1914-18. If the same applies, in greater
or lesser degree, to the rest of the United States, the
change is more marked in the South, where the once
grievously excessive illiteracy rate has been brought
down to fairly respectable levels. As a result of the
wider diffusion of knowledge which has followed the
more adequate development of the public school system, Southern newspapers now have a bigger, better-
educated, and more articulate audience than they
enjoyed a generation ago. In addition, the radio provides a new medium of public information which did
not exist at the time of the first World War. Another
factor in the general improvement has been the development of university extension courses.

Last, but not least, in this array of elements tending
to give the South a better understanding of foreign
affairs, is the Southern Council on International Relations of Chapel Hill, North Carolina. President Frank
P. Graham of the University of North Carolina is
chairman of the council, with Dr. Keener C. Frazer as

secretary. For two years, the council issued a fortnightly mimeographed bulletin bearing upon the South's rôle in the world, and then in 1941, the bulletin was expanded into *The South and World Affairs,* an attractive monthly magazine. The council, with state and local branches throughout the South, also operates a speakers' bureau, which recommends speakers and discussion leaders; a press service which supplies newspapers with pertinent material on international relations; a program service, to assist groups in securing materials for forums, conferences, and study programs, and sponsors an annual conference on "The South in International Affairs."

The first of these conferences took place in the spring of 1940 at Nashville, and the second was held a year later in Atlanta. Each was attended by about one hundred leaders from the Southern states in the fields of education, religion, journalism, law, and finance. Many facets of the South's relation to the international scene, and particularly to the second World War, were examined realistically and intelligently. A great majority of the conferees favored the Roosevelt Administration's foreign policy *vis-a-vis* the Axis; endorsed the "good neighbor" attitude toward Latin America; approved the Hull reciprocal trade agreements, and urged participation by this country in any post-war world conference designed to build a just settlement, plus acceptance by the United States of its rightful share of responsibility in any international organization for the maintenance of peace set up after the conflict is over. While the foregoing attitudes were expressed by an assemblage of selected leaders, and not by run-of-the-mine citizens, it seems likely that a preponderant majority of the Southern rank and file would sanction this program as not only desirable, but necessary.

Since events beyond the seas have never in our history been of such vital and patent concern to us all, the South, with its greater awareness of the crisis, naturally is more alive than any other section to the war's urgent imperatives. When it looks abroad, it sees a conquering tyrant bestriding Europe from the Norwegian fjords to the Athenian acropolis, and a horde of fanatical yellow men seeking to fasten their particular brand of slavery upon all the peoples on both shores of the Pacific. As civilization itself totters under the battering of the totalitarian legions, the land which gave George Washington, Andrew Jackson, Sam Houston, and Robert E. Lee to the nation can be counted on to play a worthy rôle in the great struggle for the preservation of western civilization and the democratic way of life.

XII

THE SOUTH AND THE FUTURE

ONLY a reckless man would attempt to offer a detailed blueprint for the future of any country, or any region in these grave days. The titanic forces which are shaking the world in this cataclysmic war may leave even the wisest prophet wholly without honor. I shall make no effort, then, to draft minute specifications for the South's development in the coming years, but shall merely indicate, in broad outline, some of the directions which seem consonant with the region's best interests. I am postulating, of course, an ultimate Allied victory over the Axis. Otherwise it is impossible to envision any future for the South, for America, or for the hemisphere, except one set in a framework of unrelieved blackness.

But taking for granted a to-morrow in which Hitlerism and its concomitant obscenities will somehow be sent rocketing into oblivion, what should the South do now, what should it plan to do a few years hence, when the carnage has ended?

First on any list of the South's problems must necessarily be those having to do with its preponderantly rural civilization. A large segment of Southern country life has been described as "a miserable panorama of unpainted shacks, rain-gullied fields, straggling fences, rattle-trap Fords, dirt, poverty, disease, drudgery and monotony that stretches for a thousand miles across the cotton belt." If this vignette seems to accent all the worst features of the rural South, and to omit the rest, as it does, one must concede its applicability to thousands of farmers and farm homes in the cotton states.

Indeed, if there is one element in the Southern economy which retards its development more than the others, it is this large group of marginal and submarginal people who have been so long without opportunity or hope. Reliable estimates have it that no fewer than eleven million Southerners are members of families with annual cash incomes of $250 or less. Most of them are tenants, sharecroppers and farm laborers, both white and black.

While the New Deal's agricultural program had many serious imperfections in its early stages, some of which remain, its general direction is sound. The one-gallus farmers, "peckerwoods" or "red necks" of the cotton and tobacco states need this type of assistance, if they are to be made useful and self-respecting members of the community. If some are beyond redemption, others respond to the kind of rehabilitation which the federal farm agencies have made available to them. The fact that so large a percentage of the loans advanced to them are being repaid, is evidence of this. Within the limits of the badly overburdened federal treasury, this species of aid should be continued. It helps toward the erection of a stable economy in a region which can never be more than second-rate, so long as millions of its citizens are poverty-stricken and on the border line of malnutrition and disease.

The health problem is one of the most fundamental of all, and it is far from solved. United States Surgeon-General Thomas Parran estimates that the annual

economic loss to the South from malaria alone is $500,-
000,000. A major element in his computation is the
lag in industrial efficiency as a consequence of this
malady. Operators of textile mills in the South say
that their output is one-third less than it should be,
solely because of malaria. Many Southerners are wholly
unaware of this, and they also are hugging the com-
fortable delusion that hookworm was eradicated from
the South some decades ago by Dr. Charles W. Stiles,
with the aid of funds provided by John D. Rockefeller.
The work of Stiles was, indeed, monumental, and in
1926 the International Health Board was able to announce that "hookworm disease has almost disappeared
from the United States." Yet about a decade later, Alabama completed a state-wide intestinal parasite survey
and found that in certain counties, from 60 to 70 per
cent of the school children were infected. In 1939 and
1940, the Farm Security Administration sponsored sur-
veys in certain sections of Alabama and Georgia, in
coöperation with state and county health departments.
In Alabama, ten counties were included, and of the
10,000 persons examined, 28 per cent had hookworm.
In Georgia, examination of approximately the same
number of subjects showed 38 per cent positive. So the
rural South still contains many anaemic-looking, inert,
shiftless, mentally sluggish citizens, some of whom even
eat clay, dirt, or charcoal, and all of whom have been
written down as hopelessly unambitious and worthless,
when simple medical treatment to rid their bodies of
the parasite responsible for their condition would soon
make them whole both physically and mentally. Another health problem which confronts the region revolves about pellagra, which is due to deficiencies in the

diet. The death rate from this malady is eight times as high in the South as in the rest of the country. Once Southern tenants and sharecroppers raise such vegetables as carrots, spinach, and turnips, and keep poultry and dairy cows, pellagra will disappear. And then, of course, there are syphilis and gonorrhea, which are altogether too prevalent in the South, as well as in other parts of the United States. These venereal diseases have a much greater incidence among Negroes than among whites, and are factors in the segregation of the races in public places and industrial plants.

The farmers of the rural South can never become sturdy, self-reliant and solvent until their physical ills are remedied. All the rehabilitation loans or grants in the world will not benefit men and women who are too sick to work. They should receive not only more adequate public health services, but better-rounded schooling, both in educational fundamentals and in agricultural and vocational spheres. They must be taught the basic matters affecting rural living, such as the value of conserving the soil. Once they are impressed with the essential importance of soil conservation, the South, with one-fifth of the nation's wealth, no longer will have to pay three-fifths of the nation's fertilizer bill. Southern top-soil which would cover the entire state of South Carolina has been needlessly allowed to wash into the rivers and the oceans, while an area several times as large has been seriously damaged. Once the tenant or 'cropper acquires sufficient stability to remain on the same farm year after year, he will have an incentive to conserve the soil, instead of to waste and exhaust it.

There is such a thing, of course, as the government's

giving unduly preferential treatment to farmers, at the expense of other members of society, and that is what had happened by early 1942, when 16-cent cotton and 25- to 35-cent tobacco helped to set highly inflationary forces in motion throughout the country, with potentially disastrous consequences. This accelerating trend promised not only to disrupt our domestic economy and to increase the cost of living, but it also jeopardized the opportunity of the United States after the war to lead a prostrate Europe back to prosperity through lowered trade barriers and a rapidly expanding foreign commerce. There was great danger that prices in the United States would go so far above world prices, as to force us to adopt a two-price system almost totalitarian in character. The Southern cotton bloc was credited with a major share of responsibility for furthering these ominous tendencies, and for influencing the refusal of Congress to adopt prompt and effective counter measures. Some of its members were wildly resentful of the national administration's reluctance to put a ceiling on industrial wages. They professed not to believe that an even more basic cause of inflation is zooming prices for farm products, which force labor to pay more for food and hence to demand higher pay, thus inaugurating a vicious cycle, the necessary consequence of which is greatly increased living costs all along the line.

What bearing, if any, the Federal wage and hour law will have on this dangerous inflationary trend is not clear, but there may be peril for the South in the seemingly fixed policy of the Wage and Hour Division in Washington invariably to establish the same minimum wage for the South as for the North in any given industry, thus wiping out the differentials which have stood for decades, and under which the South has managed to achieve a fair degree of prosperity, in the face of such discriminatory national policies as the tariff and adverse freight rates. If the defense boom absorbs virtually all criticism to-day, and Southern industry is temporarily so prosperous that the absence of minimum wage differentials presents no problem, the day of reckoning may be only a few years distant, when the well-nigh inevitable post-war depression makes the Southern manufacturer more conscious of his handicaps. The least the nation should do, in view of the rapidly vanishing minima which formerly operated in the South's favor, is to abolish the freight differentials against the South which in the past have served as a partial offset to the North's higher wages. While the average wage scale in a given industry usually is substantially higher in the North, the elimination of the lower minimum in the Southern underwear and shirt factories, for instance, when combined with the higher freight charges they must pay, may wreck them in the post-war era, when underwear and shirts, in all likelihood, will not be as widely worn as they are to-day. The same principle may operate at that time with respect to many other products manufactured below Mason and Dixon's line.

The South of the future must concern itself with this vital problem, and it may have to insist upon some modifications of the industrial minima, in order to survive. In England after the first World War, a good many employers even reduced wages below the legal limit, in order to stay in business in a period of severe deflation, and the courts refused to convict them.

But if the effect of the Federal wage and hour law may be hurtful to the South in the coming years, the region could use additional state minimum wage laws to advantage, in order to prevent the exploitation of laundry and restaurant workers, for example, at well-nigh incredibly low pay. These and certain other classes of labor are not covered by the Federal law, since they are not producing goods for interstate commerce, and they sorely need protection. Women workers in most Southern states, whose hours in stores, laundries, restaurants, and similar establishments are not limited effectively, likewise are exploited. Child labor laws also need strengthening, a condition not limited to the South. For example, Connecticut's labor commissioner complained in 1941 that children as young as nine years of age spend as much as thirteen hours a day harvesting the state's tobacco crop, and that conditions are "intolerable and disgraceful." There is also the complete absence of any State Labor Department or workmen's compensation law in Mississippi, while such departments and laws in certain other Southern states are too weak to afford much protection.

There has been a heavy reaction of late against labor unions both in the South and elsewhere, because of the ruthlessness and extremism of a minority of labor leaders and the dishonesty and racketeering of others. The synchronization of these phenomena with the national emergency heightened the public's resentment and cost the organized workingmen of the country much of the sympathy they had gained during the period when certain elements of industry and business were denying them their legitimate rights, firing them for joining the union, and even shooting them down. But despite the justified disgust of many Southerners and other Americans over the unpatriotic attitude manifested by a coterie of labor leaders and laboring men in a time of crisis, the fact remains that workers have certain legitimate rights, and those rights ought not to be taken away, unless this is essential to national survival. In the South, unionization is less advanced than in other sections, and the unions are weaker. Such resentment against all organized labor has been aroused in the minds of employers and the public generally by the efforts of powerful unions to club the country into granting exorbitant demands, as an alternative to shutdowns of vital defense industries, that years may elapse before industrial relations return to anything approaching normalcy. But it is important to the welfare of the South as a whole that both sides eschew further swaggering and bluster, and that employer-employee attitudes be divested of acrimony and bitterness at the earliest possible moment. Such legislation as the "anti-violence bill" which Governor O'Daniel of Texas pushed through the legislature of that state in 1941, is of distinctly dubious value. Frederick W. Bliss, chairman of the committee on industrial relations of the Boston Chamber of Commerce, called this bill, with its prison terms for even "threats" of violence by strikers, "as out of date as wooden battleships."

Whatever the ultimate posture of industrial relations below the Potomac, it seems fairly clear that the working men and women of the South will be given the benefit of large-scale slum-clearance, both urban and rural, when the defense boom is deflated, and business goes into the expected tailspin. This would appear to be one of the obvious means whereby the Federal Government can cushion the blow which will fall when American industry no longer is geared to supplying the war machines of the Allies, and useful peacetime construction work is being sought. It may well be that the substantial Federal investment which already has been made in public housing in the South, will be greatly exceeded in the postwar era. There is a well-nigh limitless opportunity for such a program, especially in the rural areas, a field which is as yet almost untapped.

A future-piercing view of the industrial housing problem in the South must take note of the trend toward liquidation of the company-owned mill village. This trend is expected to become accelerated hereafter, terminating, perhaps, in the eventual elimination of all such housing arrangements. Various reasons are assigned. For one thing, the feudalistic mill village, which gave the company such a hold upon the lives of its employees, usually has been operated at a financial loss. With the arrival of labor legislation protecting workers against many varieties of paternalism and exploitation, this financial liability retained few compensatory advantages. Besides, a mill hand who purchases a home in the village from the company, thereby ties himself and his family more closely to the company, and is perhaps less apt to move away or to become an "agitator." Furthermore, for those who prefer to live elsewhere, modern transportation makes it less necessary than formerly that the worker's home be in the shadow of the mill, while his 37½-cent minimum wage in the textile industry makes it more feasible for him to buy a home than was the case when hourly pay was one-half, or well below one-half that figure.

Perhaps too, in future years, the mill hands and the

other laborers and farmers in eight Southern states will
be relieved of the necessity of paying an annual levy
in order to vote. The poll-tax is under attack to such
a degree to-day that its retention for an indefinite period, in its present form, hardly seems likely. In states
where outright repeal appears to be only a remote
possibility, modification or enforced collection might
provide fairly satisfactory alternatives. Abolition of the
cumulative provision, whereby in certain states back
poll-taxes can be assessed for several years as a prerequisite to a single exercise of the voting prerogative,
seems the minimum which ought to be demanded in
the way of liberalization. It also is desirable that payment of the tax be permitted up to, say, thirty days
before the election, instead of requiring it from three
to nine months in advance, as several states do now.
The amount of the levy also should be reduced to $1
in each state which retains it. Some, or all, of these
modifications might be combined with the passage of
legislation requiring uniform collection of this admission fee to the ballot-box, like any other tax. To-day
it is a payment made voluntarily by those who desire
to vote or who, in at least one state, pay it in order to
get a state license of any sort, but practically no serious
effort at uniform collection is made. If such an effort
were mandatory in all cases where there was ability to
pay, revenue from the tax would be much greater than
at present, the number of voters would be correspond-
ingly increased, but reliefees and other largely destitute
persons still would be voteless. At all events, efficient
collection of the levy from relatively solvent citizens
would be an improvement over the existing dispensa-
tion. Incidentally, literacy requirements should be

maintained under this or any other system, to the end that voters who cannot read and write may be kept from the polls. A successfully functioning democracy must be based upon a reasonably informed electorate.

These considerations bring sharply into focus the present status of the Negro below the Potomac. In this group is one-third of the entire Southern population, enjoying greatly inferior educational facilities, too often pushed onto the poorest farm land, excluded from many labor unions, and otherwise suffering from discrimination. Ultra-conservative Southerners whose chief thoughts on the race problem revolve about the business of "keeping the Negro in his place," seem unable to explain how the white population is ever to be reasonably healthy and prosperous if for every two white persons there is a diseased, poverty-stricken and illiterate, if not criminally inclined, Negro. While this description does not fit anything like all the Negroes in the South, under existing circumstances, it would very nearly do so, if the policies of the most zealous advocates of "keeping the Negro in his place" were to prevail. One is reminded of the observation uttered shortly after the turn of the present century by Edgar Gardner Murphy of Alabama:

The poor Negro! The man who would keep him in ignorance and then would disfranchise him because he is ignorant must seem to him a paragon of erect and radiant consistency, when compared with the man who first tells him he must work, and then tells him he must not learn how. He tells the Negro he must make shoes, but that he must not make shoes which people can wear; that he may be a wheelwright, but that he must make neither good wheels nor salable wagons; that he must be a farmer, but that he must not farm well.

Obviously if levels of Southern living are to be raised substantially, the Negro must be given an opportunity to earn a respectable livelihood in both agriculture and industry, to say nothing of the professions. Those who persist in the view that the colored man or woman should be contented to exist forever in dirt and squalor, and who proclaim with great regularity that the Negro's record with respect to crime, poverty and disease shows that he is good for nothing and undeserving of better treatment, ought to clarify their thinking. No informed person could deny that there is a high percentage of anti-social behavior among Negroes, but how much lower would it be among whites who had to live under similar conditions, and who were only a few generations removed from slavery? The excellent record as to citizenship and law observance of Negro college graduates is evidence of what opportunity and favorable surroundings can mean. Such considerations have nothing to do with that oft-debated, and somewhat nebulous concept, "social equality." The giving to the Negro of a chance to better himself, to make himself a useful and informed citizen, and to dress decently, has no bearing upon whether or not he intermarries with whites—the ultimate consequence and consummation of true "social equality," a consummation which the white South rejects emphatically, and in which the black South has no serious interest. Even if outmoded ante-bellum notions with respect to the Negro's proper rôle and function in society were tenable to-day in the forum of public opinion, and they aren't, the United States Supreme Court is pronouncing one after another of these concepts in conflict with the organic law. Recalcitrant white Southerners may as well bow to the inevitable. The fact that a good many white Northerners have not done so is evident. For example, Federal Security Administrator Paul V. McNutt said in an address at Philadelphia in the late summer of 1941 that prejudice against using Negroes in defense industries was much worse in Philadelphia "and generally north of the Mason-Dixon Line," than in the South.

Justice for the Negro in the Southern courts would go far to remove some of the disabilities from which he suffers in that region, and justice here connotes, among other things, harsher penalties for Negroes who slay other Negroes. Moreover, Negro policemen in the colored districts of Southern cities undoubtedly could do more effective work than white policemen, who tend either to excessive brutality when handling colored defendants, or excessive leniency. It is natural that they do not inspire the same confidence among Negro citizens that a respected and level-headed member of that race would enjoy.

In the sphere of education, the Southern Negro elementary and secondary schools must be improved, and the colored teachers' salaries placed on the same level as those of the whites. As for Negro education at the collegiate level, it should include regional institutions operated exclusively for Negroes, financed by appropriations from each of the states served. This is the best answer to the problem of how to provide adequate graduate and professional schooling for the colored race, and at the same time to avoid the clashes which would occur, particularly in the Deep South, if there was insistence upon admitting Negroes to the white universities. Moreover, it not only would provide the South's Negro population with professional and graduate instruction of the highest excellence, but the Negro faculties of the institutions offering these courses would afford opportunities to colored scholars which are quite limited in America to-day, and are not likely to be available at white institutions in any section of the country in the measurable future.

The idea of regional centers of instruction has distinct possibilities, too, for white institutions, both inside and outside the South. Why, for example, should Mississippi try to maintain a medical school, when an act of Congress would constitutionally validate the appropriation of funds from the Mississippi treasury to the Tulane or L.S.U. medical schools in Louisiana, or to the Vanderbilt school in Tennessee? Why should South Carolina wrestle with the same problem, and try to raise the enormous sums required, when either Emory in Georgia or Duke in North Carolina could be made to serve that commonwealth far more adequately now that transportation presents so few problems? The same argument applies, in general, to all graduate and professional work in the South. A much better grade of instruction and far more complete and up-to-date laboratory and clinical facilities can be provided by several states, acting jointly, particularly when they help to underwrite an institution already well-established, than any single state could possibly make available. This is especially applicable to schools of medicine and engineering, with their costly and elaborate plants, and to graduate schools with research facilities leading to the Ph.D. Moreover, the idea ought to be as useful to the sparsely settled and impecunious Western states and to some New England states as to those in the South. There is at the present time an excessive prevalence in all three regions of what the late

President Edwin A. Alderman of the University of Virginia liked to call "monohippic" institutions. The South needs one or more universities with graduate and professional instruction comparable to the best in America, and one or more colleges of similar rank. Its best chance of getting them lies in a congressional enactment empowering State legislatures to appropriate funds toward the support of colleges or universities in other states. Even if Congress is unwilling to authorize the establishment of regional institutions for Negroes, it is impossible to see what objection any member could have to allowing his state legislature, in its discretion, to appropriate state funds to an institution in another state. Members of these legislatures ought to rejoice in such a law, since it would relieve them of serious financial worries, at a time when taxes are sky-rocketing, and also would offer much wider educational opportunities to their constituents.

If Southern legislatures contained more Republicans —if, in other words, there were a substantial minority party in every former Confederate state—the chances of achieving this and many other advances in the fields of education, health, agriculture, industry, and welfare, would be measurably increased. As matters stand, the Republicans are too weak nearly everywhere to have even a nuisance value. With strong Democratic monopolies functioning almost universally below the Potomac and the Ohio, the issue in political contests usually resolves itself into whether this or that Democratic faction is to control. Such inbreeding and lack of competition is bad, irrespective of whether one regards the Republican party under its present leadership as even faintly stimulating or arresting. Its obstructionism in Congress almost throughout 1941, when the country was faced with the gravest crisis in its history, was more than ordinarily depressing.

The lack of an effective political minority in the South is one of the major reasons why it has been said hyperbolically that "Southern hospitality has never extended to ideas." Moreover, the monopoly which the Democrats enjoy has a large measure of responsibility for the too frequent emergence of political warlocks below Mason and Dixon's line. True, it took Kansas to threaten the elevation of "Doc" Brinkley, the eminent goat-gland specialist, to a governorship, but Dixie has plenty to answer for in the same sphere, and it would profit substantially from the catharsis of inter-party debate.

A more vigorous Republican minority in the region also would tend to hasten the demise of sectionalism. The Democratic press in the South no longer terms Republican conventions in the region "the semi-annual gathering of the federal pie brigade," nor does it refer to the delegates as "old moss-backs," "revenue doodles," and "bung-smellers," as one leading paper did immediately after the turn of the century, but Republicanism, as well as all other forms of political dissent, are too much frowned on among us, even to-day. And if Northerners no longer are openly assailed in the South as "blue-bellies," certain lingering traces of intersectional animosity are in need of eradication.

Another obviously desirable step in the direction of a more civilized South would be the repeal of the anti-evolution laws which still make Tennessee, Mississippi, and Arkansas ridiculous wherever educated men and women gather. It is hardly surprising that many Europeans envision America as a land of wild Indians, two-gun cowboys, and pineapple-tossing gangsters, when three American state legislatures have solemnly out-lawed a scientific hypothesis which is taken for granted by all the enlightened nations of the earth. The fact that the laws are largely nullified and disregarded in all three commonwealths, makes it the more remarkable that they have not been repealed. At least two Southern states finally have got around to passing legislation for-bidding the handling of snakes at religious services, owing to the frequent fatalities which were occurring as a consequence of this species of zealotry. Is it more ab-surd to wrap a writhing rattler around one's neck, in response to imagined scriptural exhortations, than it is to insist on the historicity of Genesis?

The steady improvement of Southern education in all categories should make such grievous phenomena increas-ingly rare in the future. It is only in the remoter dis-tricts, usually the mountains, that snake-handlers hold their weird rites, and it is inconceivable that hereafter any other Southern state will so much as consider the adoption of an anti-evolution statute.

Educational processes in the region have progressed with accelerated rapidity in late years because of a re-newed disposition on the part of Southerners to view their shortcomings realistically. There are agencies and organizations to-day, both statewide and Southwide in scope, which address themselves to those shortcomings without inhibitions, and in a manner which augurs well for the future.

Important among them is the Southern Policy Com-mittee, with subsidiary bodies in the various states. It was founded in 1935 through the indefatigable efforts of

Francis P. Miller of Virginia, a former Rhodes Scholar and world-traveler who conceived of these scattered groups as being somewhat analogous in function to the Committees of Correspondence of more than 150 years ago. They have been significantly influential. The Southern committee has met at periodic intervals, and usually has adopted resolutions effectively focusing attention upon pressing issues. For example, the need for adequate Federal tenancy legislation was brought to national notice by the first Southern Policy Committee meeting, held in Atlanta in 1935. It is believed the emphasis given by the gathering to the problem played a part in the subsequent passage of the Bankhead-Jones farm tenancy act. The state committees have convened more often than the parent body, and some have attacked problems inside their borders with notable results. The Arkansas Policy Committee, for example, formulated a report on farm tenancy in that state which played an indubitable rôle in the subsequent passage by the Arkansas Legislature of a land law which Edward J. Meeman of the Memphis *Press-Scimitar* said should be substantially copied throughout the South. The Alabama Policy Committee, which shares with that of Arkansas the distinction of being one of the two most conspicuously active and successful state committees, has issued a long list of publications dealing with political, educational, industrial, agricultural and social issues in Alabama. The Committee was influential in the passage of the state civil service law, in the adoption of legislation providing a minimum program fund for public education, and in securing a law designed to equalize property tax assessments among the various counties, although this last did not pass in the form desired.

The Southern Policy Committee is set up on an informal basis, with an extremely limited budget. The state committees have practically no funds. Yet this loosely knit agency has made it possible for thoughtful Southerners to exchange ideas, to rub elbows, and to learn about regional and state problems. Most of those who participate in these deliberations are called "liberals," for want of a more precise term. But it should be stressed that there is no set of principles or objectives to which regional or state policy committees are bound, and that one of the most stimulating things about them is the fact that they include men and women of varying points of view. An interest in public affairs, a willingness to be tolerant of disagreement, and, above all, a belief in the democratic way of doing things—the "democratic process," in Francis Miller's favorite phrase—are the only prerequisites.

Significant as are the tangible consequences of the policy committee's operations, the intangible ones are equally so. These conclaves have influenced many of the participants in subtle ways, have brought leaders in various Southern fields into ideological rapport, and have set in motion trains of thought which are having their impact in unexpected places. The South of the future is apt to be influenced in no small degree by this manifestation of the democratic process.

A couple of years after the policy committee idea was launched, Georgia decided to have an indigenous movement of its own, organized pursuant to the novel notion that the people of that state ought to know the facts concerning its affairs. "After trying the nostrums of local cut-rate statesmen, old-time religion, corn-whiskey sprees, and treatments in the emergency ward of the

New Deal, Georgia is trying—truth," David L. Cohn wrote in the *Atlantic*. The search for truth went forward under the ægis of the Citizens' Fact Finding Movement of Georgia, as it is called, certainly one of the most notable movements of its kind in any American state.

In thorough and discriminating fashion it sponsored twelve reports on that many aspects of Georgia civilization, during the first year of its existence. Civic, educational and professional groups enjoying a total membership of 250,000 coöperated and many experts donated their services. The facts as to such subjects as penology, taxation, agriculture, politics and natural resources were carefully scrutinized and incisively presented. Possible solutions were projected in a subsequent series. But Eugene Talmadge was elected Governor almost simultaneously, and the civilized forces in Georgia soon were badly on the defensive. While the setback seemed merely temporary, the violent Negrophobia of the Governor, and his bigoted and bumptious behavior were severely discouraging to all persons of independent mind. Fortunately it does not appear probable that a movement with as much robust force and as deeply rooted democratic origins as this one, can be permanently crushed. However, the C.F.F.M. would be still more representative of the state as a whole, if organized labor were among the coöperating citizens' groups.

The Southern Governors' Conference, formed in 1937 by the chief executives of all the former Confederate states except Virginia, with Oklahoma thrown in, is another agency which is addressing itself to the problems which confront the region. Early in 1940, it adopted a ten-point program for the South's development, a program drafted by a committee among whom Dr. Clarence Poe, editor of the *Progressive Farmer,* President Frank P. Graham of Chapel Hill, and Dean Paul W. Chapman of the University of Georgia College of Agriculture, were preëminent. This excellent program called for balancing the following factors at the end of ten years:

> Money crops, including forest products, with food, feed and fertility crops
> All crops with livestock, consistent with land use
> Production progress with marketing and transportation opportunity, free of trade barriers
> Farms with factories
> Land, water, and mineral resources with population needs
> Work with thrift and local investments
> Owner prosperity with worker prosperity
> Increasing income with increasing home ownership
> Wealth with beauty and culture
> Economic gains with advances in moral values and human welfare

After adopting this ambitious set of broadly-stated objectives, the Southern Governors' Conference seemed for a time to pigeonhole some of the most important, and to concentrate its efforts in the fields of industrial development, freight rate revision and labor relations. But since most of the governors are hardly more than window-dressing for the conference, the real work of which is carried on by the various state chairmen, the organization is not as circumscribed by political considerations as one might imagine.

While the entry of the United States into the war necessarily has tended to divert public attention from domestic to foreign problems, and it may make realization of the foregoing "Decade of Progress" program much more difficult than it would otherwise have been, the tremendous dislocations which surely will take place during and after the war both in the South and everywhere else, serve to accent the importance of some such carefully devised and nicely articulated plan. Because of the varied political predilections and individual complexes and prejudices of the governors comprising the conference, it remains to be seen how effective an agency it will be. Yet some things of consequence already have been accomplished. For example, the conference has been instrumental in improving the South's relative position with respect to freight rates, and in the agricultural sphere, distinct achievements are to be recorded. Dr. Poe feels, indeed, that the "food and feed campaigns," designed to promote the raising of home-grown food and feed on Southern farms, and the South-wide Rural Survey, which provides a score-card whereby the average rural family can record its year-by-year improvement in balanced, intelligent, diversified farming, "amply justify all the time and labor" given to the governors' conference movement.

While the conference is equipped in some respects to deal with the tremendous problems which are sure to present themselves in the South when peace returns, there are skeptics concerning its ability to handle such matters in a non-political and broad-visioned manner. John Temple Graves, II, the columnist, has suggested that "reconstruction committees" be named by the various Southern governors to plan now for the economic and social convulsions which are bound to come with the close of hostilities. Governors Homer Adkins of Arkansas and James H. Price of Virginia promised at once to follow his advice, and Mr. Adkins said he would write the other Southern governors in support of the scheme. It appears to have much merit. The objectives Mr. Graves has in mind probably can be pursued successfully by the Southern Governors' Conference, if that agency gives evidence of a capacity for bold and progressive pioneering, and of a desire to follow the recommendations of its thinkers and planners. The fact that Mr. Graves proposed the setting up of other machinery for the task was a clear indication of his doubt concerning the adequacy of a conference which may be dominated by a heterogeneous group of political leaders.

The problem of our post-war civilization is perhaps more important in the case of the South than in that of any other American region, since the South has the greatest abundance of undeveloped natural resources, the greatest surplus of man-power and the most arresting potentialities for the future. Properly guided and stimulated, the South can be transformed from Economic Problem No. 1 into Economic Asset No. 1.

It is a notable fact that no other section of America is the subject of so much intelligent analysis, the scene of so much earnest searching after truth. The groups already mentioned as concerning themselves actively and constantly with Southern phenomena are only a few of the most important. Ideas are germinating from the rocky pinnacles of the Blue Ridge to the international bridges over the Rio Grande. Civic leaders, clubwomen, business men, industrialists, lawyers, doctors, educators, and newspapermen, not to mention the man and woman in the street, the worker and the farmer, are thinking of the South's place in the nation as never before. Something significant and constructive is sure to emerge, soon or late, from this concentration of thought and effort. Its emergence is rendered the more certain by the unprecedented emphasis which Washington is placing upon the Southern scene, even though that emphasis is not always in the right place.

Dr. Howard W. Odum of the University of North Carolina is one of those who may be expected to play a conspicuous and important rôle in the development of a dynamic program for Southern progress, both during the hiatus of wartime and when peace returns. His numerous books and brochures on the region have furnished us with many of the basic facts, and he launched a plan a few years ago for a Council on Southern Regional Development which seemed to have great possibilities, but which failed, at least temporarily, because of unanticipated difficulties. This concept now has been expanded by Dr. Odum into a more ambitious blueprint covering the entire country, with a National Research and Planning Council over all, together with regional councils for the eight regions, and separate councils for each of the forty-eight states. Termed by him a "fourth balance wheel of government," the national council would require congressional implementation, as well as enactments by the various state legislatures, although most of them have state planning boards already, and these would be utilized. Whether anything so ambitious will be feasible in the post-war world, remains to be seen, but it appears certain that the scholarship and vision of men like Odum will be needed in that possibly chaotic time. Undoubtedly the lately perfected art of planning will be essential in the development of the South when this holocaust of blood is ended.

Moreover, there is reason to believe that wider horizons may open before the South after the war than

before any other American region. Among certain industrialists, for example, there is the feeling that the
plant expansions they are carrying forward South of
Mason and Dixon's line, as part of the defense boom,
will be permanently valuable, because of the relatively
undeveloped nature of the area, and the prospects there
for greatly augmented mass purchasing power and
higher levels of living. It is important to note too that
throughout history, material advances generally have
gone hand in hand with advances in cultural and intellectual realms. It was so in Athens during the Age
of Pericles, in Florence under the Medici, and in Eliza-
bethan England.

One of the principal agencies for Southern progress
during the coming era of which we are speaking will be
the press. The press of the South is not appreciated in
other sections, for the reason that Southern newspapers
circulate in minuscule quantities in the North and
West. Indeed they probably are not fully appreciated by
Southerners, since much that they do for community
and state and national advancement seems to be taken
largely for granted by those who are the beneficiaries.
The Southern press, like that of other areas, has its
venal and selfish and cowardly elements, of course.
There is no intention here of pretending that all newspaper publishers and editors in Dixie, or anything like
all of them, are white knights riding forth to slay the
dragon of untruth. Yet the level of merit is surprisingly
high, and the volume of achievement gratifyingly large.
How, for instance, would Louisiana have got rid of the
Huey Long machine, and its assorted crooks and thieves,
without the courageous New Orleans newspapers? Who
but the Atlanta press is leading the opposition to Tal-

madge in Georgia? Where in the South does one find a more insistent and effective advocate of fairness and justice for the Negro than in the white press? Where have better schools, better roads, better health, and better penal institutions more tenacious champions than among Southern publishers and editors? There are anti-social elements among them, of course, including those whom Tom Wallace, editor of the Louisville *Times*, has described as thinking that the constitutional guarantee of freedom of the press connotes the right to send a circulation truck through a red traffic light. Nevertheless the press of the South frequently is the spearhead leading the advance to new frontiers, the panzer division which breaks a path for the slogging infantry. There is at least one large, influential, and forward-looking news-paper in nearly every Southern state.

In that great future which awaits the South, its alert and uninhibited editors may be expected to join with its colleges and universities, its public-spirited professional men, its socially-conscious women, and its articulate and progressive business and labor leaders in building below the Potomac and the Ohio a grander civilization than that storied land has ever known. The structure cannot be fashioned out of reaction by Bourbons "fumbling their flyblown phylacteries" with eyes fixed on the past. Imagination and vision, resourcefulness and daring are essential ingredients of the South which must arise after Western civilization has been cleansed of the swastika's dark shadow.

The South which is to be must have the kinetic force to build for the future, and the leisure to enjoy the edifice, after it is done; it must be a wholly American South, a South of liberty and learning, of human dignity and devotion to democracy. It must be willing, if necessary, to seal its allegiance to principle in fire and steel and blood, as did another South, and it must learn to combine an ante-bellum love of gracious living with a post-bellum determination to erect a new and more virile and more humane society upon the wreckage of the old. When these desiderata are achieved, there will have been forged from Virginia to Texas a civilization worthy of the men who have made America the hope of the world in this, the crisis of the centuries.

INDEX

Academic freedom, 174-176

Accent, 15-17

Adkins, Homer, 311

Agnes Scott College, 141, 163, 166-167

Agricultural Adjustment Administration, 65-66, 132, 273

Agricultural and Mechanical College, 150, 160

Agricultural and Technical College, 227

Agriculture, dangers of preferential treatment of, 294; education for, 232-233; effect of war on, 273-279; rehabilitation by the New Deal, 59, 87, 291

Alabama, 27, 68, 72, 76, 79, 89-90, 109, 110, 115, 117, 121, 134, 148, 207-208, 239, 240, 247, 280, 283, 292. *See also* University of Alabama.

Alabama Policy Committee, 307

Alabama Polytechnic Institute, 120, 160

Alabama State Prison Farm, silk industry at, 277

Alcohol, Virginia study of effects of, 241-244

Alcorn Agricultural and Mechanical College, 233

Alderman, Edwin A., 304

Alexander, Will W., 183

Alldredge, J. Haden, 92

Aluminum Company of America, 84-85

American Civil Liberties Union, 127-129, 174

American Cotton Manufacturers' Association, 73

American Council on Education, 146

American Federation of Labor, 98-100, 131

American Medical Association, 230

American Mercury, 1939, on diet and cookery, 9

American Sugar Cane League, 150

Ames, Mrs. Jessie Daniel, 183, 188

Amidon, Beulah, 209

Anderson, Charles W., 199

Anti-Catholicism, 137-138

Anti-evolution laws, 134-135; and education, 248-255; need for repeal of, 305-306

Anti-Saloon League, 241, 242, 244

Medical schools, 158-159; Negro, 230

Meeman, Edward J., 307

Meharry Medical College, 228, 230

Mellett, Lowell, 59

Memorials, incident of the Appomattox, 260-265

Memphis, 103, 121-124, 128-129, 191, 198, 213-214

Memphis *Commercial Appeal,* 75

Mennet, Overton H., 268

Meyers, Rodes K., 128-129

Middle American Research Institute, 156

Migratory labor, 75, 97

Miller, Francis P., 307-308

Mississippi, 63, 74, 75, 76, 79, 89, 104, 109, 112, 114, 117, 120, 133, 134, 148, 185, 202, 214, 235, 246-247, 249, 296

Missouri, 75, 121, 133

Mitchell, Margaret, 2, 16

Molyneaux, Peter, 274

Monroe, James, 12

Morehouse College, 228

Morris Brown College, 228

Mound Bayou, 196

Murchison, Claudius T., 73

Murphy, Edgar Gardner, 300

Murray, Philip, 102

Music, 8

Myrick, Susan, 15

Nance, Steve, 99

Nashville, 228

Natchez, 203

National Association for the Advancement of Colored People, 180, 182-184, 188-189, 190-191, 200-201, 206-208, 215, 223-224, 234

National Bureau of Economic Research, 210

National Child Labor Committee, 96-97

National Defense Mediation Board, 100-101

National Education Association, 206

National Emergency Council, 59, 61

National Industrial Conference Board, 23

National Labor Relations Board, 101

National Recovery Administration, 87-88, 89, 98, 179

National Research and Planning Council, 313

Negro colleges, and universities, argument for regional, 215-223; eminent scholars in, 233-235; graduate and professional training in, 225-233

Negroes, as political issue, 28; birth rate, 25; crime record of, 191-196; disease among, 292; disfranchisement of, 110; eminent scholars, 233-235; graduate and professional education for, 225-233; homi-

(i)